T0214635

Lecture Notes in Computer Science 11392

Commenced Publication in 1973
Founding and Former Series Editors:
Gerhard Goos, Juris Hartmanis, and Jan van Leeuwen

Editorial Board

More information about this series at http://www.springer.com/series/7407

Zhenhua Duan · Shaoying Liu
Cong Tian · Fumiko Nagoya (Eds.)

Structured Object-Oriented Formal Language and Method

8th International Workshop, SOFL+MSVL 2018
Gold Coast, QLD, Australia, November 16, 2018
Revised Selected Papers

 Springer

Editors
Zhenhua Duan
Xidian University
Xi'an, China

Cong Tian
Xidian University
Xi'an, China

Shaoying Liu
Hosei University
Tokyo, Japan

Fumiko Nagoya
Nihon University
Tokyo, Japan

ISSN 0302-9743   ISSN 1611-3349   (electronic)
Lecture Notes in Computer Science
ISBN 978-3-030-13650-5   ISBN 978-3-030-13651-2   (eBook)
https://doi.org/10.1007/978-3-030-13651-2

Library of Congress Control Number: 2019931947

LNCS Sublibrary: SL1 – Theoretical Computer Science and General Issues

This Springer imprint is published by the registered company Springer Nature Switzerland AG
The registered company address is: Gewerbestrasse 11, 6330 Cham, Switzerland

Preface

Research on formal engineering methods is ready to show how specific formal techniques can be easily and effectively utilized to deal with practical software development. The Structured Object-Oriented Formal Language (SOFL) has fulfilled this goal by providing a comprehensible specification language, a functional scenario-based modeling, verification, and validation techniques, and efficient tool support through effective integration of formal methods with conventional software engineering techniques. The Modeling, Simulation and Verification Language (MSVL) is a parallel programming language. Its supporting toolkit MSV has been developed to enable us to model, simulate, and verify systems formally.

Following the success of the previous SOFL+MSVL workshops, the 8th International Workshop on SOFL+MSVL 2018 was jointly organized, on the Gold Coast, Australia, by Shaoying Liu's research group at Hosei University, Japan, and Zhenhua Duan's research group at Xidian University, China, with the aim of bringing together industrial, academic, and government experts and practitioners of SOFL, MSVL, or other formal engineering methods to communicate and to exchange ideas. The workshop attracted 21 submissions on software construction monitoring and predicting for human–machine pair programming, formal specification, modeling, model-checking, testing, and formal methods application. Each submission was rigorously reviewed by three Program Committee (PC) members on the basis of its technical quality, relevance, significance, and clarity. In total, 11 papers were accepted for publication in the workshop proceedings and the acceptance rate is approximately 52%.

We would like to thank the ICFEM 2018 organizers for supporting the organization of the workshop, and all of the PC members for their great efforts and cooperation in reviewing and selecting the papers. We would also like to thank all of the participants for attending the presentation sessions and actively joining the discussions at the workshop. Finally, our gratitude goes to Alfred Hofmann and Anna Kramer of Springer for their continuous support in the publication of the workshop proceedings.

November 2018

Zhenhua Duan
Shaoying Liu

Organization

Program Committee

Zhenhua Duan (Program Chair)	Xidian University, China
Shaoying Liu (Program Chair)	Hosei University, Japan
Cong Tian (Organizing Co-chair)	Xidian University, China
Fumiko Nagoya (Organizing Co-chair)	Nihon University, Japan
Yuting Chen	Shanghai Jiaotong University, China
Busalire Emeka	Hosei University, Japan
Colin Fidge	Queensland University of Technology, Australia
Huaikou Miao	Shanghai University, China
Weikai Miao	East China Normal University, China
Shin Nakajima	NII, Japan
Kazuhiro Ogata	JAIST, Japan
Shengchao Qin	Teesside University, UK
Wuwei Shen	Western Michigan University, USA
Xinfeng Shu	Xi'an University of Posts and Telecommunications, China
Rong Wang	Hosei University, Japan
Xi Wang	Shanghai University, China
Jinyun Xue	Jiangxi Normal University, China
Xiaobing Wang	Xidian University, China

Contents

Programming and Testing

Software Construction Monitoring and Predicting for Human-Machine Pair Programming

Shaoying Liu[✉]

Department of Computer Science, Hosei University, Tokyo, Japan
sliu@hosei.ac.jp

Abstract. Pair programming is one of the promising techniques advocated in agile development paradigm, but it tends to be more costly than one person-based programming and to lack a rigorous principle for governing the cooperation of the two programmers. In this paper, we put forward a novel technique called *Software Construction Monitoring and Predicting* to study an intelligent and automatic approach to *human-machine pair programming*. Its aim is to automatically, dynamically monitor the process of software construction for fault detection and to predict the possible future contents of the software towards its error-free completion. We describe the theoretical foundation and frameworks for Software Construction Monitoring (SCM) and Software Construction Predicting (SCP), respectively. We also discuss how SCMP can support the *Specification-Based programming* paradigm. Finally, we use simple examples to illustrate how SCM and SCP can be supported.

Keywords: Software Construction Monitoring ·
Software construction predicting · Agile ·
Specification-based development

1 Introduction

We have been longing for a process of software construction that can timely indicate faults in the current version of software as it is being constructed and predict the possible future contents of the software towards its error-free completion, simply because it can significantly improve software quality, reduce construction cost, and enhance software productivity.

Pair programming is a promising technique that is advocated in eXtreme Programming [1], which is an agile development paradigm, but it tends to be more costly than one person-based programming and to lack a rigorous principle for governing the cooperation of the two programmers [2]. On the other hand, specification-based programming is a rigorous, systematic technique suggested in the SOFL formal engineering method [3] that has a firm theoretical foundation in the refinement calculus [4]. Since specification-based programming is unlikely

© Springer Nature Switzerland AG 2019
Z. Duan et al. (Eds.): SOFL+MSVL 2018, LNCS 11392, pp. 3–20, 2019.
https://doi.org/10.1007/978-3-030-13651-2_1

to be fully automated in general, an efficient and effective support for the process of program construction will become important and beneficial.

In this paper, we put forward a novel technique called *Software Construction Monitoring and Predicting* (SCMP) to support *human-machine pair programming* (HMPP). This technique is expected to benefit both specification-based programming and programming in general.

By software construction monitoring (SCM), we mean that the process of software construction is automatically and dynamically observed and verified to detect faults in the current version of the software. In other words, as the software is constructed by a human developer, its current version is always being observed and checked by a software tool, and faults are reported timely if any. The targeted faults are primarily semantic faults, not syntactical faults which can be found by a complier. The theoretical foundation and the related topics for research are detailed in Sect. 2.

By software construction predicting (SCP), we mean that the process of software construction is automatically and dynamically observed and analyzed to suggest possible future contents towards the error-free completion of the software under construction. The application of SCP will strengthen the interaction between the human developer and the supporting tool. The human is primarily responsible for creating ideas and constructing software, while the tool is responsible for suggesting the possible future contents necessary for dealing with potential defects based on the human's input and for completing the software. The suggested contents can be adopted without changes or with necessary changes based on the developer's judgement. The theoretical foundation and relevant research issues are discussed in detail in Sect. 3.

Since both SCM and SCP require the syntactical analysis of the current version of the software to extract necessary information and the result of SCM can be the basis for SCP, SCM and SCP can be researched and supported together in an integrated tool, but of course, they can also be studied separately. In fact, each of them involves many technical details to be explored.

Note that this paper is unlike a usual technical paper describing some well developed technique possibly with hard evidence to evaluate its effectiveness. Instead, its purpose is to propose new research directions and topics in order to encourage more researchers to work on for more efficient and effective software engineering in the future. We believe that this kind of contribution is also important for workshops because it can timely circulate the new ideas in the research community.

The rest of the paper is outlined as follows. Section 2 describes SCM. Section 3 discusses SCP. Section 4 briefly shows an integraed framework for SCMP. Section 5 discusses the related issues. Section 6 explains how SCM and SCP can be supported with examples. Section 8 briefly reviews related work. Finally, in Sect. 9 we conclude the paper.

2 Software Construction Monitoring (SCM)

We describe the theoretical foundation, main challenges to be addressed, and a framework for realizing SCM, respectively.

2.1 Foundation and Challenges for SCM

Let S be the software under construction. Let P_1, P_2,..., P_n are properties S must possess in order to ensure that S is correct (e.g., requirements in the specification are implemented; guard conditions can evaluate to both true and false, respectively; loop body must include a variant to make the loop terminate) or satisfies the required quality standards (e.g., the standard for naming variables, style of code, readability, code structures). The technique SCM aims to automatically, dynamically check whether the current version of S (incomplete in most cases), represented by CV_S, satisfies these properties. Such a check must be performed in the background mode with a software tool, which should not affect the human developer's current activity of constructing the software. If one of the properties is not satisfied, faults must be reported properly for the developer to easily understand them.

There are following primary challenges:

- Since CV_S is usually impossible to meet all of the possible properties P_1, P_2,..., P_n defined for the completed software S, how should an appropriate subset of the properties be chosen to ensure that the real faults in CV_S are reported?
- Given a relevant property P_i ($i \in \{1, 2, \ldots, n\}$), how can CV_S be *automatically* and *efficiently* checked to find out whether it satisfies P_i or not?
- Assume that a fault report is produced, how can all of the reported faults be ensured to be real faults for CV_S and in what format should the faults be presented to allow the developer to easily understand them?

Since CV_S is dynamically changed as the construction of the software progresses, the subset of the properties to be chosen for checking will also be dynamically changed. Whether such a change can be defined in advance is a question. If there is a solution to this question, what should it be? We believe that this problem can be addressed using the *Dynamic Set Theory* proposed in [5] and the details need to be worked out in the future.

To automatically check whether a given property is satisfied, we can use the automatic testing for theorems proposed in [6]. The essential idea is to convert the property into a theorem and then carry out an automatic testing of the theorem. But the challenge is how many and what kind of test data should be produced to ensure all real faults will be revealed.

As far as the format of fault report is concerned, perhaps the most helpful format would be the one that directly indicates the location of the faults and gives a brief description of the nature of the faults. The editing tools in the Eclipse environment can be a reference for developing this idea.

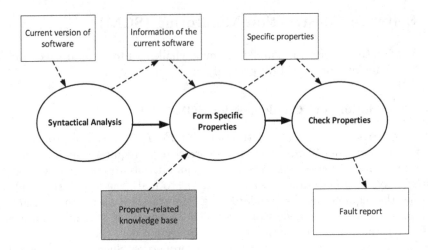

Fig. 1. Basic framework for SCM

2.2   Framework for Realizing SCM

Figure 1 shows a basic framework for realizing SCM that includes essential activities and data. The *Syntactical Analysis* provides the information of the current software CV_S for determining specific properties to be checked. This would require the knowledge about what properties can be formed. The *property-related knowledge base* is a pre-prepared knowledge base to keep all of the interesting properties of software that are defined in a manner suitable for application to CV_S. The knowledge base can be established based on the language used for writing the software, software development conventions or standards, and the most common faults occurred in the past. Of course, the knowledge base can be updated over the time. We do not explain the other parts of the framework since their roles can be easily comprehended according to their name.

3   Software Construction Predicting (SCP)

Similarly to the introduction of SCM, we also discuss the theoretical foundation, main challenges to be addressed, and a framework for realizing SCP, respectively.

3.1   Foundation and Challenges for SCP

Suppose a completed software S is composed of n fragments f_1, f_2,...,f_n. Abstractly, it is represented as $S = \{f_1, f_2, \ldots, f_n\}$. Each fragment can be interpreted into different software unit depending on the type of the software. For example, a fragment for a specification can be a formal declaration or logical expression, but for code, it can be one line of code, a statement, a sequence of statements, or a subroutine. At this point, our discussion is not affected without substantiating the fragment. A current version CV_S of S, which is usually incomplete, can be regarded as a subset of S, i.e., $CV\_S \subset S$.

On the basis of CV_S, SCP aims to automatically suggest a set of fragments, say P_c (predicted contents), which is a subset of S. Ideally, P_c can be used without change in the finally completed software S, but in many cases, some fragments of P_c may need to be modified in order to make them suitable for the final software. The predicted fragments are expected to play some of the following roles:

- Resolve the potential faults in the current version of the software CV_S. For example, when a statement converting an input number-string into an *int* type number is written in Java, the corresponding exception handling code (*try-catch* fragments) would be suggested to write in the next version. Another example is when an assignment $x = y/z$ is written in the current version, the fragment for ensuring that z is not zero will be predicted properly.
- Develop the content of CV_S towards the completion of the final software S. For example, in ATM software, after a method called *withdraw* is defined in a class called *BankAccount* by the developer, another method called *Deposit* will be automatically suggested to define next by the SCP tool (if it is already built). Of course, such a suggestion obviously needs sufficient knowledge about the ATM system. We will discuss this point further later.

To realize the goals of SCP, we must attack the following challenges:

- How should the knowlege-base be built in advance? Two essential issues need to be addressed. One is about the contents of the knowledge on the application domain, the development method used for software construction, and their possible combinations. Another issue is how existing techniques for representing domain knowledge and method-based knowledge can be utilized and/or improved to suit for software prediction. Moreover, how to expand the knowledge-base dynamically by accepting more knowledge on predicting and how to effectively and efficiently apply the knowledge-base for prediction will also be important topics to study.
- What are the effective and efficient methods for predicting? One possibility is to make good use of specifications, in particular formal specifications, for software prediction. The specification may define the functionality, safety, security, or any other important properties of the software. Another possibility is domain-specific or method-specific predicting techniques that use domain knowledge, method knowledge or both.
- Building a software tool is essential to realize SCP in an intelligent and automatic manner, but how to fulfill this goal? The focus should be put on how the knowledge-base is supported and how communications between the developer and the tool can be efficiently done through an appropriate human-machine interface.

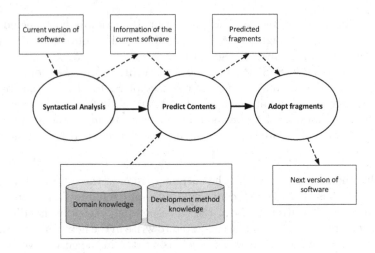

Fig. 2. Essential framework for SCP

3.2 Framework for Realizing SCP

A framework for realizing the SCP technology is shown in Fig. 2. Given the current version of the software under construction, a syntactical analysis will first be carried out to collect the necessary information. Then, on the basis of this information and the knowledge stored in the knowledge-base the future fragments will be suggested to the developer. Finally, the suggested fragments will be modified, if necessary, and adopted in the next version of the software by the developer.

In order to make the prediction as useful as possible, the key part of the framework is the knowledge-base, which should store sufficient rules indicating what kinds of fragment should be predicted under what condition of the software. The knowledge can be the one on application domain (e.g., banking system, railway control system), on the development method used for constructing the software (e.g., model-driven, agile, SOFL, MSVL), or on the way of combining them together.

4   Framework of SCMP

In addition to being able to applying SCM and SCP individually for different purpose, we can also combine them together to establish an integrated technology called software construction mointoring and predicting (SCMP). The framework of SCM and SCP can be integrated properly to form a framework for SCMP. Such a framework is shown in Fig. 3. Since all of the interesting issues involved in this famework have been discussed previously, we omit further discussion about this integrated framework here.

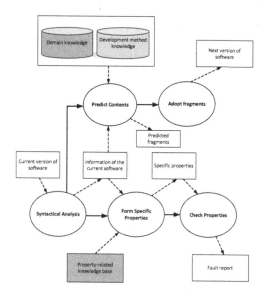

Fig. 3. Framework for SCMP

5 Discussions on Application of SCMP

For the sake of space, this section only discusses the essential ideas of how to apply SCMP to *agile* and *specification-based development* paradigms.

We believe that SCMP has a great potential to help us realize the agile development paradigm with much lower cost than that for *pair programing* in the *eXtreme Programming* (XP) paradigm. We provide a special "pair programming" in which one person is human developer and the other "person" is computer. The major role of the human developer is to create the algorithm (or similar, such as architecture) and data structures necessary for the software, while the role of computer is to point out defects or violation of relevant standards in the algorithm and to act as an assistant to suggest fragments necessary for completing the software with high quality.

In the specification-based development paradigm, building a high quality specification (which can be informal, semi-formal, or formal) is extremely important for the success of the specification-based programming. Our SCMP approach can be applied in both processes.

For constructing the specification, it can be done in the manner that the specification content is basically created by human developer while the defect detection and specification fragment predicting are done by computer as the construction proceeds. We have worked out a predicting method and a prototype tool to support an scenario-based formal specification approach to defining the functionality of a single operation in [7]. The specification is expressed using pre- and post-conditions in SOFL. The basic idea is described briefly as follows. To write the post-condition of a given operation, the user first enters one functional scenario that is represented by the conjunction of a guard condition G and a defining condition D, i.e., $G \wedge D$. Such a scenario reflects a functional requirement: if G holds, the output of the operation must be defined based on D. Then, the tool will analyze the structure of the scenario, focusing on the guard condition G, and then predict the other functional scenarios that will form a logically complete specification for the operation. After the user selects and accepts some or all of the predicted functional scenarios, the tool will automatically predict the other scenarios again if necessary. Such a process is repeated until a consistent and complete specification is constructed.

We can apply this principle to the process of constructing a program based on the specification. Instead of giving a complicated discussion on the principles, we use two examples to illustrate the ideas next.

6   Example 1

We now use a comprehensible example to illustrate how SCMP can support human-machine pair programming in specification-based program construction.

Figure 4 shows a module written in the SOFL specification language for an IC card known as Suica Card for using railway services. In this module, two operations (called processes in SOFL) are specified using pre- and post-conditions. One is *Charge_with_Cash*, describing the service of charging card with cash, and the other is *Charge_from_Bank*, describing the service of charging card directly from the customer's valid bank account. For brevity, we focus on the discussion of how to use human-machine pair programming to construct a program to implement the operation *Charge_with_Cash*.

6.1   For SCM

We require the machine to check the following properties as the program is being constructed:

(1) All items in the specification are properly implemented.
(2) All of the guard conditions in the program can evaluate to true and false, respectively.
(3) All of the loops in the program has an variant to ensure its termination.

To check these properties, they are stored in the knowledge base beforehand. When the program is constructed, the formal specification, the encountered guard conditions and the body of loops in the program will be treated as the relevant information sources that are dynamically obtained either from the specification or from the constructed program fragment. These information sources will be selectively used when a designated property needs to be checked by computer.

For property (1), the data reification laws [8] and the refinement laws [4] are properly applied. Specifically, for each type and operator defined in the specification language, a set of checking rules is defined. Whenever a variable

```
module Charge_Suica_Card;

type
BankAccounts = set of CurrentAccount;

CurrentAccount = composed of
                    account_name: string
                    account_no: seq of nat0
                    password: nat0 * nat0 * nat0 * nat0
                    address: string
                    tel: seq of nat0
                    balance: nat0
                    end;

SuicaCard = composed of
            name: string
            address: string
            tel: seq of nat0
            status: {<student>, <ordinary>, <pensioner>}
            card_no: seq of nat0  /*unique card ID number*/
            start_date: Date  /*issue date */
            commutation_ticket: CommutationTicket  /*for commuting ticket*/
            card_type: string /*e.g., "Suica", "Pasmo", "Icoca" */
            buffer: nat0   /*no greater than 50000 JPY*/
            entrance_station: string  /*recording the station from where the customer entered the station*/
                exit_station: string /*recording the station from where the customer went out the station*/
            end;

var
buffer: nat0;
ext #bank_accounts_file: BankAccounts

process Charge_With_Cash(amount1: nat0, card: Register_Suica_Card.SuicaCard)overlimit_msg1: string | charged_card:
Register_Suica_Card.SuicaCard
ext wr buffer: nat0
pre buffer < 50000   /*the card buffer must be less than50,000 JPY */
post card.buffer + amount1 > 50000 and
     overlimit_msg1 = "Amount is over limit"
     or
     card.buffer + amount1 <= 50000 and
     charged_card = modify(card,  buffer -> card.buffer + amount1)
end_process;

process Charge_From_Bank(password: BankPassword, amount2: nat0, card: seq of nat0)password_wrong_msg: string |
overlimit_msg2: string | charged_card: Register_Suica_Card.SuicaCard
ext wr buffer: nat0
    wr bank_accounts_file: BankAccounts
pre buffer < 50000      /*the card buffer is less than50,000 JPY*/
post (not exists[ acc: bank_accounts_file] | acc.pass_word = password and
     acc.card_no = card.card_no) and password_wrong_msg = "Password is wrong"
     or
     (exists[acc: bank_accounts_file] | acc.pass_word = password and
     acc.card_no  = card.card_no) and
     amount2 + card.buffer > 50000 and
      overlimit_msg2 = "Charge amount is over limit"
     or
      (exists[acc: bank_accounts_file] | acc.pass_word = password and
     acc.card_no  = card.card_no) and
     amount2 + card.buffer <= 50000 and
     charged_card = modify(card, buffer -> card.buffer + amount2)

end_process;
end_module
```

Fig. 4. A module in an IC card system written in SOFL

declared with a type in the specification is declared with a concrete type in the programming language, the corresponding rule will be automatically checked. This principle can be formalized as follows:

$$C_r : S_{items} \to R$$

where S_{items} is the set of all type names and operator names defined in the specification language, R is a power set of rules specifying what to be checked in the corresponding program in the format $condition \to action$, and C_r denotes the mapping from S_{items} to R.

Let us take the type $nat0$ (including zero and positive integers) for example. we can define its rule set as follows:

$C_r(nat0) = \{$

(1) The variable in the program corresponding to the variable declared with $nat0$ in the specification is declared with a concrete numeric type $\to$ Check whether its value is not negative before it is used,

(2) The corresponding variable in the program is declared with non-numeric type $\to$ Issue an warning message,

(3) The corresponding variable is not declared at all in the program $\to$ Issue an warning message.

$\}$

For instance, these rules can be applied for checking in the process of constructing the program for the operation $Charge\_with\_Cash$. Figure 5 shows a snapshot of reporting a potential defect after the line *if (card.getBuffer() + amount1 > 50000) {* is read by the SCM tool on the Eclipse platform. The potential defect is the lack of checking whether the value of variable *amount1* is not a negative integer before this line in the program. To remind the programmer of the potential defect, the SCM tool automatically produces a comment */ * ... * /* starting with a question mark "?", indicating the nature of the defect.

These rules are implemented in the SCM tool based on automatic program analysis techniques [9]. For some rules in the mapping C_r, the checking may not be fully automated. In that case, a lightweight approach will be taken to only issue the warning message for the possibility of potential defects.

For property (2), automatic predicate-based test generation techniques [6] can be used to check whether the guard condition of interest can evaluate to true and false, respectively.

For property (3), program analysis techniques can be applied to check whether a variant updating the loop variables exists or not. For brevity, we omit the examples.

6.2   For SCP

To realize the functionality of SCP, the knowledge base needs to store a set of knowledge expressions in advance. The knowledge base can be perceived as a mapping from the set of program fragment patterns to another set of program

Fig. 5. Snapshot of montoring in constructing the program of operation Charge_with_Cash

fragment patterns that should be more complete towards the final program. Formally, the knowledge base can be abstractly expressed as:

$$K_b : PFP \rightarrow PFP$$

where PFP denotes the set of all possible program fragment patterns. Each pattern shows a certain structure of program fragment. Below will show three examples, respectively.

6.2.1 Predicting for Constructs

Suppose that the user has written the conditional statement like *if (A and B) {...};* which is treated as a program fragment pattern. Based on this pattern, another pattern, such as *if (A and B) {...}; if (A and not B) {...}; if (not A and B) {...}; if (not A and not B) {...};,* can be predicted. Thus, the program is ensured to deal with all of the possible cases started from the initial condition *A and B.* The knowledge can come from specifications, coding standards, coding experience, and the programming language semantics. Of course, the challenge is how to build sufficient knowledge into the knowledge base for all of the possible varieties of program fragment patterns. An incremental approach can be taken to gradually build up such a knowledge base for a specific SCP tool.

Let us use the same operation *Charge_with_Cash* mentioned above as an example to illustrate what can be done by an SCP tool. Suppose the programmer has just written the following line of code:

Fig. 6. Snapshot of predicating in constructing the program of operation Charge_with_Cash

if (card.getBuffer() + amount1 > 50000) {...},

as shown in Fig. 6, the SCP tool will automatically propose the following lines of code as the result of code prediction:

if (card.getBuffer() + amount1 = 50000) {}

if (card.getBuffer() + amount1 < 50000) {}.

The two conditional statements can be merged to form the following line of code if the programmer finds it appropriate:

if (card.getBuffer() + amount1 < = 50000) {}.

The similar approach can be taken to deal with construction predicating of other aspects in programs, such as exception handling and the class structure for enforcing the principle of information hiding in object-oriented programming languages.

7   Example 2

We give two simple examples to show how SCMP can be used to support programming in general.

7.1   Predicting for Exception Handling

The similar approach can be taken to deal with construction predicting for exception handling in programs. As is well known, exception handling is an important mechanism to enhance the robustness of programs, but writing the corresponding program fragments, i.e., *try-catch* statements in programming languages such as C++, Java, C#, can often be forgotten, especially for unexperienced programmers, due to the fact that it does not deal with the main functionality of the program. Further, since writing the corresponding *try-catch* code fragments is also time consuming, many programmers may deliberately avoid writing them. If the *try-catch* statements can be automatically provided by the machine, the programmer's burden will be considerably reduced and the reliability of the program can be significantly improved.

The key to realize this goal is whether the places to produce exceptions and the nature of the exceptions can be automatically identified only based on the program code, because the places are the basis for forming the *try* statement and the nature of the exceptions is the basis for forming the *catch* statements. According to our study of the programming languages mentioned previously, this can be done in most possible situations.

For instance, when the following C++ code is written, the SCMP tool finds that in the *for* loop, the maximum number of loops is represented by variable n whose value is supplied by the user of the program. Also, in the body of the loop, the reference to the vector elements is represented by $x.at(i)$ in which the index i may exceed the size of the vector defined in the declaration of variable x previously. According to C++, the method $at(i)$ is possible to cause the *out_of_rang* exception to occur. Therefore, the SCMP tool can automatically predict the code as shown in Fig. 7 with *try-catch* exception handling statements. In general, such a predicted program fragment needs to be confirmed and possibly be revised by the programmer.

```
#include <vector>
#include <iostream>
#include <stdexcept>
using namespace std;
int main() {
        int a[] = {1, 2, 3, 4, 5};
        vector < int > x(a, a + sizeof(a) / sizeof(a[0]));
        cout < < "Input a number to explore the vector:";
        int n;
        cin > > n;
            for(vector < int > ::size_type i = 0; i < = n; i++) {
                cout < < "x[" < < i < < "] = " < < x.at(i) < < endl;
            }
}
```

7.2 Predicting for Information Hiding

Defining *getter* and *setter* methods (or member functions) for accessing and updating the member variables of a class is a desirable style in object-oriented programming, but when the number of the member variables becomes large, doing so may be time consuming and too tedious for programmers to work

Fig. 7. Snapshot of predicted code for an exception handling

on. To ensure the nature of information hiding for object-oriented programs, the SCMP tool can automatically predict program fargments for the following tasks:

- Set the access restriction of all member variables of a given class to *private*.
- Define a *getter* function for every member variable that returns its value.
- Define a *setter* function for every member variable that updates its value.
- Set the access restriction of every member function of the class to *public*.

After producing the program fragments for these tasks, the programmer should be allowed to modify the code, since some aspects of its details, such as *error messages*, may not be appropriate enough for the tool to produce.

Let us consider the following program fragment as an example. When the writing of this program fragment is finished, the SCMP tool will automatically predict the program fragment as shown in Fig. 8.

```
class BankAccount{
  string id;
  string password;
  int balance;

  BankAccount(){
  id = "";
  password = "";
  balance = 0;
  }
}
```

Fig. 8. Snapshot for predicting information hiding code fragment

8   Related Work

To the best of our knowledge, no research has been proposed or undertaken on
SCMP proposed in this paper. There are some reported work on software project
or progress monitoring, but its focus is on the analysis of project progress, risks,
and other elements in relation to software management rather than verification
of software under construction. There are also some reported studies on software related predicting, but they are concerned with software project budget
predicting or software bug predicting, rather than software fragment predicting
for constructing error-free software.

Having said the above, it does not mean that our idea of SCMP receives
no influence from other people's work. In fact, the principal ideas of SCMP
have benefited from specification-based testing and agile development methods.
The contribution of our SCMP is to form a systematic approach to support
specification-based programming in the *human-machine pair programming* fashion. Therefore, we only give a brief review of the work in relation to the above
topics.

Specification-based testing is mostly explored in test case generation from
formal specifications. Gannon *et al.* proposed a fundamental principle for testing the implementation under test based on algebraic specifications, which is to
choose some instantiations of the axioms and to check whether an execution of
the implementation makes the terms occurring in the instantiations yield results
that satisfy the corresponding axioms [10]. The same principle was also studied
by Bouge et al. [11] and later developed by Bernot *et al.* [12]. Dick and Faivre
proposed an approach to generating test data based on partitioning the conjunction of pre-condition, post-condition, and invariant for a VDM operation of
interest into disjoint sub-relations by means of Disjunctive Normal Form (DNF)

[13]. The similar principles are applied by Legeard *et al.* for test data generation from B or Z notation [14–16], and has been adapted in many test data generation tools, some of which use interactive theorem prover [17,18] and others are fully automated with constraint-logic programming [19] or with heuristics algorithms driven by the syntactical form [20]. TestEra [21] accepts representation constraints for such data structures and generates non-isomorphic test data by using a solution enumeration technique to use propositional constraint solver or SAT engine [22].

Agile development methods emphasize the importance of evolutionary prototyping in order to demonstrate working software to the user as early as possible to allow the user to "join" the development process for decision making and to avoid unnecessary configuration management cost. They support the user-centered, testing-driven, and pair-programming principles and quick releases of software products [1,23,24]. Our studies over the last ten years find that all of the agile methods lack a theoretical foundation and they are heavily dependent on human skills and experiences.

The aim of SCMP is to establish a theoretical foundation to govern the process of human-machine pair programming for specification-based programming or programming in general, and to build efficient tool support based on techniques in artificial intelligence and software engineering. There are many challenging issues to address along this line, but we believe that continuous research and development in this direction will lead to a breakthrough in tackling software crisis we have been experiencing so far.

9   Conclusion and Future Work

Software Construction Monitoring and Predicting (SCMP) for pair programming we proposed in this paper offers a novel and urgently needed technology for improving software productivity and quality. We have discussed its theoretical foundations, challenges, and frameworks. We have also pointed out its potential application in the specification-based programming paradigm. We believe that with the progress of research on SCMP, today's software development will enter a new era that will be characterized by intelligence and automation for significant enhancement of software productivity and quality.

Apart from developing the theoretical and technical details for SCMP, we also believe that extending the capability of SCM to support automatic reverse-engineering for producing documentation of programs under construction will provide considerable benefit for communication between programmers and other stakeholders and for software maintenance. This area is exciting because it is extremely useful for real software development and faces many challenging problems to deal with. Further, the current SCMP technology can be extended to support *pseudocode-based programming* approach. That is, before writing code, a pseudocode reflecting the main and abstract idea of what to be done in the algorithm should be first constructed and then it will be gradually and incrementally refined into code. This is an efficient programming style and therefore should be supported by SCMP as well.

Acknowledgement. *This work was supported by JSPS KAKENHI Grant Number 26240008.*

References

1. Beck, K.: Embracing change with extreme programming. IEEE Comput. **32**(10), 70–77 (1999)
2. Cockburn, A., Williams, L.: The costs and benefits of pair programming. In: Extreme Programming Examined, pp. 223–243. Addison-Wesley Longman Publishing Co., Inc. (2001)
3. Liu, S.: Formal Engineering for Industrial Software Development Using the SOFL Method. Springer, Heidelberg (2014). https://doi.org/10.1007/978-3-662-07287-5. ISBN 3-540-20602-7
4. Morgan, C.: Programming from Specifications. Prentice Hall, Upper Saddle River (1990)
5. Liu, S., McDermid, J.A.: Dynamic sets and their application in VDM. In: Proceedings of 1993 ACM Symposium on Applied Computing, pp. 187–192. ACM Press, February 1993
6. Liu, S.: Testing-based formal verification for theorems and its application in software specification verification. In: Aichernig, B.K.K., Furia, C.A.A. (eds.) TAP 2016. LNCS, vol. 9762, pp. 112–129. Springer, Cham (2016). https://doi.org/10.1007/978-3-319-41135-4_7
7. Li, S., Liu, S.: A software tool to support scenario-based formal specification for error prevention. In: Tian, C., Nagoya, F., Liu, S., Duan, Z. (eds.) SOFL+MSVL 2017. LNCS, vol. 10795, pp. 187–199. Springer, Cham (2018). https://doi.org/10.1007/978-3-319-90104-6_12
8. Jones, C.B.: Systematic Software Development Using VDM, 2nd edn. Prentice Hall, Upper Saddle River (1990)
9. Weiser, M.: Program slicing. IEEE Trans. Softw. Eng. **10**(4), 352–357 (1984)
10. Gannon, J., McMullin, P., Hamlet, R.: Data abstraction implementation, specification and testing. ACM Trans. Program. Lang. Syst. **3**(3), 211–223 (1981)
11. Bouge, L., Choquet, N., Fribourg, L., Gaudel, M.-C.: Test set generation from algebraci specifications using logic programming. J. Syst. Softw. **6**(4), 343–360 (1986)
12. Bernot, G., Gaudel, M.C., Marre, B.: Software testing based on formal specifications: a theory and a tool. Softw. Eng. J. **6**(6), 387–405 (1991)
13. Dick, J., Faivre, A.: Automating the generation and sequencing of test cases from model-based specifications. In: Woodcock, J.C.P., Larsen, P.G. (eds.) FME 1993. LNCS, vol. 670, pp. 268–284. Springer, Heidelberg (1993). https://doi.org/10.1007/BFb0024651
14. Legeard, B., Peureux, F., Utting, M.: Automated boundary testing from Z and B. In: Eriksson, L.-H., Lindsay, P.A. (eds.) FME 2002. LNCS, vol. 2391, pp. 21–40. Springer, Heidelberg (2002). https://doi.org/10.1007/3-540-45614-7_2
15. Legeard, B., Peureux, F., Utting, M.: Controlling test case explosion in test generation from B formal models. Softw. Test. Verif. Reliab. **14**, 81–103 (2004)
16. Utting, M., Legeard, B.: Practical Model-Based Testing: A Tools Approach. Morgan Kaufmann, Burlington (2007)
17. Helke, S., Neustupny, T., Santen, T.: Automating test case generation from Z specifications with Isabelle. In: Bowen, J.P., Hinchey, M.G., Till, D. (eds.) ZUM 1997. LNCS, vol. 1212, pp. 52–71. Springer, Heidelberg (1997). https://doi.org/10.1007/BFb0027283

18. Burton, S.: Automated Testing from Z Specifications. TR YCS-2000-329. University of York, UK (2000)
19. Lúcio, L., Samer, M.: 12 technology of test-case generation. In: Broy, M., Jonsson, B., Katoen, J.-P., Leucker, M., Pretschner, A. (eds.) Model-Based Testing of Reactive Systems. LNCS, vol. 3472, pp. 323–354. Springer, Heidelberg (2005). https://doi.org/10.1007/11498490_15
20. Donat, M.R.: Automating formal specification-based testing. In: Bidoit, M., Dauchet, M. (eds.) CAAP 1997. LNCS, vol. 1214, pp. 833–847. Springer, Heidelberg (1997). https://doi.org/10.1007/BFb0030644
21. Khurshid, S., Marinov, D.: TestEra: specification-based testing of java programs using SAT. Autom. Softw. Eng. **11**(4), 403–434 (2004)
22. Khurshid, S., Marinov, D., Shlyakhter, I., Jackson, D.: A case for efficient solution enumeration. In: Giunchiglia, E., Tacchella, A. (eds.) SAT 2003. LNCS, vol. 2919, pp. 272–286. Springer, Heidelberg (2004). https://doi.org/10.1007/978-3-540-24605-3_21
23. Manifesto for agile software development, August 2001
24. Abrahamsson, P., Salo, O., Ronkainen, J., Warsta, J.: Agile software development methods: review and analysis. Espoo 2002, vol. 478. VTT Publications (2002)

Dataset Diversity for Metamorphic Testing of Machine Learning Software

Shin Nakajima[✉]

National Institute of Informatics, Tokyo, Japan
`nkjm@nii.ac.jp`

Abstract. Machine learning software is non-testable in that training results are not available in advance. The metamorphic testing, using pseudo oracle, is promising for software testing of such machine learning programs. Machine learning software, indeed, works on a collection of a large number of data, and thus slight changes in the input training dataset have a large impact on training results. This paper proposes a new metamorphic testing method applicable to neural network learning models. Key ideas are *dataset diversity* as well as *behavioral oracle*. Dataset diversity takes into account the dataset dependency of training results, and provides a new way of generating follow-up test inputs. Behavioral oracle monitors changes of certain statistical indicators as training processes proceed and is a basis of metamorphic relations to be checked. The proposed method is illustrated with a case of software testing of neural network programs to classify handwritten numbers.

1 Introduction

Machine learning using statistical methods, such as a deep neural network (DNN) [10], is basically searching for appropriate learning parameter values with respect to a given set of data, a training dataset. Machine learning programs are solving numerical optimization problems, and it is not easy to check whether resultant parameter values are correct. Correctness, in practice usually, may be evaluated in view of inference results or service quality.

From software engineering viewpoints, product quality of machine learning software must be guaranteed. Learning parameter values may be incorrect if programs are buggy. An issue here is testing whether a machine learning program is implemented correctly with respect to its design specifications, describing functional behavior to solve numerical optimization problems. Those programs are, however, non-testable [22], because trained learning parameter values are not known in advance. If those values are already known, running machine learning computer programs, actually training programs, is not necessary. We may use such known parameter values to implement inference programs that work on new data.

Conventional software testing methods implicitly assumes that some correctness criteria are available as test oracles [2], and are not applicable to

© Springer Nature Switzerland AG 2019
Z. Duan et al. (Eds.): SOFL+MSVL 2018, LNCS 11392, pp. 21–38, 2019.
https://doi.org/10.1007/978-3-030-13651-2_2

non-testable programs in a naive manner. Alternatively, we make use of pseudo oracles [7], in which a kind of weak notion of correctness criteria plays a key role. As such weak correctness criteria, gold-standard oracles use execution results of programs other than the current test target.

Metamorphic testing (MET) [5] adapts an approach similar to the gold-standard oracle in that execution results of a program are employed as correctness criteria. The MET method is a framework of calculating a new follow-up test data from a given initial data so that two execution results, one with the initial data and another with the follow-up one, satisfy a metamorphic relation. The method is especially effective in testing of numerical computing application programs, and is also successful in testing machine learning classifiers [6,23]. Generating a set of corner-case test data systematically is effective [12] in particular for testing of support vector machines (SVM) (e.g. [3]). However, these methods are not applicable to either a DNN or even a classical neural network (NN) [11], because the optimization problem of NN is non-convex and thus oracles are not apparent. Contrarily, the optimization problem of SVM is convex and gold-standard oracles are easy to define.

This paper investigates a new MET framework applicable to NN, which involves two key ideas of *dataset diversity* and *behavioral oracle*. The proposed framework is explained by using a case of testing NN machine learning programs, written in Python, to classify handwritten numbers.

In the following, the first two sections introduce background materials; Sect. 2 explains the basic MET framework, and Sect. 3 summarizes problems of neural network machine learning. Section 4 proposes a new MET framework applicable to software testing of neural networks of non-convex optimization problem. Section 5 illustrates a case for testing NN machine learning programs. Finally, Sect. 6 presents discussions including comparison with related work, and Sect. 7 concludes the paper.

2   Metamorphic Testing

Software testing [2] is accompanied with an implicit, often forgotten, assumption that correctness criteria are known. Let $f(x)$ be a test target program or system under test (SUT)[1]. Usually, a correct value C^a for an input value of a is known from functional specification documents or as a theoretical value. Then, software testing of $f(x)$ is checking whether the computation result $f(a)$ is equal to the known expected value of C^a.

If such correctness criteria are not known, $f(a)$ may be checked against some concrete value R^a instead of C^a. Such an R^a is a *golden output*, an execution result of a certain program other than the current SUT. Because R^a is just an execution result of program, its correctness is not guaranteed, but can still be used as a certain criterion.

Several approaches are known for obtaining such a correct value R^a. An *N-version programming* approach relies on constructing multiple programs to

---

[1] Programs are regarded as functions for simplicity.

satisfy a given functional specification. Different development teams work independently, in some cases, using different programming languages, which avoids contaminating programs with similar faults, and thus raises reliability levels of R^a. The method is conceptually exploring a design space to result in variant implementations, and thus relies on *design diversity*.

Data diversity [1] is a notion orthogonal to design diversity so as to obtain input data for a given test target program $f(x)$. This is especially effective for numerical programs. For example, if $f(x)$ refers to a program to implement a trigonometric function $sin(x)$, then various input test data can be systematically derived thanks to characteristics of $sin(x)$. We consider here $sin(a + b) = sin(a)sin(\pi/2 - b) + sin(\pi/2 - a)sin(b)$. This re-expression of $sin(a + b)$ leads to four different test inputs for a certain combination of a and b. From a viewpoint of testing $sin(x)$, the above re-expression provides a way to obtain various test inputs, which can basically be considered exploring input data space. In data diversity, re-expression formulae may provide relations that execution results must satisfy. However, the notion of test oracle is not recognized explicitly; the above example involves five calls to $sin(x)$, each with a different test input data.

Metamorphic testing (MET) [5] is an alternative way for introducing pseudo oracles, which is proposed initially to conduct software testing of numerical programs as well. It is a framework of calculating a new follow-up test data from a given initial data so that two execution results, one with the initial data and another with the follow-up one, satisfy a metamorphic relation (MR). MET shares the notion of data diversity in that MET provides a method to explore input data space, but has characteristics as a testing method more usable than the data diversity proposed in [1]; the follow-up data generation takes into account of MRs, which is related to pseudo oracle. However, both the data diversity approach of [1] and the MET provide ways to exercise data space to search for various test inputs systematically. We, in this paper, call *extended data diversity*, or just *data diversity*, this characteristics of data space exploration, as compared with design diversity.

Generally, MET can be conducted iteratively to test the SUT. A new test data, a follow-up test data, is generated systematically from a current test data. Given an m-th test input $x^{(m)}$, a translation function T generates a new follow-up test input $x^{(m+1)}$ such that $x^{(m+1)} = T(x^{(m)})$. The T is derived from functional specifications of $f(x)$ such that an appropriate metamorphic relation $Rel^T(f(x^{(m)}), f(x^{(m+1)}))$ is satisfied. If the relation $Rel^T(f(x^{(m)}), f(x^{(m+1)}))$ is violated for two executions of the same program $f(x)$, one with $x^{(m)}$ and another with $x^{(m+1)}$, then the program $f(x)$ is considered to contain some faults in it. In simple cases, Rel^T can be just an equality,

$$Rel^T(f(x^{(m)}), f(x^{(m+1)})) \stackrel{def}{=} (f(x^{(m)}) = f(x^{(m+1)})).$$

We consider a trigonometric function $sin(x)$ again to explain the basic ideas of MET. For example, $sin(a) = -sin(\pi + a)$ for a certain value a. If we take a as an initial input data $x^{(0)}$ and $T(x)$ to be a function adding π to x, then

$x^{(1)} = \pi + a$. This translation function T is intended to satisfy $Rel^T(y^{(0)}, y^{(1)}) \overset{def}{=}$
$(y^{(0)} = -y^{(1)})$ where $y^{(m)} = sin(x^{(m)})$. For a given a, two executions of $sin(x)$,
one with a and another with $\pi + a$, are compared. If $Rel^T(y^{(0)}, y^{(1)})$ is violated,
we conclude that the program under test $f(x)$, $sin(x)$, contains some faults in
it, because the program does not satisfy the formula that $sin(a) = -sin(\pi + a)$.

Machine learning programs are implementing numerical optimization methods and thus are amenable to MET. MET is, indeed, successful in testing
machine learning classifiers [23], which introduces six metamorphic properties
(MPs) that translation functions satisfy. The MRs are basis of guidelines to
introduce translation functions for classification tasks.

An MP is either additive, multiplicative, permutative, invertive, inclusive, or
exclusive. A dataset, which is input to machine learning, is a set of data points,
and each data point consists of a lot of attributes. Furthermore, each data point is
assigned a supervisor tag[2] of $+1$ or -1. Additive or multiplicative MP generates
a new dataset whose data points are modified such that a constant is added or
multiplied to certain attributes. Permutative MP interchanges chosen two data
points to create a new dataset. Invertive MP inverts all the values of supervisor
tags of either $+1$ or -1. Inclusive MP adds a new data point to the current
dataset, and exclusive MP deletes an existing data point.

3   Machine Learning Problems

We briefly introduce machine learning problems that this paper considers.

3.1   Neural Network Model

A neural network learning model consists of perceptrons. As shown in Fig. 1(a),
a perceptron receives a set of weighted inputs and emits an output signal. Let
x_i be an input signal and w_i be a weight on the i-th input. An output signal y
is calculated as $\sigma(\sum_{i=1}^{d} w_i x_i)$ where an activation function σ is sigmoid.

A classical neural network is a set of perceptrons arranged in two layers.
Figure 1(b) shows such an example which receives D input signals propagated

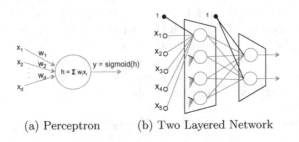

(a) Perceptron   (b) Two Layered Network

Fig. 1. Neural network

---

[2] We assume here supervised learning problems.

into M perceptrons in a middle or hidden layer. The middle layer signals are then fed into the R perceptrons in the output layer. If h and r are activation functions, the k-th output y_k is a non-linear function.

$$y_k(\mathbf{V}, \mathbf{W}; \ \boldsymbol{x}) = r(\sum\nolimits_{j=0}^{M} v_{kj} h(\sum\nolimits_{i=0}^{D} w_{ji} x_i))$$

The formula can be compactly rewritten with $\boldsymbol{x}$ being a D-dimensional vector or a $D \times 1$ matrix.

$$\boldsymbol{y}(\mathbf{V}, \mathbf{W}; \ \boldsymbol{x}) = r(\mathbf{V} \cdot h(\mathbf{W}\boldsymbol{x}))$$

$\mathbf{W}$ is a $M \times D$ matrix consisting of w_{ji}, and $\mathbf{V}$ is a $R \times M$ matrix of v_{kj}. All the elements in both $\mathbf{W}$ and $\mathbf{V}$ are collectively called *learning parameters*.

Learning with respect to a given training dataset is basically a numerical optimization problem. Let $\{\langle \boldsymbol{x}^n, \boldsymbol{t}^n \rangle\}$ be a training dataset of size N where $\boldsymbol{x}^n$ are D-dimensional vectors representing data points and $\boldsymbol{t}^n$ are R-dimensional vectors of supervisor tags. Optimal parameters are those minimizing an error function E.

$$\langle \mathbf{V}^*, \mathbf{W}^* \rangle = arg \min_{\mathbf{V}, \mathbf{W}} \ E(\mathbf{V}, \mathbf{W}; \{\boldsymbol{x}^n, \boldsymbol{t}^n\})$$

Together with obtained parameters, $\boldsymbol{y}(\mathbf{V}^*, \mathbf{W}^*; \ \boldsymbol{x})$ is a function to infer an output tag for a given data point $\boldsymbol{x}$.

In the above, E is an error function defined using another function ℓ.

$$E(\mathbf{V}, \mathbf{W}; \{\boldsymbol{x}^n, \boldsymbol{t}^n\}) = \frac{1}{2} \sum_{n=1}^{N} \ell(\boldsymbol{y}(\mathbf{V}, \mathbf{W}; \ \boldsymbol{x}^n), \ \boldsymbol{t}^n)$$

The function ℓ provides a measure to represent how much a calculated output $\boldsymbol{y}(\mathbf{V}, \mathbf{W}; \ \boldsymbol{x}^n)$ differs from an expected supervisor tag value $\boldsymbol{t}^n$. ℓ can take various forms, and one such example ℓ may be defined as a square of a distance between two vectors such that $\ell(\boldsymbol{u}, \boldsymbol{v}) = \|\boldsymbol{u} - \boldsymbol{v}\|^2$.

An inference function $\boldsymbol{y}(\mathbf{V}^*, \mathbf{W}^*; \ \boldsymbol{x})$ with obtained learning parameter values may be over-fitting to the training dataset. Therefore, another dataset, a testing dataset $\{\langle \boldsymbol{x}^m, \boldsymbol{t}^m \rangle\}$, must be prepared, which is different from the training dataset. The inference function is applied to each data point $\boldsymbol{x}^m$ to check whether an inferred tag reproduces a given tag $\boldsymbol{t}^m$. All such results produce an error rate, which describes how often the inference function miss-infers. The obtained learning parameters $\langle \mathbf{V}^*, \mathbf{W}^* \rangle$ are appropriate if an error rate is smaller than a certain given threshold value, such as 95%, demonstrating a criterion. This criterion is determined in view of required service quality.

3.2   Loss and Accuracy

An NN machine learning problem in the previous section is considered as a *declarative* functional specification of NN machine learning software; it is indeed solving a problem of finding optimal values for learning parameters. In particular, an NN learning is a non-convex optimization problem of a non-linear error function E.

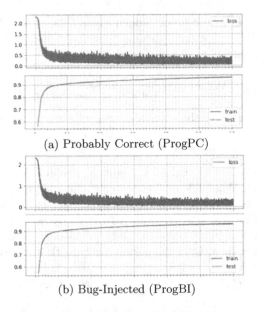

(a) Probably Correct (ProgPC)

(b) Bug-Injected (ProgBI)

Fig. 2. Loss and accuracy

Software testing works on programs, which implements algorithmic ways to solve the declarative problem. Below briefly introduces characteristics of such algorithmic solutions so as to understand why testing NN programs is difficult.

A standard approach to searching for a set of learning parameter values is a gradient decent method (e.g. [11]). The method iteratively calculates new values starting from a given initial set of parameter values, $\langle \mathbf{V}_0, \mathbf{W}_0 \rangle$.

repeat {
$$\mathbf{V}^{new} \; = \; \mathbf{V}^{old} \; - \; \eta \nabla_v E;$$
$$\mathbf{W}^{new} \; = \; \mathbf{W}^{old} \; - \; \eta \nabla_w E$$
} **until** (*converge* $\vee$ *timeout*)

where η is a learning rate and is called a hyper-parameter. Furthermore, a back-propagation method is employed to calculate $\nabla E(\mathbf{V}^{old}, \mathbf{W}^{old})$. The method is more efficient and accurate than numerical differentiations.

Because the optimization problem is non-convex, the search is not guaranteed to reach a global minimum, This characteristic is different from the other machine learning classifiers such as SVM, which is a convex optimization problem and thus is guaranteed to terminate with a global minimum (e.g. [3]).

In NN training, error rates for a training dataset provide a piece of information when to stop the iteration; namely the iteration is terminated when an error rate becomes smaller than a certain threshold. Therefore, NN training procedures usually monitor the two metrics, loss and accuracy. The loss is a graph of an error function. The accuracy, one minus an error rate, is a graph for rates of reproducing correct tags for a testing dataset. Figure 2 shows such graphs as iterations or epochs proceed.

The graphs actually demonstrate that the search converges at a certain desirable point in the solution space because the loss decreases to be almost stable below a threshold, and the accuracy reaches a satisfactory level of higher than 0.95. Figure 2 implies that loss together with accuracy may be good indicators to decide whether NN training processes behave well or not. However, the two metrics are not appropriate indicators in view of software testing.

Firstly, the learning rate η has much impact on graph shapes (e.g. [11]). If η is far from its optimum value, the accuracy, for example, is not acceptable. It implies that the graphs might take undesirable forms even if NN learning programs are correctly implemented with respect to the design specification referring to theoretically correct algorithms.

Secondly, the graphs in Fig. 2(a) and (b) are similar. However, (a) is obtained for probably correct implementation of an NN learning program, while (b) is a monitored result of a bug-injected program. This experiment shows that we can write a buggy program such that the loss and accuracy are not much different from those of a correct implementation. Furthermore, differences in graph shapes are often larger for programs with inappropriate η than the case for a bug-injected one.

Indicators other than the loss and accuracy are needed in view of software testing of NN machine learning programs.

4   Extended Metamorphic Testing

This section proposes a new MET framework applicable to software testing of neural networks of non-convex optimization problem. The framework is based on two key notions, *dataset diversity* and *behavioral oracle*.

4.1   Dataset Diversity

Machine learning programs work on a training dataset whose size is as large as more than ten thousands. Training results, learning parameter values, are sensitive to the size N. Furthermore, the results are also sensitive to *distributions* of data in the training dataset. Two datasets DS_1 and DS_2 with the same size N may lead to different training results if their distributions are different.

Software testing with a series of input dataset, that slightly differ from each other, may be effective to enable corner-case testing. Note that standard code coverages focusing on control aspects [2] are inadequate, because control flows in machine learning programs are not complicated and thus such coverages are readily satisfied with any non-trivial datasets (e.g. [12]).

Dataset diversity is a notion based on the observation that data distribution in a training dataset is significant. Imagine we have M number of dataset DS_j ($j = 1, \cdots, M$). Their sizes are all same (N), but data distribution in DS_j is not same. It introduces an idea of conducting software testing with M different datasets DS_j. In addition, corner-case testing would be possible with carefully chosen such a group of datasets. Although DS_js are not same with each other, they have to be *similar* in view of a given machine learning task at hand. Generating DS_j randomly does not make sense, because these datasets do not refer to the same learning tasks anymore. A question here is how we obtain such a *good* dataset.

Our approach is introducing the notion of dataset diversity into MET, because its follow-up test data generation method provides a systematic way to obtain appropriate new test data. In particular, we assume that metamorphic relations, which translation functions must obey, are *equality*.

A translation function T, in the case of dataset diversity, is extended as below. Let $D^{(m)}$ be a training dataset, which is also a test input to a machine learning program $f(X)$ of test target; $f(X)$ is a program to implement algorithmic solution of numerical optimization problem as discussed in Sect. 3.2. Under dataset diversity, a follow-up dataset $D^{(m+1)}$ is such that

$$D^{(m+1)} = T(D^{(m)}, f(D^{(m)})),$$

where $f(D^{(m)})$ refers to a training result for $D^{(m)}$. $D^{(m+1)}$ is so chosen to have a data distribution slightly different from $D^{(m)}$. A series of datasets can be calculated starting with a certain initial dataset $D^{(0)}$. As seen from the above discussion, dataset diversity is a kind of data diversity, which is apparent when we regard a dataset as a set-valued data. Dataset diversity, however, is important, because our focus is exploring different data distributions in dataset, but not exploring simply data values.

In our previous work on software testing of SVM [12], we adapted *reduce margin*, an instance of *inclusive* metamorphic property [23], to introduce new data points into $D^{(m+1)}$; the new data are to be located close to a separating hyper-plane for $D^{(m)}$. Such a hyper-plane can, indeed, be calculated from $f(D^{(m)})$, where $f(D^{(m)})$ is a training result and refers to a piece of information to define a separating hyper-plane. We can create a new data point x located close to a hyper-plane for $D^{(m)}$ and obtain a follow-up dataset such that $D^{(m+1)} = D^{(m)} \cup \{x\}$. Namely, the distribution of data points in $D^{(m+1)}$ is slightly modified with respect to $D^{(m)}$, and is potentially effective because such a new x close to a separating hyper-plane can be a corner-case. Note that we are able to know that a data point is, indeed, close enough to a separating hyper-plane only after we conduct classifying $D^{(m)}$.

Because machine learning problems that NN works on are different from those with SVM, we must find appropriate ways to calculate follow-up dataset $D^{(m+1)}$ with taking into account the training results for $f(D^{(m)})$. We will study in Sect. 5 an NN learning problem of MNIST dataset.

4.2 Behavioral Oracle

SVM is a convex optimization problem, formulated as Lagrangian (e.g. [3]), and the search is guaranteed to reach a global minimum. When an optimization process or training terminates, resultant Lagrange multipliers are guaranteed to provide a piece of information defining an optimized separating hyper-plane.

Therefore, after the programs terminate, metamorphic relations can be applied to comparing of those parameters defining the hyper-planes.

NN learning is, on the other hand, a non-convex optimization problem, and thus a learning program is not guaranteed to terminate with a desirable minimum. As explained in Sect. 3.2, monitoring program executions is practically an effective way to know how learning proceeds.

Recall that training is actually an iterative process of finding parameter values $\langle \mathbf{V}^*, \mathbf{W}^* \rangle$ so as to minimize an error function $E(\mathbf{V}, \mathbf{W}; \{\boldsymbol{x}^n, \boldsymbol{t}^n\})$. The multi-dimensional space to be searched is dependent on a set of $\{\boldsymbol{x}^n, \boldsymbol{t}^n\}$, particularly on the distribution of $\{\boldsymbol{x}^n\}$ in the dataset; training dataset has much impact on search space *shapes*.

The search method, SGD (e.g. [11]), is empirically known to be robust enough; an appropriate minimum, although it may be a local minimum, can be found in most cases if it starts with appropriate initial search points. A training program to implement the SGD correctly may also be robust even for a *distorted* dataset that the techniques using dataset diversity (Sect. 4.1) generates. We further expect that buggy training programs may not be robust enough because their behavior is faulty.

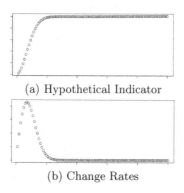

(a) Hypothetical Indicator

(b) Change Rates

Fig. 3. Shape of indicator graph

As discussed with Fig. 2, however, loss and accuracy are not good indicators. Now, an issue is to find appropriate indicators to be monitored. Imagine that a certain *good* indicator is identified. Such an indicator may qualitatively take a form of graph in Fig. 3(a) as epochs evolve, because training programs converge in a certain way. A differentiated graph (Fig. 3(b)) is easy to see changes.

Since the number of those learning parameters is quite large, choosing just a few learning parameters out of them as indicators is difficult. We choose some statistics calculated from a set of learning parameters as indicators. If $\alpha(e)$ refers to such a statistic at an epoch e, then $g[\alpha](e)$ defined below is a graph in Fig. 3(b). Recall that graphs show qualitative trends.

$$g[\alpha](e) = \alpha(e+1) - \alpha(e)$$

When a number of epochs of interest is N_E, a measure function $\mathcal{F}(g_1, g_2)$ is defined as a normalized squared distance of two such graphs.

$$\mathcal{F}(g_1, g_2) = \frac{1}{N_E} \sum_e |g_1(e) - g_2(e)|^2$$

It essentially shows how two graphs are similar. For example, two graphs are mostly identical if the value is acceptably small.

We extend equality metamorphic relations in the original MET with the above measure function. We introduce a meta-parameter ϵ referring to an upperbound reference to consider that two graphs can be considered identical. Below shows a general case of behavioral oracle where more than one statistic α make sense as indicators.

$$Rel^T(f(D^{(m)}),\ f(D^{(m+1)})) \stackrel{def}{=} \bigwedge_{\alpha} (\mathcal{F}(g[\alpha^{(m)}],\ g[\alpha^{(m+1)}]) \leq \epsilon)$$

The relation refers to graphs, not computational results returned when a program is forced to be terminated. The graphs show how indicators change their values in course of execution, or show behavioral aspects of the indicators. The relation is thus called *behavioral oracle* in this paper.

In our proposed MET framework, appropriate translation functions allowing dataset diversity is identified such that accompanied metamorphic relations refer to behavioral oracle based on the graph distances. When such an equality relation within a threshold ϵ is violated, we conclude that the machine learning program under test may have faults in it.

5   A Case Study

As a demonstration of the proposed MET framework, whose key aspects are dataset diversity and behavioral oracle, this section illustrates a case of testing NN machine learning programs.

5.1   MNIST Dataset Problem

MNIST dataset is a standard benchmark of classifying handwritten numbers. It contains a training dataset of 60,000, and a testing dataset of 10,000. The machine learning task is to classify an input sheet into one of ten categories, from 0 to 9. A sheet consists of 28×28 pixels, each taking a value between 0 and 255 to represent a gray scale. Pixels to represent ink are black, and blurry stroke is gray in particular. The others constitute white backgrounds. A handwritten number appears as a specific pattern of these pixel values.

In our experiments, NN learning model is, as in Fig. 1(b), so defined that its hidden layer is 50-dimension while the input is 784-dimension and the output is 10-dimension. Thus, the total number of learning parameters is 39,700. The matrix $\mathbf{W}$ consists of all the weights input to perceptrons in the hidden layer and $\mathbf{V}$ refers to the weights input to those in the output layer. A training program returns a set of optimal parameter values $\mathbf{W}^*$ and $\mathbf{V}^*$ to consist of 39,700 weights. Since the number is large, checking individual parameter values does not make sense. Some statistics to calculate from these learning parameter values are candidates of indicators used in metamorphic relations.

5.2   Follow-Up Input Generation

Because numbers are handwritten, some part of pen strokes is blurry, which might confuse the classification task. It implies that a new dataset $D^{(m+1)}$, which is almost the same as $D^{(m)}$, but changes some pixel values to be blurry, will be more difficult than $D^{(m)}$ to classify, and thus that such a $D^{(m+1)}$ may be appropriate as an input dataset for corner-case testing of learning programs.

This needs a systematic method to choose pixels whose gray scale values are to be changed. Those pixels are determined with an auxiliary function G_o^K in Fig. 4. Then, follow-up test input takes a form below with an appropriate translation function T and the function G_o^K.

$$D^{(m+1)} = T(D^{(m)}, G_o^K(\mathbf{V}^{(m)}, \mathbf{W}^{(m)}))$$

where $\mathbf{V}^{(m)}$ and $\mathbf{W}^{(m)}$ refer to obtained learning parameter values against the training dataset of $D^{(m)}$.

As shown in Fig. 4, the function G_o^K calls another function $top(K, \ell, \mathbf{M})$. It receives a weight matrix $\mathbf{M}$, either $\mathbf{V}$ or $\mathbf{W}$, and returns a set of indices for the K largest weight values in the ℓ-th column of $\mathbf{M}$.

In the current NN learning model, $\mathbf{V}$ refers to a matrix of weights that are input to the output layer. When o refers to one of the ten output signals $(o = 0, \ldots, 9)$, $top(K, o, \mathbf{V})$ collects indices of matrix elements whose values are

$$
\begin{aligned}
&G_o^K(\mathbf{V}, \mathbf{W}) \overset{\triangle}{=} \{ \\
&\quad H = top(K, o, \mathbf{V}); \\
&\quad \textbf{return } \bigcup\nolimits_{h \in H} top(K, h, \mathbf{W}) \\
&\}
\end{aligned}
$$

$$
\begin{aligned}
&top(\text{K}, \ell, \text{M}) \overset{\triangle}{=} \{ \\
&\quad X = \{ \, abs(M_{\ell j}) \, \}; \; Idx = \emptyset; \\
&\quad \textbf{repeat } K \textbf{ times } \{ \\
&\quad\quad A_{\ell J} = max(\, X \,); \\
&\quad\quad X = X \backslash \{ \, A_{\ell J} \, \}; \;\; Idx = Idx \cup \{ \, J \, \} \\
&\quad \} \\
&\quad \textbf{return } Idx \\
&\}
\end{aligned}
$$

Fig. 4. Pixel search

in the top K-th largest. G_o^K calls *top* again for $\mathbf{W}$, which eventually returns a set of input signal indices that have much impacts on the final classification result o.

Figure 5 depicts a small portion of MNIST training dataset. Each number sheet shows a pattern of pixels, representing ink strokes, but has some black dots superimposed on the patterns. These dots are in the resultant set of $G_4^5(\mathbf{V}^*, \mathbf{W}^*)$, where $\mathbf{V}^*$ and $\mathbf{W}^*$ refer to weight parameter values trained against the original MNIST training dataset.

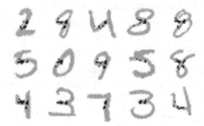

Fig. 5. Obtained pixels

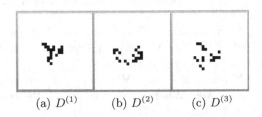

(a) $D^{(1)}$ (b) $D^{(2)}$ (c) $D^{(3)}$

Fig. 6. Changes in patterns of dots

An appropriate translation function T generates the (m+1)-th follow-up input dataset $D^{(m+1)}$ using both $D^{(m)}$ and $G_4^5(\mathbf{V}^{(m)}, \mathbf{W}^{(m)})$. For example, the input signal values identified by $G_4^5(\mathbf{V}^{(m)}, \mathbf{W}^{(m)})$ are increased by some specified amount if they are on the stroke pattern (cf. Fig. 5). We selectively choose a particular pixel or a set of pixels to change value(s). This is similar to *additive* or *multiplicative* metamorphic properties introduced in [23].

In both the SVM [12] and NN cases, distributions in training datasets used as test input are changed, which can be regarded as instances of *dataset diversity*. Note that affected distributions are different in NN case from those in SVM. In the SVM case, the distribution of data points in dataset is modified, and thus is considered as an instance of *inclusive* MP. In the NN case, the number of data points in dataset is not changed, but the distribution of a particular pixel value is affected. Roughly speaking, a mean value of such an affected pixel is changed from the one before applying the modification.

Starting with the original MNIST training dataset as $D^{(0)}$, $D^{(m+1)}$ is calculated using weight matrices of the training result for $D^{(m)}$. Figure 6 shows three patterns of identified dots. The number of dots increases and the dot patterns become spread widely. Pixel patterns in $D^{(m+1)}$, consecutively obtained, are more blurry than those in $D^{(m)}$. Therefore, some $D^{(n)}$ are expected to be effective for corner-case testing of the target training program of NN learning.

5.3   Metamorphic Relations

As mentioned in Sect. 5.1, some statistics to calculate from weight parameter values ($\mathbf{V}^*$ and $\mathbf{W}^*$) are candidates of indicators used in metamorphic relations. We may consider means or variances of weights. Such statistics are defined for $\mathbf{W}$ as below, where $w_{ji}(e)$ refers to a weight value at an epoch index e. $\mathbf{W}(e)$ is, indeed, changed as epochs proceed[3].

The number of weights is $M \times D$ because $\mathbf{W}$ is an $M \times D$ matrix. The means $\mu_w(e)$ and variances $\sigma_w^2(e)$ are below.

$$\mu_w(e) = \frac{1}{M \times D} \sum\nolimits_{j,i} w_{ji}(e)$$

$$\sigma_w^2(e) = \frac{1}{M \times D - 1} \sum\nolimits_{j,i} ((w_{ji}(e))^2 - (\mu_w(e))^2)$$

Indicator graphs, $g[\mu_w](e)$ and $g[\sigma_w^2](e)$, are constructed using the above statistics.

Specifically, after initial trial experiments, we found two indicators were useful, $\alpha \in \{\mu_w, \sigma_v^2\}$. The metamorphic relations for the behavioral oracle takes a form below.

$$R^T = \bigwedge\nolimits_{\alpha \in \{\mu_w,\, \sigma_v^2\}} (\mathcal{F}(g[\alpha^{(m)}],\ g[\alpha^{(m+1)}]) \leq \epsilon)$$

where ϵ is an externally given small value.

Figure 7 is indicator graphs[4] of $g[\sigma_v^2](e)$ for the program, a probably correct program (ProgPC), for which Fig. 2(a) is graphs of its loss and accuracy. Figure 8 is those graphs for a bug-injected program (ProgBI) showing the behavior of the program whose loss and accuracy are found in Fig. 2(b).

In both Figs. 7 and 8, the top graphs are $g[\sigma_v^2](e)$ with its input data of the original MNIST training dataset (referred to as $D^{(0)}$). The middle graphs are monitored results with the first follow-up dataset $D^{(1)}$ and the bottom refers to the case with the second follow-up dataset $D^{(2)}$. These datasets are calculated with the method described in Sect. 5.2 where the condition to obtain strengthening dots is G_4^3 (see Fig. 6).

Comparing two series of graphs indicates that the top and middle graphs take almost similar forms, but that the bottom graphs are different. Specifically,

---

[3]   Statistics for $\mathbf{V}$ are similar.
[4]   Discussions on $g[\mu_w]$ are similar.

the bottom graph for ProgBI (Fig. 8) is distorted. We may say that an indicator graph $g[\sigma_v^2](e)$ discriminates between ProgPC and ProgBI executed with the second follow-up dataset $D^{(2)}$.

This discussion is, however, inadequate in view of software testing. When we conduct software testing, only one test target program, either ProgPC or ProgBI, is available. An appropriate question is whether a series of follow-up datasets can detect some potential faults in a test target program. We compare below three graphs within Fig. 8. The graphs in Fig. 7 are mostly similar, not showing any distortion.

Of the three graphs in Fig. 8, the first and second are similar in their shapes, while the distortion in the third graph is apparent as compared with the second. ProgBI may violate the metamorphic relation $Rel^T(f(D^{(1)}), f(D^{(2)}))$, which implies that the program may have some faults in it.

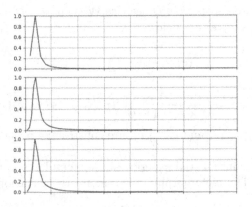

Fig. 7. Indicator graphs for ProgPC

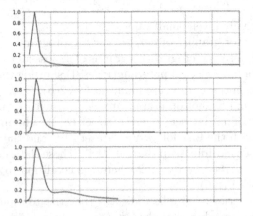

Fig. 8. Indicator graphs for ProgBI

Although the discussion is qualitative because of inspecting graphs, calculating a distance of two graphs, $\mathcal{F}(g_1, g_2)$ introduced in Sect. 4.2, allows quantitative measures. In the discussions below, α refers to σ_v^2.

For the program ProgPC, the distances between the specified indicator graphs in Fig. 7 are here.

$$\mathcal{F}(g[\alpha^{(0)}],\ g[\alpha^{(1)}]) = 0.000798$$
$$\mathcal{F}(g[\alpha^{(1)}],\ g[\alpha^{(2)}]) = 0.001544.$$

The measures for the program ProgBI (Fig. 8) are shown below.

$$\mathcal{F}(g[\alpha^{(0)}],\ g[\alpha^{(1)}]) = 0.002236$$
$$\mathcal{F}(g[\alpha^{(1)}],\ g[\alpha^{(2)}]) = 0.010771.$$

Although the absolute values are not significant, the measures for ProgPC (Fig. 7), when calculated, are small. It implies that the indicator graphs for ProgPC are almost the same, which is exactly what our inspection concludes.

For ProgBI (Fig. 8), however, $\mathcal{F}(g[\alpha^{(1)}],\ g[\alpha^{(2)}])$ is about five times larger than $\mathcal{F}(g[\alpha^{(0)}],\ g[\alpha^{(1)}])$. It indicates that the difference in shapes is large between the second and third graphs of ProgBI. If we set ϵ to 0.002, then we can say that ProgBI violates the metamorphic relation $Rel^T(f(D^{(1)}), f(D^{(2)}))$, and thus that the program may contain faults.

6   Discussions

Machine learning programs are solving certain numerical optimization problems. They fall into a category of scientific programming, which is one of the target areas of the original metamorphic testing (MET) method [5,6].

MET is, indeed, successful in testing machine learning classifiers. In particular, applying MET to testing of support vector machines (SVM) is well studied. [23] introduces six general metamorphic properties that translation functions must satisfy for machine learning classifiers. Further, [12] illustrates a systematic way to derive such translation functions from declarative SVM problem definitions. These studies show that using MET needs a thorough understanding of functional specifications of test targets. It is the same as cases of software testing in general (e.g. [2]); deriving test input data concerns much with and needs knowledge on functional specifications of programs under test.

Dataset diversity, briefly mentioned in [13], is presented clearly in Sect. 4.1. Data points in dataset take numerical values and dataset diversity changes data values as well, the latter of which essentially concerns with extended data diversity. Dataset diversity, furthermore, takes into account those characteristics of machine learning problems in that the input is a set of data, not a single data value, but consisting of a large number of data. Deriving follow-up tests in Sect. 5, indeed, concerns with functional specifications of target programs and also takes into account the machine learning tasks of interest, classifying handwritten numbers in the example.

With regard to quality of machine learning software, we may think of two distinct notions, service quality and product quality [14]. Service quality may be considered good when an accuracy of inference is better than expected, even if programs may contain faults. If our interest is service quality, then we do not care much whether training programs have faults or not. Contrarily, product quality comes from software engineering viewpoints. We eliminate faults from programs as much as possible. This paper put focus on product quality of training programs of NN machine learning and discussed a new metamorphic testing framework based on dataset diversity and behavioral oracle.

Existing work on testing machine learning software mainly concerns with service quality. DeepTest [21] takes an approach to high service quality. It employs a notion of *neuron coverage* [17] to guide generation of new training datasets. Given a training dataset, DeepTest first identifies a set of inactive neurons in a DNN model and then generates a new training dataset to activate such inactive neurons. The method is concerned with debugging *DNN models* more than implemented training programs. Identifying such metrics suitable for discussing service quality is in general an important future issue.

The follow-up input generation method discussed in Sect. 5.2 relies on finding pixels to have much impact on some specific output signals. In an extreme case, the pixel can be single, and is similar to the one pixel fooling method. The method [20] solves an optimization problem to find a particular pixel so that inference programs mis-infer in such a specified manner. The method is an instance of black-box attacks, described below, just looking at input and output signals without using any internal information of learning models. Our method is based on a deterministic graph search algorithm making use of the knowledge about the NN learning model at hand, and thus is more efficient than methods to solve optimization problems.

In machine learning research, a notion similar to dataset diversity has been studied in regard to *dataset shift* [18]. [4] uses diversity in training dataset to make active learning efficient. Research in dataset shift mainly concerns with devising robust machine learning algorithms even if training and testing datasets have different probabilistic distributions.

An adversarial example [19] is a well-elaborated data that fools DNN inference programs; they mis-infer when such an input data is given. Therefore, in general, responding appropriately to adversarial data is important in view of achieving high service quality. Existing work on adversarial attack is categorized into two [15]. The first makes use of detailed knowledge of the neural network characteristics (e.g. [9]). The second relies on input and output signals only, and is called black-box attacks [16]. Black-box attacks are more general than those using detailed knowledge, and thus are potentially applicable to a wide variety of machine learning problems. However, computational costs are high because they solve numerical optimization problems (e.g. [20]).

In summary, although motivations are different, adversarial attacks may generate exotic datasets that might be effective for corner-case testing as well. Our follow-up input generation method in Sect. 5.2 is tackling a problem similar to the one pixel fooling method [20]. It is actually demonstrating that two research areas, adversarial attacks and follow-up test generations, are quite related.

7 Concluding Remarks

The case in Sect. 5 was successful in that the proposed method was able to show some anomalies in a bug-injected program. The success is not always the case because software testing cannot guarantee that programs are free from bugs [8].

In order that software testing is a practical method for providing informal assurance on the quality and reliability of programs, we definitely need a method to generate a wide variety of test cases systematically. We conjecture that the proposed approach can be effective in software testing of machine learning programs.

Acknowledgment. The author expresses his sincere thanks to Professor T.Y. Chen (Swinburne University) for valuable comments on an early draft. The author is partially supported by JSPS KAKENHI Grant Number JP18H03224.

References

1. Ammann, P., Knight, J.C.: Data diversity: an approach to software fault tolerance. IEEE TC **37**(4), 418–425 (1988)
2. Ammann, P., Offutt, J.: Introduction to Software Testing. Cambridge University Press, Cambridge (2008)
3. Bishop, C.M.: Pattern Recognition and Machine Learning. Springer, Boston (2006). https://doi.org/10.1007/978-1-4615-7566-5
4. Brinker, K.: Incorporating diversity in active learning with support vector machines. In: Proceedings of 20th ICML, pp. 59–66 (2003)
5. Chen, T.Y., Cheung, S.C., Yiu, S.M.: Metamorphic testing - a new approach for generating next test cases. HKUST-CS98-01, The Hong Kong University of Science and Technology (1998)
6. Chen, T.Y., et al.: Metamorphic testing: a review of challenges and opportunities. ACM Comput. Surv. **51**(1), 1–27 (2018). Article no. 4
7. Davis, M.D., Weyuker, E.J.: Pseudo-oracles for non-testable programs. In: Proceedings of ACM, pp. 254–257 (1981)
8. Dijkstra, E.W.: The Humber Programmer - ACM Turing Award Lecture (1972)
9. Goodfellow, I.J., Shelens, J., Szegedy, C.: Explaining and harnessing adversarial examples. CoRR abs/1412.6572 (2014)
10. Goodfellow, I., Bengio, Y., Courville, A.: Deep Learning. The MIT Press, Cambridge (2016)
11. Haykin, S.: Neural Networks and Learning Machines, 3rd edn. Pearson India, Noida (2016)
12. Nakajima, S., Bui, H.N.: Dataset coverage for testing machine learning computer programs. In: Proceedings of 23rd APSEC, pp. 297–304 (2016)

13. Nakajima, S.: Generalized Oracle for testing machine learning computer programs. In: Proceedings of SEFM Workshops, pp. 174–179 (2017)
14. Nakajima, S.: Quality assurance of machine learning software. In: Proceedings of GCCE 2018 (2018, to appear)
15. Narodytska, N., Kasiviswanathan, S.P.: Simple black-box adversarial attacks on deep neural networks. In: Proceedings of CVPR Workshop, pp. 1310–1318 (2017)
16. Papernot, N., McDaniel, P., Goodfellow, I., Jha, S., Celik, Z.B., Swami, A.: Practical black-box attacks against machine learning. In: Proceedings of Asia CCS 2017, pp. 506–519 (2017)
17. Pei, K., Cao, Y., Yang, J., Jana, S.: DeepXplore: automated whitebox testing of deep learning systems. In: Proceedings of 26th SOSP, pp. 1–18 (2017)
18. Quinonero-Candela, J., Sugiyama, M., Schwaighofer, A., Lawrence, N.D. (eds.): Dataset Shift in Machine Learning. The MIT Press, Cambridge (2009)
19. Szegedy, C., et al.: Intriguing properties of neural networks. CoRR abs/1312.6199 (2013)
20. Su, J., Vargas, D.V., Sakurai, K: One pixel attack for fooling deep neural networks. CoRR abs/1710.08864 (2017)
21. Tian, Y., Pei, K., Jana, S., Ray, B.: DeepTest: automated testing of deep-neural-network-driven autonomous cars. In: Proceedings of the 40th ICSE, pp. 303–314 (2018)
22. Weyuker, E.J.: On testing non-testable programs. Comput. J. $25(4)$, 465–470 (1982)
23. Xie, X., Ho, J.W.K., Murphy, C., Kaiser, G., Xu, B., Chen, T.Y.: Testing and validating machine learning classifiers by metamorphic testing. J. Syst. Softw. $84(4)$, 544–558 (2011)

Research Review on Web Service Composition Testing

Zhoujie Du[1,2(✉)] and Huaikou Miao[1,2]

[1] School of Computer Engineering and Science, Shanghai University,
Shanghai, China
duzhoujie@163.com
[2] Shanghai Key Laboratory of Computer Software Testing and Evaluating,
Shanghai, China

Abstract. Web services composition is designed to achieve a more powerful and large-grained services with organic synthesis of different Web services. In order to guarantee the quality of the Web services composition, comprehensive and adequate testing of the Web services composition is required. However, the dynamic and distributed characteristics of Web services combination make its testing technology and method have big difference with the traditional software testing and bring a large of challenges. In this paper, we summarize and analyze the definition, architecture, testing methods and testing techniques of Web service composition. In addition, we also analyze and prospect the progress of Web services combination testing.

Keywords: Web service · Web service combination · Testing methods ·
Testing techniques

1 Introduction

Web service is a software system that is unified by URI (unified resource identification). As a special kind of service, Web Service not only realizes the characteristics of remote access through network, but also inherits the characteristics of autonomy, openness and self-description of general services. Different organizations have different understandings and definitions of Web service. However, there was no fixed definition of Web service so far. There are descriptions and understandings of Web service by several large enterprises and institutions in the following.

The definition of the W3C organization: Web Service was a software application that used URI to unify the identification, and used XML to defined, described interfaces and binding. Web service is found and used by other users by network, and finished interacts through XML messages at last. The definition of SUN Company: Web service should include the following five characteristics. First, it provides an external interface, which exchange data in XML format. Second, the out Web service can be access by Web. Third, the services among the systems support relationship are loosely coupling. Fourth, if Web services completed registered and the services would be located. Fifth, it supports the specification of Web service protocol and implemented message communication used XML. The definition of IBM Company: Web service is the smallest

© Springer Nature Switzerland AG 2019
Z. Duan et al. (Eds.): SOFL+MSVL 2018, LNCS 11392, pp. 39–51, 2019.
https://doi.org/10.1007/978-3-030-13651-2_3

application module that has the characteristics of self-description, self-contained and support matched with other Web service. Web service can implement description, search, publish and be called anywhere in the network environment. Whether service users asked for simple application requests or complex composite business processes, it can accomplish tasks by calling the Web Service. When a Web service deployed successfully, any other application can be discover and invoke deployed service through a UDDI service registry to accomplish the task. The definition of HP Company: Web service is a service that solves user's problems through Internet, and transacted and processed tasks on behalf of applications and users.

Web services are platform independent, low coupled, self-contained and programmable. Web applications that describe, publish, discover, coordinate, and configure them using an open XML (a subset of the standard General Markup Language) for developed distributed interoperable application. The rise of Web service has been accompanied by the introduction of service-oriented software architecture (SOA), which provided a new paradigm of standards-based, loosely coupled, cross-platform distributed computing on the Internet. Individual Web service provides specific capabilities, and in order to meet the needs of users, more and more real projects need to integrate and combine multiple Web services to provide comprehensive and complex value-added services composite Web services. Members of the service can communicate with each other and handle user operations and requests in a logical manner. With the further development of Internet application, Web service composition is bound to get concerned and applied widely. In order to ensure the quality of composite Web services, model checking is used to verify the conformance and the related properties of the model of composited Web services with its implementation [1, 2]. Comprehensive and adequate testing for the implementation of Web services composition is required. However, because of the dynamic and distributed characteristics of the Web service composition itself, many traditional software-testing technologies have lost their original effectiveness to the Web service composition. Therefore, we need to study the new testing techniques and methods for the Web service composition, to provide a powerful support for the performance, function and reliability of composite service.

At present, Web service portfolio testing has been studied and some research results have been obtained. The purpose of this paper is to systematically summarize and analyze the existing methods and techniques for the testing of Web services composition. Although some researchers have made a definite analysis and discussion about this problem, we think that this problem is still needed further investigating. Web services testing analyzed and summarized by Hong, Bozkurt and Ebrahim [2–5], however, the research status of Web services composition testing had not been emphasized. Web services composition testing has discussed by categorized the test methods completed by Rusli et al. [6] in long before. After that, there were other study results have been published. Therefore, it is necessary to make a new and comprehensive survey summary.

The structure of this paper is as follows. The first section, introduces the definition of web services in detail; The second section, analyzes and discusses Web service architecture; The third section summarizes and describes several web service composition testing methods; The fourth section, introduces and summarizes testing techniques about Web service composition; The last section summarizes and prospects about the research on web service composition testing.

2   Analyzed and Studied the Web Service Architecture

In general, Web Service used to invoke remotely. The traditional software testing technology could not be simply apply to measure tested work of Web service application system; In view of this, Zhang and Zhang [7] proposed a criteria contain J attribute indicators such as accuracy, fault tolerance and testability, which can be used to evaluate the reliability of Web services application systems. According to this reliability criterion, we can effectively eliminate inappropriate Web services.

Testing framework [8] based on JUnit used in unit testing of application system widely. Therefore, Zhang et al. [9] had attempted to propose a suitable unit test framework for BPEL, which included Composition Model, test architecture, life cycle management and so on. In this framework, the test function divided into several test process (TP) and control TP process (CP), with the life cycle of TP be controlled by TP provided beginTest and endTest.

Dong et al. [10] put forward an automated testing framework based on WSDL. Given that the message contained in WSDL didn't fully assist the test work, so the WSDL extension specification was referenced in this framework, it included four other extensions such as into/output (I/O) dependency. According to these extensibility, this test framework could deduce test data and operation flow, formed a complete test case at last.

Akehurst et al. [11] defined constraint for each object in BPEL based on the Object Constraint Language (OCL), and implement the Java classes of verification based on these restrictions. At the same time, Akehurst established a Meta-model based on specification of BPEL, and the associations in objects defined by BPEL were represented as UML diagrams.

Looker et al. [12] put forwarded a test method based on Fault-Injection. Because of the SOAP packet format used by Web services to exchange messages was based on XML, Looker was able to add an injector server between the service provider and the service requester by modified the container of the Web service, to monitor all messages exchange between the service provider and the service requester, and according to the setting of test cases insert a message that might cause an error into a normal message, and observed whether the Web service under tested could correctly correspond to messages with exceptions, such as error content, missing content, and so on.

Offutt et al. [13] proposed to use data disruption to generated different SOAP parameter data, and analyzed the messages in response to verified correctness of the peer-to-peer Web service. Offutt et al. [13] proposed three methods of disruption message: Data Value Perturbation (DVP), RPC Communication Perturbation (RCP), and Data Communication Perturbation (DCP). DVP was mainly based on the parameter message format defined by WSDL, such as string or numeric value, through the method of boundary value analysis to generate different parameter messages. RCP used mutation operators to calculated parameters to generate different new parameter messages. DCP is a Web services testing that used XML messages to send messages. Offutt et al. [11] modified the contents of XML messages in SOAP by some rules, These XML messages are used to test the access to a Web service's database whether correct or not.

Chen, Li and Zhang [14] proposed a development and test environment that could flexibly define the process – WSCE, which enables the combination of Web services to carry out in a very convenient way. In this architecture, Yu proposed two mechanisms such as virtual partner and inspector service, to help developers verify the correctness of the process or not.

Tsai and Paul et al. [15] put forwarded a test framework of WSTF (Web Services Testing Framework). This framework was based on agent technology and could be applied to SOA architecture system.

3   Web Service Composition Testing Methods

Web services testing methods had many similarities to traditional software testing and there are differences of them. Web service testing required service requesters, service providers, and UDDI accomplished together. The comparative results between Web service testing and traditional software testing were shown in Table 1.

Compared with the traditional software testing and the characteristics of the Web service composition itself, the tester could not have all the test information, because of the component service is black box test, the tester could not have the source code of the component service, so it was unable to get all the features of a component service and build a rich test model. Therefore, in the test of Web service composition, some scholars have studied how to expand document parsing or build model technology to obtain sufficient test information. Furthermore, the dynamic binding of Web service composition makes it difficult to predict the operating environment and behavior of the combined service, the generation of test prediction was difficult, however, traditional software testing techniques target and software behavior were predictable, static, and non-distributed, so it could not be applied to Web service composition testing. As with traditional software, the compositional Web service also has a software evolution process, but the evolution process was dynamic, the changes didn't limited to internal structure or variable of the program. Instead, component services are upgraded or replaced, business processes are replaced, and interface information for component services is changed, and these evolutionary processes exist throughout the operation of the system, so additional information is needed to support the regression test. As we could see from the comparison above, the difference between Web service comparison testing and traditional software testing exists in the whole process of testing. According to the testing process, this paper summarized and analyzed the technologies and methods of Web composite service testing in different stages.

Table 1. Traditional software testing and web service composition testing

Item	Traditional software testing	Web services composition testing
Testers	Dedicated test team or software developer	Service integrator
Regression testing	Offline, static evolution; can sufficient understand software changes and regression testing timely	Online; dynamic evolution; difficult to grasp the evolve situation of component services, and there will also be evolution in the process of regression testing; additional information is needed to support regression testing
Software evolution	Static evolution, changed internal structure or variables of program	Dynamic evolution, component services upgraded or replaced, business processes changed, and component service interface information changed
Test client	Software itself	Built component service, such as proxy, etc.
Test coverage	White-box testing and black-box testing for software	Black-box testing for component services; white-box testing for BPEL documents
Test distribution	Centralized, multi-stage testing	Distribute, remote, multi-stage testing
Test execution	Off-line test	Runtime test
Test model	Have software code and could build rich test model according to software characteristic	Do not have source code of component services, testers could build controlled and observable test models only
Test prediction	The behavior of software is predictable, and it is easier to generate test predictions	It is difficult to predict state and behavior of composite services and generate test predictions difficultly
Test type	Unit test, integration test, system test, acceptance test, regression test, etc.	Unit test, integration test, system test, regression test

4   Web Service Composition Testing Techniques

One of the major features of Web services testing is that most testers do not gain the source code. Therefore, all white-box testing relevant techniques are not used. How to test Web services effectively is becoming a hot issue in Web services research.

4.1   Web Service Composition Testing Based on EH-CPN

The Web composite service testing technology based on EH-CPN mainly have the following steps: First of all, we analyzed the data flow in the extended colored Petri net through OWL-S document transformation, and find the used pairs for all of the variable definitions and the used chains for the definitions of corresponding input and output. Next, the definition that all input and output used chain extended to get an executed test sequence. The above test sequences meet the full definition of use coverage criteria. The test data was generated by the test case generated method that combined the equivalence class partition and condition constraint, then combined test data and test sequences to generated test cases. Input the OWL-S document in the developed test tool of TWCS, and TWCS would generated a colored Petri net that extended levels corresponding to OWL-S, then find out used chains that all the input and output of all variables and extend it to an executable test sequence. Input the number of test cases corresponding to each test sequence, and completed the generated the number of test cases was same. Using the proxy occupancy program in .NET Framework SDK to generated proxy for each Web service; finally, the proxy service be used to completed the call of the corresponding Web service, executed the test case and completed the test of the Web service.

4.2 Web Service Composition Testing Based on Mutation

The idea of mutation testing was to detect the effectiveness of test cases by embedded errors in the program and guided the generation, selection and reduction of test cases, and to achieve the purpose of tested at last. It was a test method based error. The idea of mutation testing was proposed based on white box testing first, and the object of mutation testing was program code. With the development of mutation testing, the idea of mutation testing could be using for Web services testing, and guided test cases generation, selection and reduction of test cases [16].

There were a lot of research in Web service mutation test [17]; this section introduced the mutation-based Web service composition testing, which takes following steps to test the Web composite service workflow: Firstly, parsed OWL-S document and extracted information such as the type, format, and etc. input format accepted by the composite Web service to be tested and workflow. Generated the initial test data set based on the type, format, and other information of the input format, and test data could be generated randomly or by the usual methods of boundary value analysis or equivalence class division. At the same time, the workflow information of Web composite service is analyzed and found nodes that meet the variation conditions in the workflow. According to the corresponding change rules, changed the OWL-S document information to generate new mutant that injected the wrong to the original composite service to be wrong version of service composition.

After completed the above work, entered the same test data should be returned different test results executed the original service composition and the variant Web service composition, because of the workflow of the service composition was changed. If the output was different, the variant was killed and the test data could identify the wrong Web service combination and it was an effective test data. The test data should be retained and added an effective test data set for later test data selection. It indicated that the test data is invalid if the output results were same, the new test data should be redesigned or repeated above tests and expanded the effective test data set [18].

4.3   Web Services Testing Based on Interactive Behavior Specifications

This section introduces test problem of service interaction from the service requester's point of view. A Web service tested method that leverages interaction behavior specification. The main steps were as follows:

Firstly, the behavior specification of Web service should be described correctly. UML is widely used in system modeling in industry and academia because its simplicity and standardization, using sequence diagrams of UML and the behavior rules of Web services described by OCL. It is provided to the service requestor in the form of an XML file (XML metadata interchange) together with WSDL document, and XML documents could be generated automatically by existed UML modeling tools.

Secondly, used an extended state machine model of ELTS described the behavior rules of the service. Added semantic information based on traditional LTS generated extended ELTS to strengthen the function of LTS described data flows. ELTS was based on the implementation relationship in a certain formal defined, and introduced a new implementation relationship through generated algorithm of traditional LTS. Through this new relationship given corresponding test data generated algorithm and test cases with test coverage. It used to test whether the interaction behavior specification was consistent with service implementation or not [19].

4.4   Testing Techniques Based on Formal Methods

Test case generated based on formal method divided into model detector and formal analysis technology. The test case generation method based on model detector was an input model, which converts the service combination described of BPEL into a certain detector, and used formal method to describe the demand model that the composite service should satisfy, used them as input of the model detector to produces test cases. Most of the detectors used in the study included Nu SMV, SPIN and BLAST [20–23]. Test case generated method based on formalized analysis technology, which described by BPEL through a formal method or other formalization methods, such as Petri nets, automata or process algebra, then use existed analytical techniques of the formalized method to generated test cases, such as references [24–26].

Petri net was a modeling and analysis tool for distributed systems. It was a directed graph composed of repository, change, and directed arc. It was easy to described sequence, concurrency, conflict and synchronization of the processes and components in the system. Compared with other system models, true concurrency was a unique advantage of Petri network. The modeling method based on Petri net could described all kinds of control flow in the combinatorial process, but it could not reflect overall state of composited service directly.

Automaton was a mathematical model with clear semantics. It was suitable for describing discrete input and output systems. The system has a limited state, different states represent different meanings. In actual needs, the system could complete prescribed tasks in different states and transfer to another state. The automaton modeling method could described internal state of Web service composition directly, but it could not described interaction behavior between two services. The ability to described concurrent activities in composite process was limited, and there was a space explosion problem. Process algebra was a formal modeling language based on algebraic methods. A group of operators was used as a process component in grammar. The semantics of the operator was defined by a structured operating semantic method. In this way, a process could be regarded as label transition system (LTS). A significant feature of process algebra was attributed concurrency to non-deterministic, that is, considered the behavior of concurrent processes as all possible interlace behavior of each process. The behavior of concurrent execution was suitable for described concurrent interactive systems. The modeling method of process algebra had strong description ability and rigorous computational reasoning ability, but its expression was more complicated, not intuitive and difficult to understand.

Miao and Chen et al. [27] proposed a testing approach to model-based testing for Web applications, which designed and implemented a web application testing system based on this model. Taking the UML state diagram of Web application as system test model, used UML sequence diagram described test target, and the FSM test model is constructed by transformation and combination, automate generate test case; test model visualization and automation of test execution were come true. It mainly focused on functional testing in article: Model-Based Testing for Web Applications. The performance tests, load testing, usability testing, compatibility testing and security testing not verified.

Qian and Miao et al. [28] proposed a test path generate approach, which illustrated by SWLS (Simple Web Login System) as an example and presented an effective Web testing model for Web software testing. One of the main advantages of this approach is that you did not need to access back-end source code. In order to get PTT from PFD, they proposed a transformation algorithm by this method. They obtained test path from PTT by constructing path expression, and gave a possible way to describe test path in XML. Qian and Miao, which were full link coverage and full-page coverage, also proposed two important concepts. It is possible that a particular link will appear on a page only if provided a specific input in tested. But this web test method is not necessarily adaptable in new case, so it needs to further improve test path generation method, and develop new prototype to re-validate this web test model proposed.

Above several kinds of formal model could described the behavior of the Web service combination well and have relevant technical and tools support, there were some differences only in computational complexity. However, these methods required staff with relevant professional background knowledge and ignored data flow information modeling in combination process. Therefore, the non-formal test case generated method was discussed below.

4.5 Testing Techniques Based on Informal Methods

The informal method [29–51] that it converted control flow, data flow, message flow, behavior, etc. in a composite service described by BPEL and others into a graph model and used search technology and constraint analysis technology generated test cases.

The steps of test case generated method as follows: Firstly, build a model based on some features of Web service composition. Secondly, generated test paths based on model traversal. Thirdly, generated test cases based on constraint condition in above path. The following research work falls into this category.

On studied of test case generated problem in Web service combination, some researchers focus on control flow characteristics of Web service composition. Yuan et al. [29] proposed a BPEL test case generation method based on graph search, which used to deal with concurrent semantics of BPEL. This method described the WS-BPEL program by defined control flow graph (BPEL flow graph, BFG). BFG contained control flow and data stream of BPEL program. Generated test paths by traversed the BFG model, the constraints in test path as the input of constraint parser generated abstract test data and converted it into executable test cases automatically. However, the process of converted BPEL documents to BFG and test paths search process were done manually.

The method proposed by Yan et al. [30] was similar to Yuan's method [29]. They converted the WS-BPEL program into an extended control flow graph (XCFG) and generated test paths based on XCFG, and then used a constraint parser generated test data from test path. However, it is different from the Yuan et al. method that Yan and others used symbolic execution methods to obtain a series of constraints from the test path by invoked component services, but this method produced abstract test case that it needed to be converted to an executable test case manually.

Mei and others proposed a test method based on XPath Rewrite Graph (XRG) [31, 32] that it combined the control flow graph (CFG) and XRG to solved possible integration problem caused by XPath in BPEL process. With the gradual deepening research, some scholars believed that the model based test cases produce techniques same as the method based on path generated test case. This method represents the test data by generated message parameters, but the generated test cases were high redundancy and low error rate. Hou [33] and Ni et al. [34] applied test technology based on message flow in Object Oriented Program (OOP) to Web service combination test first time. Wu and Huang [35] thought that binding internal state of single service, execution sequence among services and behavior of service closely related in runtime. Therefore, references [36–38] proposed an EDSM sequence test model (EFSM-SeTM) for Web service composition. They studied runtime test from the point of workflow view and proposed a scenario-based testing framework for Web service composition.

We summarized and analyzed informal testing method based on model. As shown in Table 2. It is shown that most of above test case generation techniques are semi-automated, even include the technology proposed in running test. Therefore, firstly, How to achieve full automation is a problem that can be further studied. Secondly, no test case generated technology involved Web services and the quality of Web services determined the correctness of entire Web service composition, so it is necessary to test the Web service.

Table 2. Classification of informal methods

References	Model	Focus	Quality of test case	Type	Automated testing
Reference [34]	Message sequence graph	Message flow	Test case accurate, error detect capability low; high redundant	Runtime test	Semi-automatization
				Runtime test	
Reference [35]	State transition diagram; message exchange sequence diagram	Service interchange and dynamic behavior	Without considering the constraint conditions in the path; test case with practical significance can not be obtained	Runtime test	Semi-automatization
Reference [36]	BPEL model	Scene-based	Testing is only based on path; test cases inaccurate; high redundant; error detect capability low	Runtime test	Automation
Reference [37]				Runtime test	Automation
Reference [38]				Runtime test	Automation
Reference [30]	Extended control flow graph	Control flow	Abstract test cases	Static test	Semi-automatization
Reference [31]	Rewrite the graph of Xpath	Data flow	Abstract test cases	Static test	Semi-automatization
Reference [32]			Abstract test cases	Static test	Semi-automatization
Reference [33]	Message sequence graph	Message flow	Higher detection rate than RAND and GS; redundancy is higher	Static test	Semi-automatization

5   Summary and Outlook

It can be known from above analysis that some problem of Web service combination need to be research, although some results have been achieved in this area, which were mainly reflected in the following aspects.

Formal modeling technology of Web services combination need to be developed and researched deeply, such as research on the correlation, fairness and applicability of formal model, further research on the property analysis technology of Web services formal model. It is necessary to research Web services technologies made formal technology provide services and support better.

The quality of test cases was fundamental condition for effective Web service combination testing, which shown that high error rate, low redundancy and high coverage. How to obtain more constraints that can enrich test information generating test cases is a problem needed to be solved in academia and industry today.

Some researchers have been concerned about the runtime binding problem of Web service composition, Ni [34], Wu [35] and Sun et al. [38] designed test automation prototype tools, but they did not elaborated automation level of test technology, or did they verify the relationship between automation and runtime binding issues.

Acknowledgement. This paper is supported by National Natural Science Foundation of China (NSFC) under Grant No. 61572306.

References

1. Duan, Z., Yang, X., Koutny, M.: Framed temporal logic programming. Sci. Comput. Program. **70**(1), 31–61 (2008)
2. Tian, C., Duan, Z., Duan, Z.: Making CEGAR more efficient in software model checking. IEEE Trans. Softw. Eng. **40**(12), 1206–1223 (2014)
3. Hong, Z., Feng, Z.Y.: Collaborative testing of web services. IEEE Trans. Serv. Comput. **5**(1), 116–130 (2012)
4. Bozkurt, M., Harman, M., Hassoun, Y.: Testing and verification in service-oriented architecture: a survey. Softw. Test. Verif. Reliab. **23**(4), 261–313 (2013)
5. Ebrahim, S.M.: A survey of service-oriented architecture systems testing. J. Softw. Eng. Appl. (IJSEA) **3**(6), 19–27 (2012)
6. Rusli, H.M., Puteg, M., Ibrahim, S., Tabatabaei, S.: A comparative evaluation of state-of-the-art web service composition testing approaches. In: Proceedings of the 6th International Workshop on Automation of Software Test (AST), pp. 29–35 (2011)
7. Zhang, J., Zhang, L.-J.: Criteria analysis and validation of the reliability of web services-oriented systems. In: Proceedings of the IEEE International Conference on Web Services, pp. 11–15 (2005)
8. Toure, F., Badri, M., Lamontagne, L.: A metrics suite for JUnit test code: a multiple case study on open source software. J. Softw. Eng. Res. Dev. **2**(1), 1–32 (2014)
9. Zhang, X., Sun, W., Jiang, Z.B.: BPEIAWS unit testing: framework and implementation. In: Proceedings of the IEEE International Conference on Web Services, pp. 103–110 (2005)
10. Dong, W., Tasi, W.T., Chen, Y.: WSDL-based automatic test case generation for web services testing. In: IEEE International Workshop, pp. 215–220 (2005)
11. Akehurst, D.H.: Validating BPEL specifications using OCL. Technical report, University of Kent at Canterbury (2004)
12. Looker, N., Xu, J.: Assessing the dependability of SOAP RPC-based web services by fault injection. In: The Ninth IEEE International Workshop on Object-Oriented Real-Time Dependable Systems, pp. 165–172 (2003)
13. Offutt, J., Xu, W.: Generating test cases for web services using data perturbation. In: ACM SIGSOFT Software Engineering Notes, vol. 29, pp. 1–10 (2004)
14. Chen, Y., Li, Y., Zhang, L.: WSCE: a flexible web service composition environment. In: Proceedings of the IEEE International Conference on Web Services, pp. 428–435 (2004)
15. Tsai, W.T., Paul, R., Yu, L., Saimi, A.: Scenario-based web service testing with distributed agents. IEICE Trans. Inf. Syst. **86**, 2130–2144 (2003)
16. Jiang, Y.: Research on web service workflow variation test technology. Southeast University (2011)
17. Wang, R., Huang, N.: Requirement model-based mutation testing for web service. In: Proceedings of the 4th International Conference on Next Generation Web Services Practices, pp. 71–76 (2008)

18. Bruno, M., Canfora, G., Di Penta, M., Esosito, G., Mazza, V.: Using test cases as contract to ensure service compliance across releases. In: The 3rd IEEE International Conference on Service-Oriented Computing, Amsterdam, Netherlands (2005)
19. Li, B., Zhang, P.: Modeling. Testing and Verification of Combined Services. Science Press, Henderson (2013)
20. Huang, H., Tsai, W.T., Paul, R.: Automated model checking and testing for composite web services. In: Proceedings of the IEEE International Symposium on Object-Oriented Real-Time Distributed Computing, pp. 300–307 (2005)
21. Garcia-Fanjul, J., de La Riva, C., Tuya, J.: Generating test cases specifications for BPEL compositions of web services using SPIN. In: Proceedings of WS-MaTe 2006, pp. 83–94 (2006)
22. Garcia-Fanjul, J., de La Riva, C., Tuya, J.: Generation of conformance test suites for compositions of web services using model checking. In: Testing: Academic and Industrial Conference - Practice and Research Techniques, pp. 127–130 (2006)
23. Zheng, Y.Y., Zhou, J., Krause, P.: A model checking based test case generation framework for web services. In: Proceedings of the International Conference on Information Technology, pp. 715–722 (2007)
24. Li, B., Zhang, W.S., Zhang, X.G.: Describing and verifying web service using CCS. In: Proceedings of the International Conference on Parallel and Distributed Computing, pp. 1571–1576 (2006)
25. Long, H.Y., Ma, D.: Checking compatibility of BPEL4WS based on CCS. In: Proceedings of the International Conference on System Science, Engineering Design and Manufacturing Informatization, pp. 255–258 (2011)
26. Du, Y.H., Tan, W., Zhou, M.C.: Timed compatibility analysis of web service composition a modular approach based on Petri nets. IEEE Trans. Autom. Sci. Eng. **11**(2), 594–606 (2014)
27. Miao, H.-K., Chen, S.-B., Zeng, H.-W.: Model-based testing for web applications. Chin. J. Comput. **34**(06), 1012–1028 (2011)
28. Qian, Z., Miao, H.: Efficient web software testing method. Comput. Sci. **38**(02), 152–155+159 (2011)
29. Yuan, Y., Li, Z., Sun, W.: A graph-search based approach to BPEL4WS test generation. In: Proceedings of the International Conference on Software Engineering Advances (ICSEA), pp. 1–14 (2006)
30. Yan, J., Li, Z., Yuan, Y., Sun, W., Zhang, J.: BPEL4WS unit testing: test case generation using a concurrent path analysis approach. In: Proceedings of the 17th International Symposium on Software Reliability Engineering (ISSRE), pp. 75–84 (2006)
31. Mei, L., Chan, W.K., Tse, T.H.: Data flow testing of service choreography. In: Proceedings of the 7th Joint Meeting of the European Software Engineering Conference and the ACM SIGSOFT International Symposium on Foundations of Software Engineering (ESEC), pp. 151–160 (2009)
32. Mei, L., Chan, W.K., Tse, T.H.: Data flow testing of service oriented workflow applications. In: Proceedings of the 30th International Conference on Software Engineering (ICSE), pp. 371–380 (2008)
33. Hou, S.S., Zhang, L., Lan, Q., Mei, H.J., Sun, S.: Generating effective test sequences for BPEL testing. In: Proceedings of the 5th International Conference on Quality Software, pp. 331–340 (2009)
34. Ni, Y., Hou, S.S., Zhang, L., Zhu, J., Li, Z.J., Lan, Q.: Effective message-sequence generation or testing BPEL programs. IEEE Trans. Serv. Comput. **6**(1), 7–19 (2013). https://doi.org/10.1109/TSC.2011.22

35. Wu, C.S., Huang, C.H.: The web services composition testing based on extended finite state machine and UML model. In: Proceedings of the IEEE International Conference on Service Science and Innovation, pp. 215–222 (2013)
36. Sun, C.A., Shang, Y., Zhao, Y., Chen, T.Y.: Scenario-oriented testing for web service compositions using BPEL. In: Proceedings of the 12th International Conference on Quality Software (QSIC), pp. 171–174 (2012)
37. Zhang, P.C., Leung, H., Li, W.R., Li, X.D.: Web services property sequence chart monitor: a tool chain for monitoring BPEL-based web service composition with scenario-based specifications. IET Softw. **7**(4), 222–248 (2013)
38. Sun, C., Zhao, Y., Pan, L., Liu, H., Chen, T.Y.: Automated testing of WS-BPEL service compositions: a scenario-oriented approach. IEEE Trans. Serv. Comput. **11**, 616–629 (2015)
39. Li, Q., et al.: Service composition and interaction in a SOC middleware supporting separation of concerns with flows and views. J. Database Manag. (JDM) **22**(2), 32–63 (2011)
40. Belli, F., Endo, A.T., Linschulte, M., Simao, A.: A holistic approach to model-based testing of web service compositions. Softw.: Pract. Exp. **44**(2), 201–234 (2014)
41. Herbold, S., Harms, P., Grabowski, J.: Combining usage-based and model-based testing for service-oriented architectures in the industrial practice. Int. J. Softw. Tools Technol. Transfer **19**(3), 309–324 (2017)
42. Chen, C., Zaidman, A., Gross, H.G.: A framework-based runtime monitoring approach for service-oriented software systems. In: Proceedings of the International Workshop on Quality Assurance for Service-Based Applications, QASBA 2011, pp. 17–20. ACM, New York (2011)
43. Gao, H., Li, Y.: Generating quantitative test cases for probabilistic timed web service composition. In: Proceedings of the APSCC, pp. 275–283 (2011)
44. Hallé, S., La Chance, E., Gaboury, S.: Graph methods for generating test cases with universal and existential constraints. In: El-Fakih, K., Barlas, G., Yevtushenko, N. (eds.) ICTSS 2015. LNCS, vol. 9447, pp. 55–70. Springer, Cham (2015). https://doi.org/10.1007/978-3-319-25945-1_4
45. Elqortobi, M., Bentahar, J., Dssouli, R.: Framework for dynamic web services composition guided by live testing. In: Belqasmi, F., Harroud, H., Aguech, M., Dssouli, R., Kamoun, F. (eds.) AFRICATEK 2017. LNICST, vol. 206, pp. 129–139. Springer, Cham (2018). https://doi.org/10.1007/978-3-319-67837-5_13
46. Mei, L., Cai, Y., Jia, C., Jiang, B., Chan, W.K.: Test pair selection for test case prioritization in regression testing for WS-BPEL programs (Report). Int. J. Web Serv. Res. **10**(1), 73(30) (2013)
47. Petrova-Antonova, D., Ilieva, S., Manova, D.: TASSA: testing framework for web service orchestrations. In: 2015 IEEE/ACM 10th International Workshop on Automation of Software Test, pp. 8–12, May 2015
48. Cao, D., Félix, P., Castanet, R.: WSOFT: an automatic testing tool for web services composition. In: 5th International Conference on Internet and Web Applications and Services (2014)
49. Xu, C., Qu, W., Wang, H., Wang, Z., Ban, X.: A Petri Net-based method for data validation of web services composition. In: 2010 IEEE 34th Annual Computer Software and Applications Conference (COMPSAC), pp. 468–476, July 2010
50. Zhang, J., Yang, R., Chen, Z., Zhao, Z., Xu, B.: Automated EFSM-based test case generation with scatter search. In: Proceedings of the 7th International Workshop on Automation of Software Test, 02 June 2012, pp. 76–82 (2012)
51. Shan, N.: Applications research in ultrasonic testing of carbon fiber composite based on an optical fiber F-p sensor. In: Proceedings of SPIE - The International Society for Optical Engineering, 25 October 2016, vol. 9685, pp. 968511–968511-6 (2016)

Verification and Validation

Runtime Verification Method for Social Network Security Based on Source Code Instrumentation

Xiaobing Wang[1], Wenxuan Guo[1], Liang Zhao[1]([✉]), and Xinfeng Shu[2]([✉])

[1] Institute of Computing Theory and Technology and ISN Laboratory,
Xidian University, Xi'an 710071, People's Republic of China
`xbwang@mail.xidian.edu.cn`, `gentlewx@foxmail.com`, `lzhao@xidian.edu.cn`
[2] School of Computer Science and Technology,
Xi'an University of Posts and Communications,
Xi'an 710061, People's Republic of China
`shuxf@xupt.edu.cn`

Abstract. Security of social network is a serious issue that cannot be ignored. In order to improve the situation that most traditional verification methods are not real-time and too complicated, this paper proposes a runtime verification method based on source code instrumentation for social network systems. First, a property related to a social network system's characteristics is formalized as a three-valued propositional projection temporal logic ($PPTL_3$) formula, and based on the formula a monitor is constructed. Then, probes are instrumented into the source code of the system, which capture events and generate the execution trace of the system. The trace is dealt with by the monitor in real-time to check whether the system satisfies or violates the desired property. To illustrate the effectiveness of this method, a case study of an open-source social network system is provided.

Keywords: Runtime verification · Monitor · $PPTL_3$ ·
Social network · Source code instrumentation

1 Introduction

With the development of Internet technology and the growing number of Internet users, people's online social needs are increasing. Social network (SN) has become an important part of people's work and daily life, and SN platforms such as Sina Weibo, WeChat, Facebook, Twitter, Instagram and LinkedIn are well known. As a virtual style of social medium, SN provides people a convenient way of communication and information sharing and greatly reduces the cost of

This research is supported by the NSFC Grant Nos. 61672403, 61272118, 61402347, 61420106004, and the Industrial Research Project of Shaanxi Province No. 2017GY-076.

Z. Duan et al. (Eds.): SOFL+MSVL 2018, LNCS 11392, pp. 55–70, 2019.
https://doi.org/10.1007/978-3-030-13651-2_4

information transfer. With the rapid development of SN, the number of SN users also surges in recent years. According to the second quarter earnings report of Sina Weibo in 2018, the platform's monthly active users had increased to 431 million by the end of June 2018.

The wide use of SN brings a lot of problems concerning security. In fact, SN has the hardest hit by various cyber attacks. As we all know, SN users are likely to share a large amount of information through the platform, including text, pictures, videos and addresses. In certain platforms, it is not difficult for attackers to obtain the information and then use it to perform malicious behaviors. In addition to intentional attacks, security problem of SN may also be caused by the fact that users are not vigilant enough to protect their own privacy. For example, one may set a public view access to personal profile or a too simple password.

So, it is important to ensure security of SN systems. For this reason, we propose an online runtime verification method based on source code instrumentation which aims at improving the correctness and security of SN systems. Runtime verification is a kind of lightweight verification technique. It is only concerned with the execution trace of the system at runtime [1], without the need to model the entire system. Although the technique of runtime verification is relatively novel, it has been applied to various fields such as Web Service [2], the vehicle bus systems [3] and C program's memory overflow detection [4]. For runtime verification of an SN system, we first characterize a desired system property as a $PPTL_3$ [5] formula and construct a monitor according to the property formula. Then, we adopt the technique of source code instrumentation and use probes to capture information of the system's runtime trace. Through monitoring the trace, the monitor reports in real-time if the property is satisfied or violated by the system.

The rest of the paper is organized as follows. The logic $PPTL_3$ and the definition of property monitor are briefly introduced in the next section. Then, Sect. 3 illustrates the specific implementation of the runtime verification method based on source code instrumentation. As a case study of the method, Sect. 4 presents the process of verifying properties of an open-source social network system. Finally, Sect. 5 discusses related work and Sect. 6 suggests future work.

2   Preliminary

Let *Prop* be a finite set of atomic propositions, $B = \{true, false\}$ the Boolean domain and $\Sigma = 2^{Prop}$. An element a of Σ represents a set of holding propositions, e.g. $a = \{p, q\}$ represents that p and q hold while other propositions do not hold. The sets of finite traces $\langle a_1, a_2, \ldots, a_n \rangle$ and infinite traces $\langle a_1, a_2, \ldots \rangle$ on Σ are denoted as Σ^* and Σ^ω, respectively. Let u, v range over finite traces Σ^* and w range over finite or infinite traces $\Sigma^* \cup \Sigma^\omega$. The concatenation of u and w is simply denoted as uw.

$$\varepsilon \stackrel{def}{=} \neg \bigcirc true \qquad more \stackrel{def}{=} \neg\varepsilon$$

$$P;Q \stackrel{def}{=} (P,Q)\, prj\, \varepsilon \qquad \Diamond P \stackrel{def}{=} true; P$$

$$len(0) \stackrel{def}{=} \varepsilon \qquad len(n) \stackrel{def}{=} \bigcirc len(n-1)(n>0)$$

$$\Box P \stackrel{def}{=} \neg\Diamond\neg P \qquad fin(P) \stackrel{def}{=} \Box(\varepsilon \to P)$$

Fig. 1. Derived formulas

Generally, we use capital letters P and Q, possibly with subscripts, to represent PPTL formulas. The syntax of PPTL is defined as followed:

$$P, Q ::= p \mid \neg P \mid P \wedge Q \mid \bigcirc P \mid (P_1, \ldots, P_m)\, prj\, Q$$

where $p \in Prop$, $\bigcirc$ (next) and prj (projection) are temporal operators. As the semantics of PPTL, a formula P may hold on a trace w, denoted as $w \models P$, which is also called w satisfies P. The detail of the semantics is provided in [6]. It is worth pointing out that the express power of PPTL is the same as that of the full regular expressions [7], which is strictly greater than that of LTL.

For convenience, some derived formulas are defined, shown in Fig. 1. The abbreviations $true$, $false$, $\vee$ and $\to$ are defined as usual. The chop construct $P;Q$ holds on a trace that can be divided into two sub-traces where P and Q respectively hold.

Given a PPTL formula P and a trace w, there are only two cases: $w \models P$ or $w \not\models P$. However, this mode of two valued logic is not suitable for the runtime verification scenario. Runtime verification verifies whether a system satisfies a given property, which can be formalized as a logic formula P, by a single execution of the system. At each execution point of the system, obviously, we can only obtain a finite prefix u of the system execution trace, while possible execution traces of the system may be arbitrary extension uw of u. The information of u itself may not be adequate to decide whether or not each possible execution uw satisfies P. For example, a property $Q \stackrel{def}{=} \Box p$ indicates that a proposition p holds all the time. In certain case, like $u = \langle \{p,q\}, \{q\} \rangle$, it can be decided that Q is not satisfied. But in other cases, like $u = \langle \{p,q\}, \{p\} \rangle$, it is not sufficient to make the decision.

To enable runtime verification, we extend the domain of PPTL with an additional truth value $inconclusive$. The extended three valued logic is called PPTL$_3$ [5] and its semantics is defined as follows.

$$[u \models P]_3 = \begin{cases} true, & \text{if } \forall w \in \Sigma^* \cup \Sigma^\omega : uw \models P; \\ false, & \text{if } \forall w \in \Sigma^* \cup \Sigma^\omega : uw \not\models P; \\ inconclusive, & \text{otherwise} \end{cases}$$

To realize runtime verification, we use a $monitor$ to observe finite execution traces and decide whether a given property is satisfied, violated, or uncertain yet. Specifically, a monitor is defined as a finite state machine (FSM).

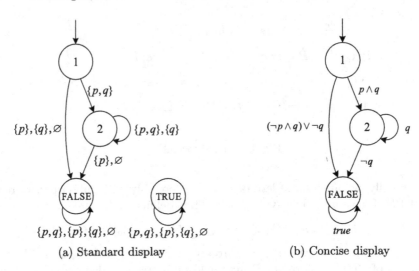

(a) Standard display   (b) Concise display

Fig. 2. Monitor of $p \wedge \Box q$

Definition 1. *A monitor M is a 6-tuple* $(S, \Sigma, \delta, s_0, s_{TRUE}, s_{FALSE})$, *where*

- *S is the state set, which contains two special states* s_{TRUE} *and* s_{FALSE},
- $\Sigma = 2^{Prop}$ *is the alphabet,*
- $\delta : S \times \Sigma \rightarrow S$ *is the transition function, satisfying* $\delta(s_{TRUE}, a) = s_{TRUE}$ *and* $\delta(s_{FALSE}, a) = s_{FALSE}$ *for any* $a \in \Sigma$,
- $s_0 \in S$ *is the initial state, and*
- s_{TRUE} *and* s_{FALSE} *are the accepting states.*

A monitor can accept a finite trace $u \in \Sigma^*$ by one of the two accepting state. For the purpose of runtime verification, we discriminate the two accepting states so that a monitor has two accepting languages. Specifically, the *true language* $L_t(M)$ of a monitor M is the set of traces M accepted by the state s_{TRUE}, and the *false language* $L_f(M)$ of M is the set of traces M accepted by the state s_{FALSE}. A monitor M is called the *property* monitor of a PPTL$_3$ property P, denoted as M^P, if $L_t(M) = \{u \mid [u \models P]_3 = true\}$ and $L_f(M) = \{u \mid [u \models P]_3 = false\}$.

The property monitor M^P of an example property $P \stackrel{\text{def}}{=} p \wedge \Box q$ is depicted in Fig. 2(a) with $Prop = \{p, q\}$. Suppose a system executes for the first two steps and the execution trace observed is $u = \langle \{p, q\}, \{q\} \rangle$. With this trace, the monitor moves to State 2 which is not an accepting state. This means from the current trace u, it is inconclusive whether the system satisfies the property. Then, if the system executes for one more step and the trace becomes $v = u\langle \{p\} \rangle$, the monitor moves to State s_{FALSE} which indicates $v \in L_f(M^P)$. So, it is sufficient to conclude that the system does not satisfy P, no matter how it executes in further steps.

The display of a monitor can be simplified for conciseness. First, the label of each transition, i.e. one or more sets of propositions, can be represented by an

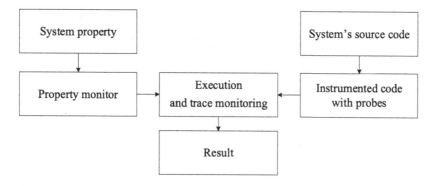

Fig. 3. Process of online runtime verification

equivalent propositional logic formula. By equivalent, we mean the models of the formula are exactly the sets of propositions. In addition, if a state is not reachable from the initial state, we do not need to draw it. The concise presentation of the monitor in Fig. 2(a) is shown in Fig. 2(b).

3   Online Runtime Verification

Generally, runtime verification has two modes: online and offline, which are different in the way how the system's execution trace is constructed. The online mode usually uses source code instrumentation to obtain the trace, while the offline mode constructs the execution trace from offline data of the system. In this paper, we use online runtime verification and monitor the system in real-time. The overview of our verification process is shown in Fig. 3.

This section introduces details of the verification process, which consists of three main steps.

(1) Formalize a desired property of the system as a PPTL$_3$ formula and construct its property monitor;
(2) Insert probes into appropriate positions of the system's source files, which capture events relevant to the property, such as values of relevant variables, and based on these information generate the system's execution trace;
(3) As the system executes, monitor its execution trace constantly with the property monitor and report if the property is satisfied or violated.

3.1   Property Monitor Construction

A property monitor is constructed from a desired system property. Such a property may reflect some rules that the system should follow when executing, or some behavioral specifications of users. Since natural language is sometimes ambiguous in property description, formal languages are used to characterize properties for further verification. In this work, we characterize a system property as a PPTL$_3$ formula. Then, we construct a property monitor based on the

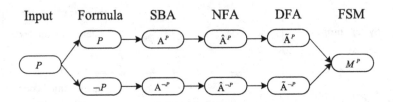

Fig. 4. Process of property monitor construction

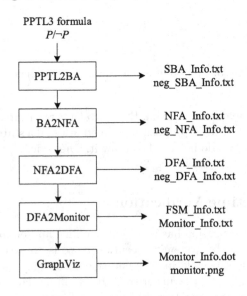

Fig. 5. Sketch of PMG_PPTL

PPTL$_3$ formula. Figure 4 shows the process of the construction, which consists of the following steps. Details of the construction steps are illustrated in [5].

(1) Consider two PPTL$_3$ formulas: the system property P and its negation $\neg P$.
(2) Transform the two formulas into corresponding Stuttered Büchi Automata (SBA) [7,8] A^P and $A^{\neg P}$, respectively, using the theory of normal form.
(3) Construct two Nondeterministic Finite Automata (NFA) $\hat{A}^P$ and $\hat{A}^{\neg P}$ based on the SBA, respectively.
(4) Convert the two NFA to equivalent Deterministic Finite Automata (DFA) $\tilde{A}^P$ and $\tilde{A}^{\neg P}$, respectively.
(5) Multiply the two DFA and make necessary simplification, obtaining the property monitor M^P, which is an FSM.

In order to convert a PPTL$_3$ formula P into its property monitor M^P automatically and reduce errors that may occur during manual conversion, we have developed a tool PMG_PPTL (Property Monitor Generation of PPTL property) that implements the above process. The tool is written in Java and its sketch

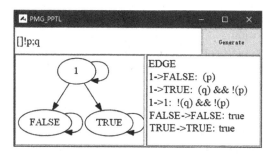

Fig. 6. Interface of PMG_PPTL

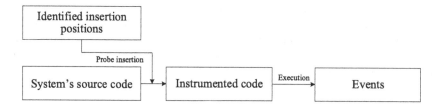

Fig. 7. Flow chart of source code instrumentation

is shown in Fig. 5. The tool saves all generated automaton information in corresponding files, where information of the result property monitor is stored in Monitor_Info.txt.

The tool uses GraphViz to draw the information in the Monitor_Info.txt into the corresponding image. The result of property monitor generation of an example $PPTL_3$ property $\Box \neg p; q$ is presented in Fig. 6.

3.2 Source Code Instrumentation

To enable runtime verification with the property monitor, we need to obtain the execution trace of the system which contains information relevant to the property. For this, we adopt the technique of source code instrumentation.

The source code of the system can be considered as a set of source files. Source code instrumentation is a technique that inserts code fragments, also called probes, into the appropriate positions of appropriate files. The probes capture information needed to verify the system property, and organize the information into a fixed format. The flow chart of source code instrumentation is shown in Fig. 7.

In source code instrumentation, the choice of appropriate positions for probe insertion is very important. We must collect information accurately and minimize the impact of probes on the execution efficiency of the original system. In our method, we first define *events* related to specific aspects of the system property and locate the position of events in the source code. Events are used to determine truth values of atomic propositions in the $PPTL_3$ formula. Then, we insert probes into the corresponding positions of source files so as to obtain the relevant information.

Suppose $Sys = \{file_1, file_2 \ldots\}$ is the set of source files of the system, $Probe = \{probe_1, probe_2, \ldots\}$ is a set of probe names, and $Flag$ is a set of binary variables.

Definition 2. *An event e is a triple $(probe, file, flag) \in Probe \times Sys \times Flag$.*

An event $e = (probe, file, flag)$ indicates that a probe named $probe$ is inserted into the file named $file$ in Sys, and the value of event is captured by a binary variable $flag$. The binary variable is used to determine the truth value of atomic propositions.

When successfully capturing an event, the probe uses the socket interface to transmit it to the property monitor. Specifically, a communication function $send\_rv\_data$ is encapsulated into the source code of the system. Its functionality is to use the socket to send information of the event data, in the form of the above string, to the monitor.

3.3 Runtime Verification

When the instrumented system executes, an execution trace is generated step by step in the form of an event sequence. In each step, the property monitor, which is an FSM, may changes its state according to the event it receives. Once the accepting state s_{TRUE} (resp., s_{FALSE}) is arrived at, the verification terminates and the result is reported that the system satisfies (resp., violates) the property.

As the implementation of runtime verification, we have developed a tool named RV_PPTL (Runtime Verification of PPTL property). The tool is programmed in JAVA and its sketch is shown in Fig. 8.

RV_PPTL reads information of a property monitor, including states and transitions of the FSM, from the output of PMG_PPTL. On the other hand, it receives the sequence of events generated by probes through the receiving server, and translates it into a combination of atomic propositions. According to the state changes of the FSM as the atomic propositions are input, RV_PPTL monitors the execution of the system in real-time. Once an accepting state is arrived at, it terminates and outputs the corresponding verification result.

4 Case Study

In this section, we present a case study of an SN system to illustrate the practicality of the runtime verification method based on source code instrumentation. Since most popular SN platforms such as Facebook and Twitter are not open-source, it is infeasible to insert probe codes. In this case study, we select an open-source SN platform named Elgg, which is developed by PHP+Mysql. The source code of Elgg can be obtained from www.elgg.org. Elgg has basic functionalities as most popular SN platforms, such as tweeting, blogging and adding

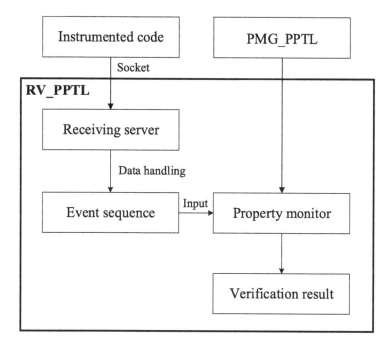

Fig. 8. Sketch of RV_PPTL

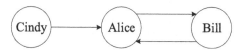

Fig. 9. Relationship of users in the Elgg system

friends. It also allows plugin customization and has good extensibility. So, we consider an Elgg system as the system to be verified.

The Elgg website is deployed in the experimental environment Wampserver and we register 3 users on the website. The relationship between 3 users in the system is shown in Fig. 9. User relationship in Elgg is similar to Twitter's weak relationship that following a user does not require the user's consent, different from Facebook's strong relationship that adding a user as friend needs the user's consent. In Elgg, if Cindy adds Alice to her friend list, then Alice is a friend in Cindy's perspective, but Cindy is not a friend in Alice's perspective. The arrow from Cindy to Alice in Fig. 9 represents this relationship.

With the weak relationship, we can perform runtime verification on some privacy properties of the SN system. If a user does not want to publish some blog to public, or does not expect strangers to see information of his personal profile, he can set the corresponding view access as Friends or Private. However, it is possible that he sets a wrong view access (e.g. Public) because of negligence, and thus a stranger can see the information. To verify whether a user's privacy is leaked, this case study verifies two properties concerning view accesses to user's blog and profile, respectively.

4.1 View Access to User's Blog

Property 1: Alice saves a blog. Then, if and only if a user is Alice's friend, he can view the blog.

The property is relevant to a few events, described informally as follows.

$$e_1 : Alice\ saves\ a\ blog$$
$$e_2 : User\ is\ a\ friend\ of\ Alice$$
$$e_3 : User\ can\ view\ the\ blog\ published\ by\ Alice$$

To capture these events, we insert probes into the source code of the Elgg system. Specifically, we insert probes into save.php (relative path: elgg\mod\blog\actions \blog) and all.php (relative path: elgg\mod\blog\views\default\resources\blog). So, the events are formalized as follows.

$$e_1 = (probe_1, save.php, flag_1)$$
$$e_2 = (probe_2, all.php, flag_2)$$
$$e_3 = (probe_3, all.php, flag_3)$$

Among the probes, $probe_2$ calls the Elgg's function *check_entity_relationship ($guid_one, $relationship, $guid_two)* to check whether the relationship between two users is $relationship (such as 'friend') or not, and assigns a value to $flag_2$. So, it is a universal probe. According to the above events, two atomic propositions p, q are defined as follows.

$$p \stackrel{\text{def}}{=} flag_1 = 1$$
$$q \stackrel{\text{def}}{=} flag_2 = flag_3$$

The truth of the propositions depends on the values of variables $flag_1$, $flag_2$ and $flag_3$. With these propositions, Property 1 is formalized as the following PPTL$_3$ formula.

$$P_1 \stackrel{\text{def}}{=} p \wedge \bigcirc \Box q$$

We input the formula into the tool PMG_PPTL and obtain a property monitor as shown in Fig. 10.

After generating the property monitor and inserting probes into the Elgg system, we use RV_PPTL to read information of the property monitor and monitor the execution of the system. In Elgg, we simulate user operations with registered users: Alice posts a blog but (wrongly) sets its view access as Public, Bill tries to view the blog, and then Cindy tries to view the blog. The event trace is expected to be $\langle e_1, e_2, e_3, e_2, e_3 \rangle$. The verification result is shown in Fig. 11.

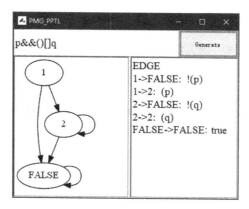

Fig. 10. Property monitor of Property 1

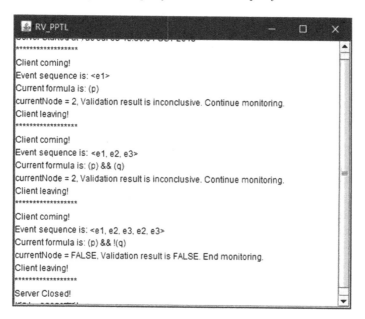

Fig. 11. Verification result of Property 1

Since Bill is a friend of Alice, he can view the blog published by Alice. At this stage, it is insufficient to determine whether the property is satisfied or violated. As the result shows, upon reading the event trace $\langle e_1, e_2, e_3 \rangle$, RV_PPTL outputs *inconclusive* and continues monitoring. Then, when Cindy tries to views the blog, she successes as its view access is Public. In this way, Alice's privacy is leaked. As the result shows, upon reading the event trace $\langle e_1, e_2, e_3, e_2, e_3 \rangle$, RV_PPTL outputs *false* and terminates. This result indicates Property 1 is violated and there are problems in the view access setting of Alice's blog.

4.2   View Access to User's Profile

Property 2: If a user who is logged in is not a friend of Alice, he can only view the Email in Alice's profile, but not other information such as phone number or address. If a logged-in user is a friend of Alice, he can view all the information of Alice's profile.

The property is relevant to the following (informally described) events.

e_2 : *User is a friend of Alice*

e_4 : *User logs in*

e_5 : *Friend can view Email, phone number and address in Alice's profile*

e_6 : *Non-friend can view Email in Alice's profile, but cannot view phone number or address*

To capture these events, we insert probes into the source file login.php (relative path: elgg\vendor\elgg\elgg\actions). So, the events are formalized as follows.

$$e_2 = (probe_2, login.php, flag_2)$$
$$e_4 = (probe_4, login.php, flag_4)$$
$$e_5 = (probe_5, login.php, flag_5)$$
$$e_6 = (probe_6, login.php, flag_6)$$

Notice that we only need to insert probes into the source file login.php, but not the viewing profile, because we invoke relevant functions in login.php to view the profile. So, the probes express the meaning "can view profile without having to wait until a user visits Alice's profile page". According to the above events, four propositions p, q, r and s are defined as follows.

$$p \stackrel{def}{=} flag_2 = 1 \ and \ flag_4 = 1$$

$$q \stackrel{def}{=} flag_5 = 1$$

$$r \stackrel{def}{=} flag_2 = 0 \ and \ flag_4 = 1$$

$$s \stackrel{def}{=} flag_6 = 1$$

The truth of the propositions depends on the values of variables $flag_2$, $flag_4$, $flag_5$ and $flag_6$. With these propositions, Property 2 is formalized as the following PPTL$_3$ formula.

$$P_2 \stackrel{def}{=} \Box((p \rightarrow \bigcirc\Box q)\&\&(r \rightarrow \bigcirc\Box s))$$

The property monitor of P_2 is shown in Fig. 12.

Similar to the verification process of Property 1, RV_PPTL reads the property monitor of Property 2 and monitors the system. We simulate user operations as: Bill logs in and views Alice's profile, then Cindy logs in and views Alice's profile, but Alice forgot to set the view access to her profile. Notice that in Elgg,

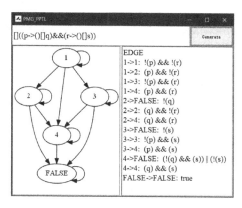

Fig. 12. Property monitor of Property 2

the view access to a user's profile is by default Public. The expected event trace is $< e_2, e_4, e_5, e_2, e_4, e_6 >$ and the monitoring result is shown in Fig. 13.

Since Bill is a friend of Alice, there is no problem that he logs in and sees all the information of Alice's profile. At this stage, therefore, it is insufficient to determine whether Property 2 is satisfied or violated. As the result shows, upon reading the event trace $\langle e_2, e_4, e_5 \rangle$, RV_PPTL outputs *inconclusive* and continues monitoring. Then, when Cindy logs in and views Alice's profile, She can also see all the information since the view access to her profile is the default value Public. In this way, Alice's privacy is compromised. As the result shows, upon reading the event trace $\langle e_2, e_4, e_5, e_2, e_4, e_6 \rangle$, RV_PPTL outputs *false* and terminates. This result indicates Property 2 is violated and there are problems in the view access setting of Alice's profile.

To sum up, this case study shows that the runtime verification method based on source code instrumentation is effective in verifying properties and finding potential security problems.

5 Related Work

As a lightweight verification technique, runtime verification is real-time and can avoid the problem of state explosion. So, it has advantages over testing and model checking in software reliability verification.

Zhou et al. propose a runtime verification method for time-critical system [9]. In their work, the runtime verification tool AnaTempura [10] is used to verify two properties (safety and activity) of a simplified mail sorter system. First, interval temporal logic (ITL) [11] is used to describe system properties and a logic program corresponding to the property is loaded into AnaTempura. Then, interceptors are deployed on the verified system to intercept messages and send messages to the monitor for validation. In the same way, Sulaiman Al Amro et al. use Anatempura to detect virus processes [12]. The logic ITL is used to describe

Fig. 13. Verification result of Property 2

the API invocation behavior, and processes in the operation system with the virus API calling behavior are identified.

JavaMOP [13] is a runtime verification framework of monitoring oriented programming (MOP) developed by the FSL Lab of Illinois at Urbana - Champaign University. It is enforceable for Java programs, supporting the use of formal logic, such as ERE, FSM and LTL, to describe properties. And the formal logic language used to describe properties can be extended by writing the corresponding module. Runtime verification in JavaMop requires writing a mop file that contains the weaved code [14], the definition of events, and a formal description of properties. JavaMop weaves code into methods of Java, instead of manually inserting code into systems. An overview of MOP is presented in [15] with examples to illustrate how JavaMop works.

Researches about runtime verification for the security of SN systems have also been developed in recent years. R. Pardo et al. propose an automata-based approach to evolving privacy policies in Online Social Networks [16]. In their works, a novel formalism of policy automata is presented, and an approach based on runtime verification techniques to defining and enforcing such policies is proposed. The policy automata are used to describe privacy policies and converted to DATEs (Dynamic Automata with Timers and Events) which are symbolic automata aimed at representing monitors in the runtime verification tool LARVA.

The approach and LARVA have been applied to an open source distributed social network Diaspora.

Both of the above methods are real-time and flexible. However, the first two methods can only monitor systems in the local machine, and JavaMop only supports the verification of Java programs. Compared with these two methods, the advantage of our runtime verification method is the support of information transmission through socket interfaces, which enables remote monitoring of systems. In addition, due to the full-regular expressiveness of PPTL, we are able to formalize and verify a larger set of system properties. The last approach also supports socket interfaces and can dynamically change privacy policies of SN systems by monitoring state changes of policy automata. DATEs are similar with property monitors in our method, but they need manual conversion while property monitors can be automatically constructed through PMG_PPTL.

6 Conclusions

With the wide and increasing use of SN, security of SN information and users is under threat and requires verification. In order to solve the problem that most traditional verification methods are too complicated for complex systems and not real-time, this paper proposes a runtime verification method for SN systems based on source code instrumentation. The method is applied to an open-source SN system Elgg and properties concerning privacy of the system are verified. The results show that the method is effective in verifying SN systems and identifying potential security problems. For future work, we are going to adapt the method and apply it to more substantial SN systems.

References

1. Bauer, A., Leucker, M., Schallhart, C.: Runtime verification for LTL and TLTL. ACM Trans. Softw. Eng. Methodol. **20**, 1–64 (2011)
2. Decker, N., Kuhn, F., Thoma, D.: Runtime verification of web Services for interconnected medical devices. In: IEEE International Symposium on Software Reliability Engineering, pp. 235–244. IEEE Press, New York (2014)
3. Zhang, S., He, F., Gu, M.: VeRV: a temporal and data-concerned verification framework for the vehicle bus systems. In: IEEE Conference on Computer Communications, pp. 1167–1175. IEEE Press, New York (2015)
4. Joy, M.M., Mueller, W., Rammig, F.J.: Source code annotated memory leak detection for soft real time embedded systems with resource constraints. In: IEEE International Conference on Dependable, Autonomic and Secure Computing, pp. 166–172. IEEE Press, New York (2014)
5. Wang, X., Liu, D., Zhao, L., Xue, Y.: Runtime verification monitor construction for three-valued PPTL. In: Liu, S., Duan, Z., Tian, C., Nagoya, F. (eds.) SOFL+MSVL 2016. LNCS, vol. 10189, pp. 144–159. Springer, Cham (2017). https://doi.org/10.1007/978-3-319-57708-1_9
6. Duan, Z.: Temporal Logic and Temporal Logic Programming. Science Press, Beijing (2005)

7. Tian, C., Duan, Z.: Expressiveness of propositional projection temporal logic with star. Theor. Comput. Sci. **412**, 1729–1744 (2011)
8. Duan, Z., Tian, C.: A practical decision procedure for propositional projection temporal logic with infinite models. Theor. Comput. Sci. **554**, 169–190 (2014)
9. Zhou, S., Zedan, H., Cau, A.: Run-time analysis of time-critical systems. J. Syst. Archit. **51**, 331–345 (2005)
10. Elkustaban, A., Moszkowski, B., Cau, A.: Specification analysis of transactional memory using ITL and AnaTempura. In: International MultiConference of Engineers and Computer Scientists, pp. 176–181. International Association of Engineers (2012)
11. Moszkowski, B.: Compositional reasoning using intervals and time reversal. Ann. Math. Artif. Intell. **71**, 175–250 (2014)
12. Al Amro, S., Cau, A.: Behavioural API based virus analysis and detection. Int. J. Comput. Sci. Inf. Secur. **10**, 14–22 (2012)
13. Jin, D., Meredith, P.O., Lee, C., Roşu, G.: JavaMOP: efficient parametric runtime monitoring framework. In: IEEE International Conference on Software Engineering, pp. 1427–1430. IEEE Press (2012)
14. Gabsi, W., Zalila, B., Hugues, J.: A development process for the design, implementation and code generation of fault tolerant reconfigurable real time systems. Int. J. Auton. Adapt. Commun. Syst. **9**, 269–287 (2016)
15. Meredith, P.O., Roşu, G.: An overview of the MOP runtime verification framework. Int. J. Softw. Tools Technol. Transfer **14**, 249–289 (2012)
16. Pardo, R., Colombo, C., Pace, G.J., Schneider, G.: An automata-based approach to evolving privacy policies for social networks. In: Falcone, Y., Sánchez, C. (eds.) RV 2016. LNCS, vol. 10012, pp. 285–301. Springer, Cham (2016). https://doi.org/10.1007/978-3-319-46982-9_18

Verification of SysML Activity Diagrams Using Hoare Logic and SOFL

Yufei Yin[1]([⊠]), Shaoying Liu[2], and Yixiang Chen[1]

[1] East China Normal University, Shanghai, China
2571603738@qq.com
[2] Hosei University, Tokyo, Japan

Abstract. During the process of utilizing Model-Based Systems Engineering (MBSE), SysML activity diagrams are often used for designing the software systems and its correctness is likely to significantly affect the reliability of the implementation. However, how to effectively verify the correctness of SysML diagrams still remains a challenge and to the best of our knowledge, there are few tools to support the verification of SysML models. Testing-based formal verification (TBFV) is designed for verifying the sequence code. To solve the problem, we creatively apply the existing TBFV approach into the verification of SysML activity diagrams and established a new approach, called TBFV-M. TBFV-M has ability to verify a SysML activity diagrams meet the user' need. We also propose a method to dealing with invocation, because invocation is very common in the model-driven development process. In this paper, we describe the principle of TBFV-M and present a case study to demonstrate its feasibility and usability. Finally, we conclude the paper and point out future research directions.

Keywords: SysML activity diagrams · TBFV · Test path generation · Formal verification of SysML diagram

1 Introduction

Model-Based Systems Engineering (MBSE) [1] is often applied to design large scale systems, because it can make sure of their reliability and save the cost of modification effectively. The systems modelling language SysML [2, 3] can support effective use of MBSE, for its well-designed mechanism for creating object-oriented models, which can be combined with software, people, material and other physical resources. In MBSE, SysML models are often used as the design for code. It means that whether the SysML model meets the users' requirement in relation to the high reliability of the code. Unfortunately, to the best of our knowledge from the literature, there are few tools to support the verification of SysML models [4, 5] in particular rigorous ways of verification.

Testing-Based Formal Verification (TBFV) proposed by Liu [6–8] shows a rigorous, systematic, and effective technique for the verification and validation of code. TBFV integrated the specification-based testing approach and Hoare logic to verify the correctness of all the traversed program paths during testing. The advantage of TBFV is

© Springer Nature Switzerland AG 2019
Z. Duan et al. (Eds.): SOFL+MSVL 2018, LNCS 11392, pp. 71–88, 2019.
https://doi.org/10.1007/978-3-030-13651-2_5

its potential and capability of achieving full automation for verification utilizing testing. However, the current TBFV is mainly designed for sequential code in which all of the details are formally expressed, and there is no research on applying it to verify SysML models yet.

In this paper, we discuss how the existing TBFV can be applied to SysML models for their verification and we use TBFV-M (testing-based formal verification for models) to represent the newly developed approach. Since SysML Activity Diagrams can model the systems dynamic behavior and describe complex control and parallel activities, our discussion in this paper focuses on the activity diagrams.

The essential idea of TBFV-M is as follows. All of the functional scenarios are first extracted from a given formal specification defining the users' requirements. And at the same time, test paths are generated from corresponding SysML Activity Diagrams waiting to be verified. Then, test paths are matched with functional scenarios by a given algorithm. After this, the pre-condition of the test path is automatically derived by applying the assignment axiom in Hoare logic based on the functional scenario. Finally, the implication of the pre-condition of the specification with the guard condition of the functional scenario to the derived pre-condition of the path is verified which concerns the accuracy of the activity diagram. And the processing method of dealing with invocation is also be proposed by TBFV-M.

The remainder of the article will detail the TBFV-M method. Section 2 presents related work we have referenced. Section 3 characterizes the definitions of basic terms and concepts. Section 4 introduces TBFV and the derivation of the main idea of TBFV-M. Section 5 describes the principle of TBFV-M, showing the core technology of TBFV-M. Section 6 uses one case study to present the key point of TBFV-M. Finally, the details of the implementation are presented in Sect. 6 and Sect. 7 concludes the paper.

2 Related Work

2.1 Testing-Based Verification

Considering the shortcoming of formal verification based on Hoare logic being hard to automate, Liu proposed the TBFV (Testing-Based Formal Verification) method by combining specification-based testing with formal verification [6]. This method not only take the advantage of full automation for testing, but also the efficiency of error detection with formal verification. Liu also designed a group of algorithms [9] for test cases generation from formal specification written in SOFL [10]. A supporting tool [8] is also developed. These efforts have significantly improved the applicability of formal verification in industrial settings.

Raimondi [11] addressed the problem of verifying planning domains written in the Planning Domain Definition Language (PDDL). First, he translated test cases into planning goals, then verified planning domains using the planner. A tool PDVer is also generated. In this paper, testing is also used during verification and the effectiveness and the usability is improved.

2.2   Test Case Generation

Lasalle [12] utilized the existing UML/OCL Model-Based Test generation tool, Smartesting Test DesignetTM. He designed rewriting rules to translate a SysML model into an equivalent UML model. The advantage of this process is that we can use the existing UML tools to handle the SysML model.

Nayak [13] introduced an approach to transform the particular Activity Diagram into a model that can be used for testing, called ITM, based on its structure characteristics. The advantage of using ITM is that it can simplify the process of extracting and analyzing test scenarios based on the coverage criteria. However, it also has limitations on processing unstructured Activity Diagram because the unstructured Activity Diagrams shape is out of structure.

Oluwagbemi [14] proposed a new concept called activity flow tree (AFT) and it can store the information obtained by traversing the activity diagram. Then, AFT is used as an intermediate expression to generate test cases automatically. They designed the transformation and generation algorithm and compared their achievement with the work done by the predecessors.

Inspired by Liu's work, we apply and extend the TBFV approach to models and propose the TBFV-M. A model is more intuitive than a formal specification because it requires less relevant background knowledge and is easier to communicate with customers. TBFV approach shows the treatment of code, while TBFV-M approach deals with SysML Activity Diagrams. And different with Feng Liang's work, TBFV-M approach do not use other supporting tools, like Modelica, we merely use Hoare Logic to do the verification. Referring to test case generation, TBFV-M approach can deal with unstructured diagrams, which may have stronger processing power than existing approaches.

3   Related Concept

3.1   Formal Definition of Activity Diagram

Activity Diagram Formal Definition [2] can be represented as:

$$AD = (Node; Edge) \qquad (1)$$

Node is a set of nodes of which definition as follow:

$$Node = \{InitialNode; FlowFinalNode; ActivityFinalNode; Action-Node; ActivityNode;$$
$$ForkNode; JoinNode; DecisionNode; MergeNode; RecieveSignaNode; SendSignalNode\}$$
$$(2)$$

InitialNode signifies the beginning of Activity Diagram, while ActivityFinalNode signifies the ending of Activity Diagram. Edges defines the relationship between nodes such that:

$$Edge = \{(x, y)|x, y \in Node\} \tag{3}$$

There are two types of edges: control flow and object flow. Control flow edges represent the process of executing token passing in AD and object flow edges are used to show the flow of data between the activities in AD.

3.2 Test Case

From a global view, test case based on the SysML activity diagram consists of test path and test data. And the definition is as followed:

$$TC(AD) = (Path;\ Data) \tag{4}$$

For Activity Diagram, test path consists of a series of actions and edges in the diagram. Based on the formal definition of the activity diagram given above, the test path is defined as follow:

$$path = \left(a'_1, a'_2, \ldots, a'_n\right) \tag{5}$$

$$a'_i = (t_n,\ a_n),\ (i = 2, \ldots,\ n) \tag{6}$$

$$t_n = a_{i-1} \rightarrow a_i,\ (i = 2, \ldots, n) \tag{7}$$

In these formulas, a_i means node, t_i means edge. In this case, a test path is a set of nodes, starting from node a_1 and ending with node a_n through the transition edges $t_2 \ldots t_n$.

Test data indicates the input information corresponding to a particular test scenario including various types of data, even user actions and so on.

3.3 Test Coverage Criteria

For software, the adequacy measurement of testing is reflected in the rate of coverage and effectiveness of the test case. These coverage criteria ensure the sufficiency of testing and provide implications for the test case generation algorithm. Here are four test coverage criteria used in our design, for test case generation of SysML activity diagram [15, 19, 20]:

- Action coverage criteria: In software testing process, testers are often required to generate test cases to execute every action in the program at least once.
- Edge coverage criteria: In software testing process, testers are often required to generate test cases to pass every edge in the program at least once.
- Path coverage criteria: These coverage criteria require that all the execution paths from the programs entry to its exit are executed during testing.
- Branch coverage criteria: These coverage criteria generate test cases from each reachable decision made true by some actions and false by others.

3.4   Hoare Logic

Hoare Logic is a formal system developed by Hoare [21, 22], and it is designed for the proof of partial correctness of a program. In Hoare Logic, the Hoare Triple [23] is best known and is also referenced in our method. The Hoare triple is of this form:

$$\{P\} \, C \, \{Q\} \tag{8}$$

P and Q are assertions and C is a command. P is named the pre-condition, which is a predicate expression describing the initial states and Q the post-condition, which is also a predicate expression describing the final states.

Hoare also established necessary axioms to define the semantics of each program construct, including axiom of assignment, rules of consequence, axioms of composition, axioms of alternation, iteration and block. Axiom of assignment is used in our work, so we will briefly introduce it:

$$\{Q(E\backslash x)\} \, x := E \, \{Q\}, \tag{9}$$

where x is a variable identifier, E is an expression of a programming language without side effects, but possibly containing x, $Q(E\backslash x)$ is a predicate resulting from Q by substituting E for all occurrences of x in Q. This axiom means that to verify the correctness of the assignment, the postcondition Q should be satisfied. This equals to $Q[E\backslash x]$ are true because x is assigned by representing E after the execution.

3.5   Functional Scenario Form

A functional scenario is a logical expression that tells clearly what condition is used to constrain the output when the input satisfies some condition. S_{pre} and S_{post} denote the pre- and post-conditions of operation S. Let:

$$S_{post} = (G_1 \wedge D_1) \vee (G_2 \wedge D_2) \vee \ldots \vee (G_n \wedge D_n), \tag{10}$$

G_i and D_i ($i \in 1, \ldots, n$) are two predicates, called guard condition and defining condition, respectively. The definition of functional scenarios and FSF (functional scenario form) are listed below:

$$Functional\ Scenario = S_{pre} \wedge G_i \wedge D_i \tag{11}$$

In the definition of functional scenario, $S_{pre} \wedge G_i \wedge D_i$ is treated as a scenario: when $S_{pre} \wedge G_i$ is satisfied by the initial state (or intuitively by the input variables), the final state (or the output variables) is defined by the defining condition D_i. The conjunction $S_{pre} \wedge G_i$ is known as the test condition of the scenario, which serves as the basis for test case generation from this scenario.

$$FSF = (S_{pre} \wedge G_1 \wedge D_1) \vee (S_{pre} \wedge G_2 \wedge D_2) \vee \ldots \vee (S_{pre} \wedge G_n \wedge D_n) \tag{12}$$

3.6   Path Triple

The path triple is similar in structure to Hoare triple, but is specialized to a single path rather than the whole program and the definition is below:

$$\{S_{pre} \wedge G_i\} P \{D_i\}, \tag{13}$$

P is called a program segment, which consists of decision (i.e., a predicate), an assignment, a return statement, or a printing statement. It means that if the pre-condition S_{pre} and the guard condition G_i of the program are both true before path P is executed, the post-condition D_i of path P will be true on its termination.

4   TBFV and TBFV-M

4.1   TBFV

TBFV is a novel technique that makes good use of Hoare logic to strengthen testing. The essential idea is first to use specification-based testing to discover all traversed program paths and then to use Hoare logic to prove their correctness. During the proof process, all errors on the paths can be detected.

Testing is a practical technique for detecting program errors. A strong point of testing superior to formal correctness verification is that it is much easier to be per-formed automatically if formal specifications are adopted [19], but a weak point is that existing errors on a program path may still not be uncovered even if it has been traversed using a test case. TBFV takes advantage of testing, realized full automation for error detection efficiency, and also overcome its weak point by making good use of relevant part of Hoare logic.

4.2   TBFV-M

In the last decade, the model-driven approach for software development has gained a growing interest of both industry and research communities as it promises easy automation and reduced time to market [17]. Because of the graphical notation for defining system design as nodes and edge diagrams, SysML model addresses the ease of adoption amongst engineers [18] (Fig. 1).

During the Model-Driven process, model is an important medium for the Model based system engineering development. The TBFV-M method takes the specification describing the users' requirements and the SysML Activity Diagram model as input and verifies the correctness of the SysML model according to the specification. The TBFV-M method is mainly used to verify whether SysML Activity Diagram model meets the user's requirements written in SOFL (Structured-Object-oriented-Formal Language).

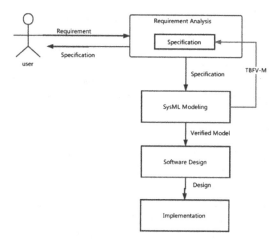

Fig. 1. TBFV-M usage scenario.

5 Principle of TBFV-M

The procedure of TBFV-M is illustrated in Fig. 2. We find that functional scenarios are derived from the specification written in the pre-/ post-condition style, while test paths are generated from the Activity Diagram and the data constraints can be extracted from each test path. Then, the extracted data constraints are used to match with functional scenarios. A matching algorithm is defined by us. We will verify the successful

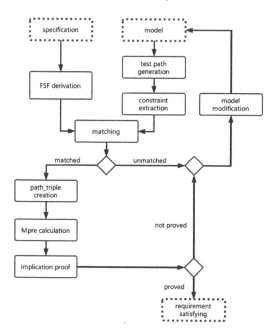

Fig. 2. TBFV-M processing procedure.

matched the test path according to the requirements represented in specification. The verification part can be separated into three parts: first, create a path triple, and then use the axiom of Hoare Logic to derive pre-assertion for each test path. Finally, prove the implication of the pre-condition in the specification and pre-assertion. If we can prove all the implication of pre-assertion of all the test paths of the model and the matching pre-condition, then we conclude that the model is to meet the requirements.

5.1 Unified Formal Expression

Using a unified formal expression can not only reduce the ambiguity during communications, but also give a possibility to automate the entire process, making analysis and verification more accurate and efficient.

We establish the unified formal expression, including specification guide and modeling guide. Specification reflects complete requirements and we chose SOFL to describe formal specification. The SOFL method intergrades formal methods, structured methods and object-oriented methodology, which not only supports requirements analysis and specifications, but also play an import role during design and implementation stages. An example specification written in SOFL is given below. It describes that if a non-negative integer a equals to zero, TRUE will be returned; otherwise return FALSE.

```
process: equal_zero (a: int) equal: bool
pre: a > 0
post: a == 0 AND equal == TURE
OR
a != 0 AND equal == FALSE
```

5.2 Functional Scenarios Derivation

The overall goal of functional scenario derivation is to extract all functional scenarios completely in "$S_{pre} \wedge G_i \wedge D_i$" form (FSF), as mentioned above in related concept section. A systematic transformation procedure, algorithm, and software tool support for deriving an FSF from a pre-post style specification written in SOFL have been developed in our previous work [16].

The below segment of the process "equal_zero", mentioned previously, shows the FSF generated from the specification described in the last one.

```
1.  S_pre: a > 0
    G_1: a == 0
    D_1: equal == TRUE

2.  S_pre: a > 0
    G_2: a != 0
    D_2: equal == FALSE
3.  ~S_pre: a <= 0
```

5.3   Test Path Generation

A test path auto-generation tool based on the SysML Activity Diagram model takes the model as input and generates test cases as outputs automatically, according to test path generation algorithms and coverage criteria chosen by test group members.

The SysML Activity Diagram test path generation includes three parts. First, we use transformation algorithm to compress the input Activity Diagram, which may contain unstructured module. The transformation is an iteration process, dealing with loop module, concurrent module and the problem of multiple starting nodes separately. After compressing, we transform this unstructured activity diagram into an intermediate representation form Intermediate Black box Model (IBM). IBM consists of one basic module and a map from black box to the corresponding original actions. The third phase of our approach is test path generation based on IBM. In this phase, two problems should be solved, which are basic module test path generation and black box test path generation. Details of automated test paths generation algorithm and imple-mentation of unstructured SysML Activity Diagram has been developed in our pre-vious work [24].

We give a motivation case to show the above process. Figure 3 is an unstructured SysML activity diagram model, which contains a concurrency module and a loop module.

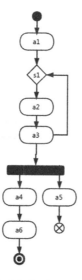

Fig. 3. Motivation example.

Figure 4 shows how to compress an unstructured activity diagram and transform the unstructured module into a black box node. Eventually the unstructured activity diagram converts into an intermediate representation of IBM. The first step is to identify the loop module and compress it into a black box node while-do loop1, shown in Fig. 4(a). The compressed black box node is the intermediate representation of the loop shown in the following Fig. 5(a).

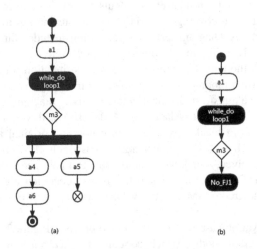

Fig. 4. Transformation process.

The second step is to identify the noJoin concurrency module and compress it into a black box node No FJ1, shown in Fig. 4(b). The compressed black box node is shown in the following Fig. 5(b).

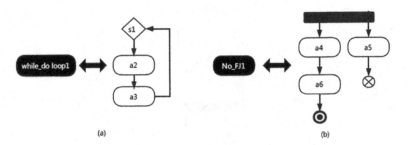

Fig. 5. Motivation example.

Figure 5(b) is a compressed and structured SysML activity diagram that can be used to automatically generate test cases. Finally, the black box module can be replaced.

5.4 Matching Algorithm

Matching the test path with functional scenario is very important for verification. In order to verify the correctness of one path in Activity Diagram, we need to match it with corresponding functional scenario. The constraints of test path can be extracted from edges of each path, which are used to compare with $S_{pre} \wedge G_i$ part of functional scenario. If unmatched test paths or functional scenarios appears, it means some errors may be exist in this model. And the model needs to be modified. The matching algorithm is given below.

Algorithm 1 Matching

Input: Edge_list, FS_list
Output: labelled Edge_list, labelled FS_list

1: **for** each edge $\in$ Edge_list **do**
2:      integration(edge.guard_collection)
3:      edge.label = unvisited
4: **for** each fs $\in$ FS_list **do**
5:      fs.label = unvisited
6: **for** each edge $\in$ Edge_list **do**
7:      **for** each fs $\in$ FS_list **do**
8:          **if** fs.$S_{pre} \wedge G_i$ == edge.guard_collection **then**
9:              fs.label = edge.ID
10:             edge.label = fs.ID
11:     **if** e thendge.label == unvisited
12:         return (edge, exist unmatched requirement);
13: **if** e thenxist FS.label == unvisited
14:     return (fs, exist unmodeled requirement);
15: **else**
16:     return Edge_list, FS_list;

Matching algorithm takes the edge list and FS_list as input. Edge list is the collection of guard conditions saved from test path and FS_list is extracted functional scenario form from specification. First, the algorithm sets the label of the two lists unvisited. And for each edge in edge list do data integration. Data integration is like data intersection. For example, if we contain two guard conditions x < 6 and x < 60, the integration of it is x < 6.

After completing the initialization step, find a matching functional scenario for each element in edge list. The specific operation is: the edge after the integration compares with $S_{pre} \wedge G_i$ in the functional scenario, if exactly the same, then we mean that we find the edge with the matched functional scenario. If there is no exact matched functional scenario, then there is an inaccurate modeling problem and needs to be refined. Therefore, immediately terminate the program, the problem of the edge will also be returned. After traversing all the edge_list, we also need to check whether each in FS_list has been visited. If there is an unvisited functional scenario, then it means that there is a requirement that the model fails to be represented in the specification, and the model needs to be refined.

5.5 Path Triple Establishment

Establish Path Triple and apply each node with the axiom in Hoare Logic. "$(S_{pre} \wedge G_i \wedge D_i)$ $(i = 2, ..., n)$" denote one functional scenario and P = [node$_1$; node$_2$; ...; node$_m$] be a program path in which each node$_j$($j = 2, ..., n$) is called a functional node, which is a DecisionNode, ActionNode, or other activity diagram nodes. Assume each path P has its own target functional scenario, which is decided utilizing matching algorithm. To verify the correctness of P with respect to the functional scenario, we need to construct Path Triple: $\{S_{pre}\}$ P $\{G_i \wedge D_i\}$.

The path triple is similar in structure to Hoare triple, but is specialized to a single path rather than the whole program. It means that if the pre-condition S_{pre} of the program is true before path P is executed, the post-condition $G_i \wedge D_i$ of path P will be true on its termination. Repeatedly apply the axiom for assignment to derive a pre-assertion, denoted by Ppre. Finally, we can form the following expression:

$$\{Spre \wedge Gi\} \rightarrow Ppre, \tag{14}$$

where S_{pre}, P_{pre} and $G_i \wedge D_i$ are a predicate resulting from substituting every decorated input variable $\sim x$ for the corresponding input variable x in the corresponding predicate, respectively. And the correctness of the specific path is transformed into the implication Spre $\wedge$ Gi $\rightarrow$ Ppre. If the implication can be proved, it means that no error exists on the path; otherwise, it indicates the existence of some error on the path.

5.6   Implication

Prove the implication. Finally, the correctness of one path whether it meets the corresponding requirement is changed into the proof of the implication "$S_{pre} \wedge G_i \rightarrow P_{pre}$". If the implication can be proved, it means that the path can model one part of the requirement; otherwise, it indicates the existence of some error on the path.

Formally proving the implication "$S_{pre} \wedge G_i \rightarrow P_{pre}$" may not be done automatically, even with the help of a theorem prover such as PVS, depending on the complexity of S_{pre} and P_{pre}. Our strategy is as follows: if the complexity of data structure is not high, we will transform the problem into solver, which can achieve full automation. Otherwise, if achieving a full automation is regarded as the highest priority, as taken in our approach, the formal proof of this implication can be "replaced" by a test. That is, we first generate sample values for variables in S_{pre} and P_{pre}, and then evaluate both of them to see whether P_{pre} is false when Spre is true.

For example, if we need to judge the validity of the implication "(price > 0) $\rightarrow$ (price < 100 AND $\sim$ price-5 = $\sim price^2$ - $\sim$ price", use the test case (price, 60) and we can easily prove the implication is not correct.

5.7   Invocation

During the process of design, especially for the complex system, modularization is very necessary when modelling, according to users' requirements. Model driven software development process often faces the problem of function or module invocation.

Because the TBFV-M method needs to deal with functional scenario derivation from specification describing users' requirement and test path generation from SysML activity diagrams, we need to take both side into account while dealing with invocation.

For specification, if a function invocation is used as a statement, it can change the current state of a program. So that, the traversed path containing the invoked function should consider in deriving the pre-assertion of the invocated function. Our solution is utilizing the sub path of the invocated function to substitute the actual traversed path, while deriving the functional scenario form. Also, we need to append the pre-condition of invocated function into the S_{pre} of particular functional scenario and during the above process parameter substitution needs to be considered.

To express the idea, we will give a motivation example.

```
function FareDiscount (age:int, fare:int) FinalPrice: int
pre: age > 0 AND .fare > 0
post: age <= 6 AND FinalPrice == 0
     OR
     age >= 70 AND FinalPrice == 0
     OR
     age > 6 AND age<60 AND FinalPrice == fare
     OR
   age >= 60 AND age<70 AND FinalPrice == HalfPrice(fare)

function HalfPrice (price: int) Half_P: int
pre: price > 0
post: Half_P = 0.5 * price
```

While deriving, we can get the below functional scenario. HalfPrice is the invocation function.

$$S_{pre}:age > 0 \text{ AND } fare > 0$$
$$G_4: age >= 60 \text{ AND } age<70$$
$$D_4: FinalPrice == HalfPrice(fare)$$

According to the solution we mentioned above, we will substitute the original form with the sub path of invocation function and the actual parameter `price` is replaced by `fare` in the invocation function. The result is shown below.

$$S_{pre}:age > 0 \text{ AND } fare > 0$$
$$G_4: age >= 60 \text{ AND } age<70$$
$$D_4: FinalPrice == 0.5 * fare$$

For Activity Diagram, "Activity" is often used to realize the hierarchy design. Our solution is also utilizing the sub path of the invocated activity to substitute the actual traversed test path, while generating test path.

6 Case Study

Now we show a motivation example to detail the process of TBFV-M method. First, we will get a requirement from the user, which consists of inform the description, may like this: "The park will give the tourist fare discount according to their age. If he is younger than 6 or older than 70, he will be free; Or if he is between 60 and 70, he can enjoy the half price, otherwise he will pay the normal price". This specification is formal and structured, as shown in the last section.

According to the specification, we can construct a set of SysML model and the Activity Diagram is shown below (Fig. 6).

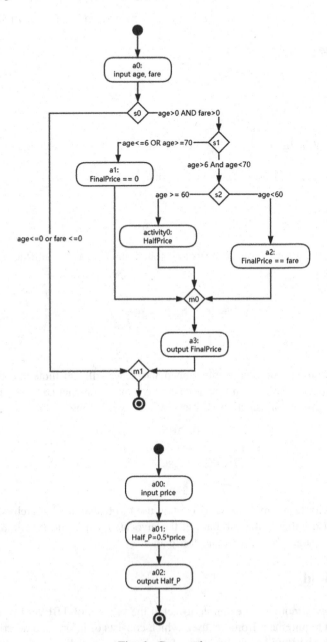

Fig. 6. Case study.

First, we derive Functional Scenarios from specification and generate test paths from Activity Diagram. The result is shown as below.

```
1.  S_pre: age > 0 AND fare > 0
    G_1: age <= 6
    D_1: FinalPrice == 0
2.  S_pre: age > 0 AND fare > 0
    G_2: age >= 70
    D_2: FinalPrice == 0
3.  S_pre: age > 0 AND fare > 0
    G_3: age > 6 AND age<60
    D_3: FinalPrice == fare
4.  S_pre: age > 0 AND fare > 0
    G_4: age >= 60 AND age<70
    D_4: FinalPrice == 0.5*fare
5.  ~S_pre: age<=0 or fare<=0
```

Because of the invoked activity, we should substitute the original test path, like T4, into the update version, T4′, by substituting activity0 with its sub actions.

```
Test Path:
T1: start →a0 → so → m1 → end
T2: start → a0 → so → s1 → a1 → m0 → a3 → end
T3: start → a0 → so → s1 → s2 → a2 → m0 → a3 → end
T4: start → a0 → so → s1 → s2 → activity0 → m0 → a3 → end

T4´: start → a0 → so → s1 → s2 → start_0 → a00 → a01 →a02
→ end_0 → m0 → a3 → end
```

At the same time, we can extract data constraints from each test scenario, which is used for matching with functional scenario. Then, the matching process is shown below.

```
Matching Result:
FSF_1 - T2
FSF_2 - T2
FSF_3 - T3
FSF_4 - T4
FSF_5 - T1
```

The blow segment chose the forth path and matched the first functional scenario as an example and shows the substitution process, from bottom to up.

```
Derivation Process:

{age> 0 AND fare > 0 AND age >= 60 AND age<70}
{0.5 *fare == 0.5*fare}
input age,  fare
{0.5 *fare == 0.5*fare}
input fare
{0.5 *fare == 0.5*fare}
FinalPrice =0.5 *fare
{FinalPrice == 0.5*fare}
output FinalPrice
{FinalPrice == 0.5*fare}
output FinalPrice
{FinalPrice == 0.5*fare}
```

Finally, we turn this verification problem into proving whether the pre-condition of specification can imply P_{pre}. If it can be proved, means that the path satisfies the requirement. As the strategy of implication mentioned before, this implication uses simple data structure, so that we use testing to access the procedure of verification. In this case, we prove it is correct.

7 Conclusion

We presented an approach, known as TBFV-M (Testing-Based Formal Verification for Model), for requirement error detection in SysML Activity Diagrams by integrating test cases generation and Hoare Logic. The principle underlying TBFV-M is first to derive functional scenarios form specification and generate test scenarios from Activity Diagrams. Then match them and verify each test scenario according to the corresponding functional scenario. Hoare logic is used during the verification process. TBFV-M method made up the limitation of TBFV, not concerning about models and solved the problem of inconsistent, incomplete, and inaccurate models. We also give a solution to deal with the invocation problem. It has advantage in reducing the probability of system error and shortening the developing time.

Acknowledgements. This work was supported by JSPS KAKENHI Grant Number 26240008, and Defense Industrial Technology Development Program JCKY 2016212B004-2. The authors would like to thank the anonymous referees for their valuable comments and suggestions.

References

1. Wymore, A.W.: Model-Based Systems Engineering: An Introduction to the Mathematical Theory of Discrete Systems and to the Tricotyledon Theory of System Design. CRC Press, Boca Raton (1993)
2. Friedenthal, S., Moore, A., Steiner, R.: A practical guide to sysml. San Francisco Jung Inst. Libr. J. **17**(1), 41–46 (2012)
3. Weilkiens, T.: Systems engineering with SysML/UML. Computer (6), 83 (2006)
4. Shah, M., et al.: Knowledge engineering tools in planning: state-of-the-art and future challenges. Computer (2013)
5. Vaquero, T.S., Silva, J.R., Beck, C.J.: A brief review of tools and methods for knowledge engineering for planning scheduling. Computer 7–14 (2011)
6. Liu, S.: Utilizing hoare logic to strengthen testing for error detection in programs. Computer **50**(6), 1–5 (2014)
7. Liu, S., Nakajima, S.: Combining specification-based testing, correctness proof, and inspection for program verification in practice. In: Liu, S., Duan, Z. (eds.) SOFL+MSVL 2013. LNCS, vol. 8332, pp. 3–16. Springer, Cham (2014). https://doi.org/10.1007/978-3-319-04915-1_1
8. Liu, S.: A tool supported testing method for reducing cost and improving quality. In: IEEE International Conference on Software Quality, Reliability and Security, pp. 448–455 (2016)
9. Liu, S.: Testing-based formal verification for theorems and its application in software specification verification. In: Aichernig, B.K.K., Furia, C.A.A. (eds.) TAP 2016. LNCS, vol. 9762, pp. 112–129. Springer, Cham (2016). https://doi.org/10.1007/978-3-319-41135-4_7
10. Liu, S., Ofiutt, A.J., Hostuart, C., Sun, Y., Ohba, M.: So: a formal engineering methodology for industrial applications. IEEE Trans. Softw. Eng. **24**(1), 24–45 (1998)
11. Raimondi, F., Pecheur, C., Brat, G.: PDVer, a tool to verify PDDL planning domains. Computer (2009)
12. Lasalle, J., Bouquet, F., Legeard, B., Peureux, F.: SysML to UML model transformation for test generation purpose. ACM SIGSOFT Softw. Eng. Notes **36**(1), 1–8 (2011)
13. Nayak, A., Samanta, D.: Synthesis of test scenarios using UML activity diagrams. Softw. Syst. Model. **10**(1), 63–89 (2011)
14. Oluwagbemi, O., Asmuni, H.: Automatic generation of test cases from activity diagrams for UML based testing (UBT). Computer **77**(13) 2015
15. Khurshid, S., Marinov, D.: TestEra: specification-based testing of Java programs using SAT. Autom. Softw. Eng. **11**(4), 403–434 (2004)
16. Liu, S., Nakajima, S.: A decompositional approach to automatic test case generation based on formal specifications. In: International Conference on Secure Software Integration Reliability Improvement, pp. 147–155 (2010)
17. Liu, S., Hayashi, T., Takahashi, K., Kimura, K., Nakayama, T., Nakajima, S.: Automatic transformation from formal specifications to functional scenario forms for automatic test case generation. In: New Trends in Software Methodologies, TOOLS and Techniques Proceedings of the SoMeT 2010, Yokohama City, Japan, 29 September–1 October 2010, pp. 383–397 (2010)
18. Kent, S.: Model driven engineering. In: Butler, M., Petre, L., Sere, K. (eds.) IFM 2002. LNCS, vol. 2335, pp. 286–298. Springer, Heidelberg (2002). https://doi.org/10.1007/3-540-47884-1_16
19. Broy, M., Havelund, K., Kumar, R., Steffen, B.: Towards a unified view of modeling and programming (track summary). In: Margaria, T., Steffen, B. (eds.) ISoLA 2016. LNCS, vol. 9953, pp. 3–10. Springer, Cham (2016). https://doi.org/10.1007/978-3-319-47169-3_1

20. Joseph, A.K., Radhamani, G., Kallimani, V.: Improving test efficiency through multiple criteria coverage-based test case prioritization using modified heuristic algorithm. In: International Conference on Computer and Information Sciences, pp. 430–435 (2016)

21. Hoare, C.A.R.: An axiomatic basis for computer programming. Commun. ACM **12**(1), 53–56 (1969)

22. Floyd, R.W.: Assigning meanings to programs. In: Colburn, T.R., Fetzer, J.H., Rankin, T.L. (eds.) Program Verification, pp. 65–81. Springer, Dordrecht (1993). https://doi.org/10.1007/978-94-011-1793-7_4

23. Pratt, V.R.: Semantical considerations on Floyd-Hoare logic. In: Symposium on Foundations of Computer Science, pp. 109–121 (1976)

24. Yin, Y., Xu, Y., Miao, W., Chen, Y.: An automated test case generation approach based on activity diagrams of SysML. Int. J. Perform. Eng. **13**(6), 922–936 (2017)

Model Checking Java Programs
with MSVL

Xinfeng Shu[1], Na Luo[1], Bo Wang[1], Xiaobing Wang[2(✉)], and Liang Zhao[2(✉)]

[1] School of Computer Science and Technology,
Xi'an University of Posts and Communications, Xi'an 710061, China
{shuxf,wangbo}@xupt.edu.cn
[2] Institute of Computing Theory and Technology and ISN Laboratory,
Xidian University, Xi'an 710071, China
{xbwang,lzhao}@mail.xidian.edu.cn

Abstract. To verify the correctness of Java programs, a novel approach for model checking Java programs with MSVL (Modeling, Simulation and Verification Language) is advocated. To this end, the rules for decoding the object-oriented semantics of Java Language with the process-oriented semantics of MSVL are defined, and the technique for automatically rewriting a Java program into its equivalent MSVL program is formalized, which in turn can be verified with the model checking tool MSV. In addition, an example is given to illustrate how the approach works. The approach fully utilizes the powerful expressiveness of MSVL to verify Java programs in a direct way, and helps to improve the quality of the software system.

Keywords: MSVL · Java · Program verification · Model checking

1 Introduction

Java [1], a famous object-oriented programming language, has been widely used in various areas of software development. Facing the generous softwares written in Java, how to ensure their correctness and reliability is of grand challenge to computer scientists as well as software engineers. To solve the problem, software testing has been developed for many years and a variety of tools has been developed to verify software systems with success. However, the method has its innate limitation, i.e., it can only prove the presence of errors but never their absence. In contrast, formal verification, which is based on the mathematical theories, can prove the correctness of the software and become an important means to verify software systems.

As an automatic formal verification approach, model checking [2] can exhaustively search each execution path of the system model to be verified, and check

This research is partly supported by the Industrial Research Project of Shaanxi Province No. 2017GY-076, No. 2016GY-123, and the NSFC Grant No. 61672403.

Z. Duan et al. (Eds.): SOFL+MSVL 2018, LNCS 11392, pp. 89–107, 2019.
https://doi.org/10.1007/978-3-030-13651-2_6

whether the desired property holds. Once the property fails, it can provide a counterexample path helping engineers to locate and fix the error, and hence is welcomed by both the academia and industry. In the early days, the research on model checking mainly focuses on verifying the analysis and designment of hardware and software systems, The kernel process of the verification is to model the system with a specific modeling language (e.g., Promela [3] and NuSMV [4]), which usually need to be finished by verifiers manually. For complex system, it is very difficult to create the model and guarantee its correctness.

In recent years, some methods for model checking C programs have been advocated, and a number of model checking tools have been developed (e.g., SLAM [5], BLAST [6], MAGIC [7] and ESBMC [8]) and employed to verify device drivers, secure communication protocols, and real-time operating system kernels with success. These tools directly take C programs as input, and often use techniques of predicate abstraction, static analysis or runtime analysis to obtain the finite state model of the program as well as alleviate the state explosion problem, and complete the verification with the model checking algorithm. Within the field of object-oriented programs, Java Pathfinder (JPF) [9] is developed based on Java Virtual Machine for directly model checking Java bytecode. The tool can alternatively examine each execution path of a Java program by trying all nondeterministic choices, including thread scheduling order. The available program model checking tools mainly focus on verifying the process-oriented C programs and cannot be directly employed to verify the object-oriented ones. Besides, the current tools can only check the safety property and dead lock of the system, but cannot verify the liveness property.

In addition to the above methods, model checking C programs with MSVL (Modeling, Simulation and Verification Language) is an important approach [10]. MSVL [11], a process-oriented logic programming based on the Projection Temporal Logic (PTL) [12], is a useful formalism for specification and verification of concurrent and distributed systems [13–21]. It provides a rich set of data types (e.g., char, integer, float, struct, pointer, string, semaphore), data structures (e.g., array, list), as well as powerful statements [22,23]. Besides, MSVL supports the function mechanisms [24] to model the complex system. Further, Propositional Projection Temporal Logic (PPTL), the propositional subset of PTL, has the expressiveness power of the full regular expressions [25], which enable us to model, simulate and verify the concurrent and reactive systems within a same logical system [26].

To solve problem of formal verifying Java programs, we are motivated to extend the MSVL-based model checking approach of C programs to Java programs. To this end, the rules for decoding the object-oriented semantics of Java language with the process-oriented semantics of MSVL are defined, and the techniques for automatically rewriting a Java program into its equivalent MSVL program are formalized. Thus, the Java program can be indirectly verified by model checking the corresponding MSVL program with the specific model checking tool MSV.

The rest of this paper is organized as follows. In the next section, MSVL and Java language are briefly presented. In Sect. 3, the rules for converting Java programs to MSVL programs are defined and the related techniques are introduced.

In Sect. 4, an example is given to illustrate how the method works in verifying Java programs. Finally, the conclusion is given in Sect. 5.

2   Preliminaries

2.1   Modeling, Simulation and Verification Language

Modeling, Simulation and Verification Language (MSVL) is an executable subset of PTL with frame and used to model, simulate and verify concurrent systems. With MSVL, expressions can be regarded as the PTL terms and statements as treated as the PTL formulas. In the following, we briefly introduce the kernel of MSVL. For more deals, please refer to literatures [11].

Data Type. MSVL provides a rich set of data types [22]. The fundamental types include unsigned character (char), unsigned integer (int) and floating point number (float). Besides, there is a hierarchy of derived data types built with the fundamental types, including string (string), list (list), pointer (pointer), array (array), structure (struct) and union (union).

Expression. The arithmetic expressions e and boolean expressions b of MSVL are inductively defined as follows:

$$e ::= n \mid x \mid \bigcirc x \mid \ominus e \mid e_0 ope_1 (op ::= + \mid - \mid * \mid / \mid \%)$$
$$b ::= true \mid false \mid e_0 = e_1 \mid e_0 < e_1 \mid \neg b \mid b_0 \wedge b_1$$

where n is an integer and x is a variable. The elementary statements in MSVL are defined as follows:

(1) Immediate Assign $x \Leftarrow e \overset{\mathrm{def}}{=} x = e \wedge p_x$

(2) Unit Assignment $x := e \overset{\mathrm{def}}{=} \bigcirc x = e \wedge \bigcirc p_x \wedge skip$

(3) Conjunction $S_1 \ and \ S_2 \overset{\mathrm{def}}{=} S_1 \wedge S_2$

(4) Selection $S_1 \ or \ S_2 \overset{\mathrm{def}}{=} S_1 \vee S_2$

(5) Next $next \ S \overset{\mathrm{def}}{=} \bigcirc S$

(6) Always $always \ S \overset{\mathrm{def}}{=} \Box S$

(7) Termination $empty \overset{\mathrm{def}}{=} \neg \bigcirc true$

(8) Skip $skip \overset{\mathrm{def}}{=} \bigcirc \varepsilon$

(9) Sequential $S_1 ; S_2 \overset{\mathrm{def}}{=} (S_1, S_2) \ prj \ \varepsilon$

(10) Local $exist \ x : S \overset{\mathrm{def}}{=} \exists x : S$

(11) State Frame $lbf(x) \overset{\mathrm{def}}{=} \neg af(x) \rightarrow \exists b:(\ominus x = b \wedge x = b)$

(12) Interval Frame $frame(x) \overset{\mathrm{def}}{=} \Box(\bar{\varepsilon} \rightarrow \bigcirc(lbf(x)))$

(13) Projection $(S_1, \ldots, S_m) \ prj \ S$

(14) Condition $if \ b \ then \ S_1 \ else \ S_2 \overset{\mathrm{def}}{=} (b \rightarrow S_1) \wedge (\neg b \rightarrow S_2)$

(15) While $while \ b \ do \ S \overset{\mathrm{def}}{=} (b \wedge S)^\star \wedge \Box(\varepsilon \rightarrow \neg b)$

(16) Await $await(b) \overset{\mathrm{def}}{=} \bigwedge_{x \in V_b} frame(x) \wedge \Box(\varepsilon \leftrightarrow b)$

(17) Parallel $S_1 \| S_2 \overset{\mathrm{def}}{=} ((S_1 ; true) \wedge S_2) \vee (S_1 \wedge (S_2 ; true))$
$\vee (S_1 \wedge S_2)$

where x is a variable, e is an arbitrary expression, b is a boolean expression, and $S_1, \ldots, S_m, S$ are all MSVL statements. The immediate assignment $x \Leftarrow e$, unit assignment $x := e$, $empty$, $lbf(x)$ and $frame(x)$ are basic statements, and the left composite ones.

For convenience of modeling complex software and hardware systems, MSVL takes the divide-and-conquer strategy and employees functions as the basic components like C programming language does. The general grammar of MSVL function is as follows [24]:

$$\text{\textit{function} funcName}(in\_type_1 \ x_1, \ldots, in\_type_m \ x_m,$$
$$out\_type_1 \ y_1, \ldots, out\_type_n \ y_m, return\_type \ RValue)$$
$$\{ \ S \ \} \qquad //\text{Function body}$$

The grammar of function call is $funcName(v_1, \ldots, v_n)$. Parameter passing in MSVL is similar to that in C, i.e. all function arguments are passed by values (call-by-value). With call-by-value, the actual argument expression is evaluated, and the resulting value is bound to the corresponding formal parameter in the function. Even if the function may assign new values to its formal parameters, only its local copy is assigned and anything passed into a function call is unchanged in the caller's scope when the function returns. Furthermore, the pointer type is also supported by MSVL, which allows both caller and callee will be able to access and modify a same variable.

2.2 Java Programming Language

Java [1] is a popular object-oriented programming language with the feature "write once, run anywhere", and hence has been widely used in web and mobile application development, big data processing, etc. It not only supports the object-oriented mechanism, but also provides multi-thread, socket and interface programming. In this paper, we only focus on the object-oriented part of java except for the override feature. In the following, we briefly introduce the grammar of the subset of Java language to verify.

Data Type. The data types of Java programming language are divided into two categories, i.e., basic data types and reference data types. Basic data types include character (char), integer (byte, short, int, long) and floating point (float, double), boolean (boolean). Reference data types include class, interface(interface), array and so on.

Expression. Let d be a constant and x be a variable respectively. The arithmetic expressions e and boolean expressions b of Java are inductively defined as follows:

$$e ::= d \mid x \mid e_1 \ op_1 \ e_2 \ (op_1 ::= + \mid - \mid * \mid / \mid \% \mid ++ \mid --)$$
$$b ::= true \mid false \mid !b \mid e_1 \ op_2 \ e_2 \ (op_2 ::= > \mid < \mid == \mid >= \mid <= \mid !=)$$
$$b_1 \ op_3 \ b_2 (op_3 ::= \&\&, ||)$$

where op_1 denotes the traditional arithmetic operators, op_2 are the relational operators and op_3 the logical operators.

Elementary Statement. Let $type$ be a data type, x be a variable, $d, d_1, \ldots, d_n$ be constants, and obj be an object. The elementary statements of Java are inductively defined as follows:

(1) Declaration statement $type\ x \mid type\ x = e \mid dcls_1, dcls_2$
(2) Assignment statement $x = e \mid obj.attr = e$
(3) Function call statement $obj.fun(e_1, \ldots, e_n)$
(4) Compound statement $\{s\}$
(5) Sequential statement $s_1; s_2$
(6) If statement $if(b)\{s\} \mid if(b)\{s_1\}else\{s_2\}$
(7) For statement $for(dcls; b; e)\{s\}$
(8) While statement $while(b)\{s\}$
(9) Do-While statement $do\{s\}while(b)$
(10) Switch statement $switch(x)\{case\ d_1 : s_1; [break]; \ldots; [default : s]\}$

where $dcls, dcls_1$ and $dcls_2$ are any declaration statements; fun is a member function of obj with $n(n \geq 0)$ parameters, and $attr$ is an attribute of obj; $e, e_1, \ldots, e_n$ are expressions; $s, s_1, \ldots, s_n$ can be any statements.

Class Definition. Java is an object-oriented programming language supporting only single inherence, i.e., each class has at most one super class. The grammar for defining a class is as follows:

[visibility] $class$ className [$extends$ superClass] {
    [visibility] [static] $type$ attrName $= [e]$;
    ......;
    [visibility] [static] $rtnType$ funcName($type_1\ v_1, \ldots, type_n\ v_n$) {
       S;   //Function body
    };
    ......;
}

where visibility can only take one of the values *public, protected* or *private*; $rtnType, type_1, \ldots, type_n$ are all Java types.

3   Model Checking Java Program

In this section, the method for model checking Java programs is presented. The basic idea is to convert the Java program into an equivalent MSVL program and then perform model checking on the MSVL program obtained.

3.1   Strategy to Convert a Java Program into MSVL

Since Java is an object-oriented programming language whereas MSVL is a process-oriented one, we need to decode the object-oriented semantics of Java programs with the process-oriented semantics of MSVL. The conversion rules from Java to MSVL are defined as follows:

R1. For each class *cls* in Java, we define a struct in MSVL with the same *cls* to that class, Besides, for each dynamic attribute *attr* of *cls*, we define a member *attr* to the struct *cls*, and translation rules for data types between Java and MSVL are depicted in Table 1.

R2. For a class *cls* having a parent class *par*, we add a new member *_parent* with the type *struct par* to the corresponding MSVL struct *cls*.

R3. For each dynamic attribute *attr* with initial value *e* of a class, we add the corresponding assignment statement *attr* = *e* to the beginning of each constructors of the class, then remove the initial values from the attribute. In case of all such dynamic attributes having been processed, then convert the constructors of the class into MSVL functions with rule R5.

R4. For each the static attributes in the Java program, We convert them to global variable of MSVL to keep their values, and then the variables are named with the concatenation of the class name which belongs to, "_" and the original variable name.

R5. For each member function *fun* of a class *cls*, we define a MSVL function named with the concatenation of the class name, "_" and the original member function name, i.e., *cls_fun*, and parameters of *fun* are also kept as the parameters in MSVL function *cls_fun*. In order to access the dynamic attributes in the MSVL function *cls_fun*, add a parameter *struct cls *this* to the head of the function's parameter list. Besides, if member function *fun* has a return value of type *rtnType*, add a new parameter *Ret* with the MSVL type corresponding to *rtnType* to the tail of the parameter list of *cls_fun*.

R6. For each overload member functions *fun* of a class *cls*, we define a MSVL function named with the concatenation of the class name, "_", function name *fun* and the type name with the suffix "_" of each parameters of *fun* in sequence. The access of dynamic and static attributes as well as handling return value are identical to rule R5.

R7. The translation rules for basic expressions and statements are given in Table 2. Besides, for any statement *stmt* in a member function accessing a dynamic attribute *attr* of class *cls*, replace all the occurrence of *attr* in the corresponding statement of MSVL function with the expression *this* → connected with the result of algorithm *find_attr(cls, attr)*. Moreover, for any statement *stmt* accessing a static attribute *attr* of class *cls*, replace all the occurrence of *attr* in the corresponding statement of MSVL function with the expression *allStVars* → *cls_attr*.

R8. For any function call statement $x := obj.fun(e\_1, \ldots, e\_n)$ (w.r.t. *obj.fun* $(e\_1, \ldots, e\_n)$) in a member function of *obj* and *obj* is an instance of class *cls*, replace the statement in the MSVL function with the result of algorithm *find_func(cls, "obj", "fun", paramTypeList)* connected with the expression ("*e_1*,..., *e_n*,&*x*") (w.r.t. "*e_1*,...,*e_n*")), where *paramTypeList* is the data type list of the parameters $e\_1, \ldots, e_n$.

R9. For each return statement *return e* in a member of Java program, replace the statement in the corresponding MSVL function with $*Ret := e$.

R10. For the object statement $obj = new\ cls(e_1, \ldots, e_n)$, we replace it in the MSVL with a variable declare statement *struct cls obj* together with initializing the struct variable *obj* by calling the MSVL function corresponding to the constructor of class *cls* if it has.

Table 1. Translation rules of data types between Java and MSVL

Java	MSVL	Java	MSVL
int	int	boolean	boolean
float	float	array	array
char	char	List	list
String	string	Set	list

Table 2. Translation rules of expression and statement between Java and MSVL

Type	Java	MSVL
Arithmetic expression	x++	x := x + 1 and skip
	x--	x := x - 1 and skip
	x[+| - | * |/|%| ! =| == | > | <]y	x[+| - | * |/|%| ! =| = | > | <]y
Boolean expression	b1 && b2	b1 and b2
	b1||b2	b1 or b2
	!x	!x
Elementary statement	x = e	x := e
	type x = d	type x and $x <= d$ and empty
	s1 ; s2	s1 ; s2

Among the above transition rules, Rule R1 keeps the object data of Java with the struct of MSVL; Rule R2 decodes the inherent attributes as a member of child class' MSVL struct; Rule R3 deals with the initialization of the attributes of a Java class; Rule R4 handels the static attributes of Java classes; Rule R5 decodes the encapsulation of member functions of Java programs into MSVL functions keeping the ability to access the dynamic and static attributes as well as to take back the computing result; Rule R6 deals with the overload of member functions of Java classes; Rule R7 and R8 decode the access of attributes and calling the member functions; Rule R9 handles the return values; Rule R10 deals with the dynamic creating objects.

According to the semantics of Java, the algorithms $find\_attr$ and $find\_func$ employed in Rules R7 and R8 to compute the appropriate attribute and function are defined in Tables 3 and 4 respectively:

For instance, as shown in Fig. 1, the Java program in left side of the figure consists of two classes A and B, and A is the super class of B. According to the Rule R1, the MSVL defines two struct A and B in correspond with, and the dynamic attributes of the Jave class is also the member of the MSVL struct, e.g., the attributes sm and x of A and B respectively. Subsequently, the super class A of B is represented as the member $\_parent$ of struct B (Rule R2).

Table 3. Algorithm for finding the appropriate attribute

```
string find_attr(class cls, string attrName){
    if(cls.hasAttr(attrName)){
        return attrName;
    }
    else if(cls.hasParent()){
        return "_parent." + find_attr(cls.getParent, attrName)
            ;
    }else{
        return "";
    }
}
```

Table 4. Algorithm for finding the appropriate function

```
string find_func(class cls, string objPath, string funcName,
    List<type> params){
    if(cls.hasFunc(funcName, params)){
        string fName = cls.getName()+"_" + funcName;
        if(cls.isOverloaded(funcName)){ //Function is overloaded
            foreach type in params{
                fName = fName + "_" + type.getName();
            }
        fName = fName + "( &("+ objPath +")");
    }else if cls.hasParent() {
        return find_func(cls.getParent, objPath+"._parent",
            funcName, params);
    }else{
        return "";
    }
}
```

Further, the static attribute s of B is taken from the struct of B and regarded as the global variable of MSVL program (Rule R4). Moreover, the overload functions *sum* of class B are named with different function names according to Rule R5 and R6, and a new parameter *this* is added to the head of the functions' parameters list. Since the two function *sum* have return values, a new parameter *Ret* is added to the tail of the MSVL functions' parameters list respectively. In addition, the access of attribute x in the function *sum* of class B is replaced with the access of the member of MSVL struct, i.e., $this- > x$ (Rule R7), and the function call *sum* of object *obj* is replace with the MSVL function call statement $B_sum_int(\&obj, this- > x, \&Ret)$ (Rule R8).

Java Program

```
public class A{
   public int sm ;
          ...
 }
public class B extends A {
    public static int s ;
    public int x;
    public int sum(int m){
          ...
     }
     public int sum(int m,int n){
          ...
          obj.sum(x);
          ...
     }
}
```

MSVL Program

```
struct A{
    int sm
};
struct B{
    struct A _parent and
    int x
 };
int B_s;

function B_sum_int(struct B *this,int m,int
*Ret){
    ...
};

function B_sum_int_int(struct B *this,int
m,int n,int *Ret){
    ...
  B_sum_int(&obj,this->x,&Ret)
    ...
};
```

Fig. 1. Class and attribute conversion

According to the transition rules above, the process for model checking a Java program is shown in Fig. 2. For a given Java program, firstly we analyze the source code by lexical analysis and parsing tools JavaCC and obtain the Object-Oriented Abstract Syntax Tree (OOAST) of the program; then transform the OOAST to the Process-Oriented Abstract Syntax Tree (POAST) and POAST to the MSVL program in sequence; finally verify the MSVL program on MSV platform. In the following subsections, we introduce the key techniques of each step in the process.

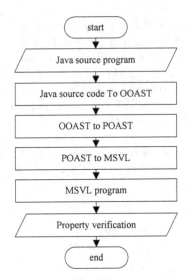

Fig. 2. The process of model checking a Java program

3.2 Java Source Code to OOAST

In order to convert Java program into MSVL, we introduce a data structure, named Object-Oriented Abstract Syntax Tree (OOAST), to analyze the syntax of Java programs. The strategy of OOAST representing the syntax of Java program can be depicted as the figure in Fig. 3. The OOAST of Java program is the set of classes, and each class consists of the set of attributes, the set of member functions, and the possible inherent relation to its super class. Besides, the technique of Hierarchical Syntax Chart (HSC) [27] is introduced to describe the syntax of each member functions. The structure of HSC is shown in Fig. 4. In first level, the HSC is the sequence of compound statements of functions, and the function body, a compound statement, is the sequence of statements in the function body. If the compound statement includes if, while or for statements, their corresponding execution breaches are also organized as the sequence of compound statements, e.g. the *if* statement in the body of function *Fun1*.

According to the above analysis, the formal definition of OOAST is as follows:

$$
\begin{aligned}
OOAST \quad &::= \; < ClassSet > \\
Class \quad &::= \; < name, [ParClass], AttrSet, FunSet > \\
Attr \quad &::= \; < [static], type, varName, [value] > \\
Fun \quad &::= \; < [static], RetType, name, ParamList, CompStmt > \\
Param \quad &::= \; < paramType, paramName > \\
CompStmt &::= \; < name, StmtList > \\
Stmt \quad &::= \; < StmtType, simpStmt > \; | \; < StmtType, CompStmtList > \\
StmtType &::= \; \text{TYPE\_COM} \; | \; \text{TYPE\_IF} \; | \; \text{TYPE\_SWITCH} \\
&\quad \quad | \; \text{TYPE\_LOOP} \; | \; \text{TYPE\_EXIT}
\end{aligned}
$$

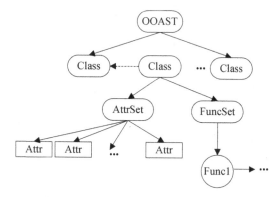

Fig. 3. Structure of Object-Oriented Abstract Syntax Tree

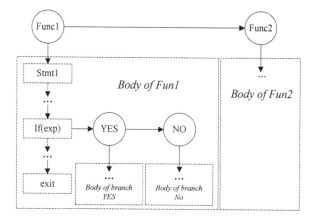

Fig. 4. Structure of Hierarchical Syntax Chart

where *type* and *RetType* are Java date types; *Fun* is a HSC which the compound statement *compStmt* describing the body of the function; *stmtType* indicates the statement is a common (TYPE_COM), branch (TYPE_IF), switch (TYPE_SWITCH), loop (TYPE_LOOP) or Exist (TYPE_EXT) statement. Note that we suppose the Java program to be verified have no syntax errors, so the visibility of the Java classes, attributes and member functions are omitted in OOAST.

To create the OOAST for the given Java program, we first need to perform lexical parsing of the program with the lexical and syntax analysis tool JavaCC. With the tool, we only need to give the lexical and syntax rules of the subset of Java language, the lexical and syntax analyzer written in pure Java code can be automatically generated. Then we employee the analyzer to process the Java program, and all the syntax elements of the program can be recognized, such as classes, date types, attributes, member functions, etc. Based on the analysis result, it is not hard to write the algorithm to create the OOAST, so the details are omitted here.

3.3   Conversion from OOAST to POAST

Once the OOAST of Java program is obtained, we then transform it into the Process-oriented Abstract Syntax Tree (POAST) which precisely describes the syntax of the MSVL program. As shown in Fig. 5, the structure of POAST is similarly to that of OOAST except that Java class is replaced with MSVL struct and the member functions in each java class are transformed into the MSVL functions. Moreover, the syntax of MSVL functions are also described in HSC. The formal definition of POAST is as follows:

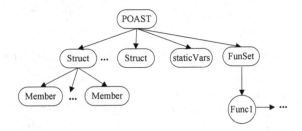

Fig. 5. Structure of Process-Oriented Abstract Syntax Tree

$$
\begin{aligned}
POAST &::= <StructSet, FunSet> \\
Struct &::= <name, MemberSet> \\
Member &::= <type, name> \\
Func &::= <name, ParamsList, CompStmt> \\
Param &::= <type, varName> \\
CompStmt &::= <name, StmtList> \\
Stmt &::= <StmtType, simpStmt> \mid <StmtType, CompStmtList>
\end{aligned}
$$

where *type* is a MSVL data type and *simpStmt* is elementary statement of MSVL.

According to the transition rules in Subsect. 3.1, the algorithm for converting OOAST into POAST consists of 10 functions whose relations are shown in Fig. 6. Function OOASTtoPOAST is the entry of the algorithm, and it traverse each class nodes in the OOAST. For each class node *cls*, function OOAST-toPOAST first calls functions Handle_Class, Handle_Parent, Handle_DynaAtts, Handle_StaticAtts to add a struct node *cls* (Rule R1), deal with the inherited attributes (Rule R2), remove the init values of dynamic attributes (Rule R3) and deal with static attributes (Rule R4) respectively, and then calls function Handle_HSC to process the HSC of the each member functions. For each member function's HSC, function Handle_HSC calls functions *Handle_FuncName*, *Replace_Vars*, *Handle_FuncCall* and *Change_RetValue* in sequence to handle the function header (Rule R5, R6), replace the access of class' attributes with members of MSVL struct (Rule R7, R10), handle the function call (Rule R8) as well as deal with the return statement (Rule R8) respectively. The code of the functions is trivial and hence skipped here.

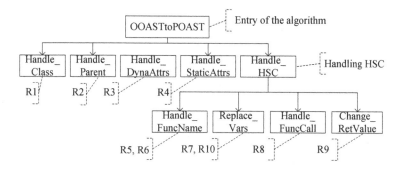

Fig. 6. Algorithm for converting OOAST into POAST

3.4 Conversion from POAST to MSVL

Now the left work is to convert the POAST to MSVL program. The algorithm POASTtoMSVL in pseudo C Language is formalized as follows, where the code of function HSC2MSVL can be found in literature [27].

```
POASTtoMSVL(POAST *ast){
    string msvlCode;
    //deal with struct
    foreach cls in ast->StructSet{
        msvlCode += ''\n struct '' + cls.name + ''{'';
        foreach mem in cls.MemberSet{
            msvlCode += mem.type +'' ''+ mem.name + '' and ''
        }
        msvlCode += ''};''
    }
    foreach fun in ast->FunSet{
        msvlCode += HSC2MSVL(fun);
    }
    return msvlCode;
}
```

4   Case Study

In following, we give an example to illustrate how our method works in verifying a Java program. The $3x+1$ conjecture is a well-known but unsolved question in number theory, which asserts that for any given positive integer x, if x is even, then let $x = x/2$, otherwise let $x = x*3+1$. If we repeat applying the calculating rule to x, then x must eventually equals 1. The implementing of $3X+1$ conjecture can be depicted as the following Java program.

```
public class PosNum {
    public int value;
```

```
    public int getValue() {
        return value;
    }
    public void setValue(int num) {
        if (num < 1)
            value = 1;
        else
            value = num;
    }
    public boolean isOdd() {
      return value % 2 == 1;
    }
    public boolean isEven() {
        return value % 2 == 0;
    }
}
public class Ques3X1 extends PosNum{
    public static int maxValue = 2147483647;
    public void run() {
        while (1 < value && value < maxValue) {
            if (isEven())
                value = value / 2;
            else
                value = value * 3 + 1;
        }
    }
    public static void main(String [] args) {
        Ques3X1 demo = new Ques3X1();
        System.out.println(''Input a positive number:");
        Scanner in = new Scanner(System.in);
        int x = in.nextInt();
        demo.setValue(x);
        demo.run();
        x = demo.getValue();
        System.out.println(x);
    }
}
```

Firstly, we analyze the lexical and syntax of the Java program to generate OOAST as shown in Fig. 7, where we only give the HSC the member function run of class Ques3X1. Then, we employ algorithm OOASTtoPOAST to transform the OOAST into the POAST as shown in Fig. 8. The object-oriented semantics of the Jave program is decoded with the MSVL semantics. Subsequently, we use algorithm POASTtoMSVL to transform the POAST into MSVL program and the result is as follows.

```
struct PosNum{
    int value
};
```

```
struct  Ques3X1{
    struct  PosNum  _parent
};
frame (Ques3X1_maxValue)  and  (
    int  Ques3X1_maxValue  and
        Ques3X1_maxValue  <==  2147483647  and  skip ;
    function  PosNum_getValue (struct  PosNum  *this , int  *Ret){
        *Ret<==this−>value  and  skip
    };
    function  PosNum_setValue (struct  PosNum  *this , int  num){
        if (num<1)then{
            this−>value<==1  and  skip
        }else{
            this−>value<==num  and  skip
        }
    };
    function  PosNum_isEven (struct  PosNum  *this , boolean  *Ret){
        *Ret<==this−>value%2==0  and  skip
    };
    function  Ques3X1_run (struct  Ques3X1  *this ){
        while ( this−>_parent . value >1  and  this−>_parent . value<
            Ques3X1_maxValue){
            boolean  Ret = false  and  PosNum_isEven (&( this−>
                _parent ),&Ret)  and  skip ;
            if (Ret)then{
                this−>_parent . value  :=  this−>_parent . value /2
                    and  skip
            }else{
                this−>_parent . value  :=  this−>_parent . value *3+1
                    and  skip
            }
        }
    };
    function  Ques3X1_main (){
        frame (demo , x)  and  (
            struct  Ques3X1  demo  and  skip ;
            int  x  and  skip ;
            Output ( ''please  input  a  positive  number :")  and  skip ;
            input (x)  and  skip ;
            PosNum_setValue (&(demo−>_parent ) , x)  and  skip ;
            PosNum_run (&demo)  and  skip ;
            PosNum_getValue (&(demo−>_parent ),&x)
            output (x)  and  skip
        )
    };
    Ques3X1_main ()
)
```

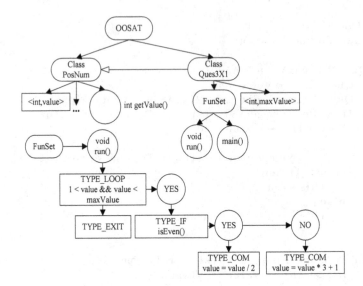

Fig. 7. OOAST of the Java program

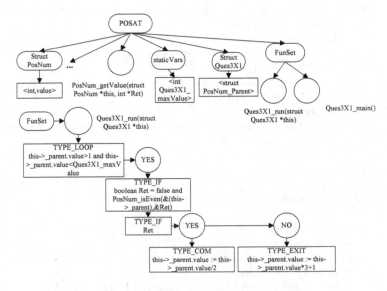

Fig. 8. POAST of the Java program

We now can verify the Java program by model checking the corresponding MSVL program with MSV tool. According to the $3x + 1$ conjecture, it is easy to figure out that the property "given a positive integer x, after calculation, the final result of x must be equal to 1" always hold, which can be describe with the following PPTL formulas:

```
</
    define p: x = 1 ;
    define q: x > 0 ;
    alw(q->stims p)
/>
```

Model checking the MSVL program on the MSV with the input integer 111, an empty LNFG with no edge is produced as shown in Fig. 9. Thus, the property holds.

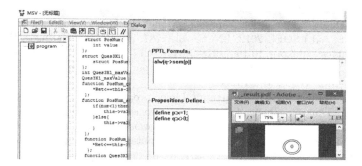

Fig. 9. Verification result of the program

5   Conclusion

In this paper, we present a novel model checking method for verifying Java programs by transforming the Java program into its equivalent MSVL program, and then verifying whether the expected property holds on the MSV platform. Compared to existing model checking method of Java, the method proposed can check more properties expressed in PPTL such as safety and liveness, etc. However, the method of this paper only concerns a subset of Java programs. In the near future, we will extend the work to more Java features such as override, multi-thread, etc.

References

1. Arnold, K., Gosling, J., Holmes, D.: Java Programming Language, 4th edn. Addison-Wesley Professional, Boston (2005)
2. Clarke, E.M.: Model checking. Lect. Notes Comput. Sci. **164**(2), 305–349 (1999)
3. Holzmann, J.: The model checker SPIN. IEEE Trans. Softw. Eng. **23**(5), 279–295 (1997)

4. Cavada, R., Cimatti, A., Jochim, C.A.: NuSMV 2.5 user manual. http://nusmv. fbk.eu/NuSMV/userman/v25/nusmv.pdf
5. Ball, T., Rajarnani, S.K.: The SLAM project: debugging system software via static analysis. In: POPL 2002, pp. 1–3 (2002)
6. Henzinger, T.A., Jhala, R., Majumdar, R., Sutre, G.: Software verification with BLAST. In: Ball, T., Rajamani, S.K. (eds.) SPIN 2003. LNCS, vol. 2648, pp. 235–239. Springer, Heidelberg (2003). https://doi.org/10.1007/3-540-44829-2_17
7. Chaki, S., Clarke, E., Groce, A., et al.: Modular verification of software components in C. In: International Conference on Software Engineering, pp. 385–395 (2003)
8. Cordeiro, L., Morse, J., Nicole, D., Fischer, B.: Context-bounded model checking with ESBMC 1.17. In: Flanagan, C., König, B. (eds.) TACAS 2012. LNCS, vol. 7214, pp. 534–537. Springer, Heidelberg (2012). https://doi.org/10.1007/978-3-642-28756-5_42
9. Brat, G., Havelund, K., Visser, W.: Java pathfinder-second generation of a Java model checker (2000)
10. Yu, Y., Duan, Z., Tian, C., Yang, M.: Model checking c programs with MSVL. In: Liu, S. (ed.) SOFL 2012. LNCS, vol. 7787, pp. 87–103. Springer, Heidelberg (2013). https://doi.org/10.1007/978-3-642-39277-1_7
11. Duan, Z., Yang, X., Koutny, M.: Framed temporal logic programming. Sci. Comput. Program. **70**(1), 31–61 (2008)
12. Duan, Z.: Temporal logic and temporal logic programming. Science Press (2005)
13. Duan, Z., Tian, C., Zhang, L.: A decision procedure for propositional projection temporal logic with infinite models. Acta Informatica **45**(1), 43–78 (2008)
14. Zhang, N., Duan, Z., Tian, C.: A cylinder computation model for many-core parallel computing. Theoret. Comput. Sci. **497**, 68–83 (2013)
15. Tian, C., Duan, Z., Duan, Z.: Making CEGAR more efficient in software model checking. IEEE Trans. Softw. Eng. **40**(12), 1206–1223 (2014)
16. Zhang, N., Duan, Z., Tian, C.: A complete axiom system for propositional projection temporal logic with cylinder computation model. Theoret. Comput. Sci. **609**, 639–657 (2016)
17. Duan, Z., Tian, C.: A practical decision procedure for propositional projection temporal logic with infinite models. Theoret. Comput. Sci. **554**, 169–190 (2014)
18. Tian, C., Duan, Z., Zhang, N.: An efficient approach for abstraction-refinement in model checking. Theoret. Comput. Sci. **461**, 76–85 (2012)
19. Duan, Z.: Modeling and analysis of hybrid systems. Science Press (2004)
20. Wang, M., Duan, Z., Tian, C.: Simulation and verification of the virtual memory management system with MSVL. In: CSCWD 2014, pp. 360–365 (2014)
21. Shu, X., Duan, Z.: Model checking process scheduling over multi-core computer system with MSVL. In: Liu, S., Duan, Z. (eds.) SOFL+MSVL 2015. LNCS, vol. 9559, pp. 103–117. Springer, Cham (2016). https://doi.org/10.1007/978-3-319-31220-0_8
22. Wang, X., Tian, C., Duan, Z., Zhao, L.: MSVL: a typed language for temporal logic programming. Front. Comput. Sci. **5**, 762–785 (2017)
23. Shu, X., Duan, Z.: Extending MSVL with semaphore. In: Dinh, T.N., Thai, M.T. (eds.) COCOON 2016. LNCS, vol. 9797, pp. 599–610. Springer, Cham (2016). https://doi.org/10.1007/978-3-319-42634-1_48
24. Zhang, N., Duan, Z., Tian, C.: A mechanism of function calls in MSVL. Theoret. Comput. Sci. **654**, 11–25 (2016)
25. Tian, C., Duan, Z.: Expressiveness of propositional projection temporal logic with star. Theoret. Comput. Sci. **412**(18), 1729–1744 (2011)

26. Duan, Z., Tian, C.: A unified model checking approach with projection temporal logic. In: Liu, S., Maibaum, T., Araki, K. (eds.) ICFEM 2008. LNCS, vol. 5256, pp. 167–186. Springer, Heidelberg (2008). https://doi.org/10.1007/978-3-540-88194-0_12

27. Shu, X., Li, C., Liu, C.: A visual modeling language for MSVL. In: Liu, S., Duan, Z., Tian, C., Nagoya, F. (eds.) SOFL+MSVL 2016. LNCS, vol. 10189, pp. 220–237. Springer, Cham (2017). https://doi.org/10.1007/978-3-319-57708-1_13

Formal Specification and Verification for Real-Time Scheduling Based on PAR

Zhen You, Zhuo Cheng$^{(\boxtimes)}$, Jinyun Xue, Qimin Hu, and Wuping Xie

State International S&T Cooperation Base of Networked Supporting Software,
Jiangxi Normal University, Nanchang 330022, China
youzhenjxnu@163.com, zhuo_cheng@126.com, jinyun@vip.sina.com

Abstract. Scheduling are playing a key role in many real-time systems. The goal of this paper is to apply PAR and its transformation rules to formal specification and verification of real-time scheduling. We formally described three constraints for uniprocessor systems and five constraints for multiprocessor systems. Furthermore, an EDF (Earliest Deadline First) program, written in Apla abstract modelling language, could be automatically transformed to an executable program. Finally, correctness of the EDF program was formally verified by using new strategies of developing loop invariant in PAR and Dijkstra's Weakest-Precondition theory. Formal specification of schedule constraints for real-time systems highlights PAR's powerful descriptive ability. Development and verification an EDF scheduling algorithm embody the efficiency and reliability role of PAR Method and PAR Platform.

Keywords: Scheduling · Real-time systems · Earliest Deadline First · Loop invariant · Formal specification · Formal verification

1 Introduction

Real-time systems are playing an important role in our society. In the last two decades, there has been a dramatic rise in the number of real-time systems being used in our daily lives and in industry production. Representative examples include vehicle and flight control, chemical plant control, telecommunications, and multimedia systems. These systems make use of real-time technologies [1].

The most important attribute that sets real-time systems apart from other systems is that the correctness of systems depends not only on the computed results but also on the time at which results are produced [1]. In other words, a task in the system is required to be completed before a specific time instant

This work was funded by the National Nature Science Foundation of China (Grant No. 61462041, 61472167, 61662036, 61462039, 61762049, 61862033), the National Natural Science Foundation of Jiangxi Province (Grant No. 20171BAB202008, 20171BAB202013) and the Science and Technology Research Project of Jiangxi Province Educational Department (Grant No. GJJ160329, GJJ150349).

© Springer Nature Switzerland AG 2019
Z. Duan et al. (Eds.): SOFL+MSVL 2018, LNCS 11392, pp. 108–122, 2019.
https://doi.org/10.1007/978-3-030-13651-2_7

which is called *deadline*. This sensitivity to timing is the central feature of system behaviors [2]. To satisfy this requirement, tasks need to be allocated sufficient resources (e.g., processor) so as to meet their deadlines. This field of study is referred to as *real-time scheduling*. With increasing complexity of real-time systems, how to guarantee the reliability of the design of scheduling is becoming a challenge for developers. To solve this problem, formal method is a promising way.

Formal method has been proposed for more than 40 years [3], and its goal is to improve the reliability, correctness and efficiency of software development [4]. Based on mathematically techniques, formal specifications is used to describe hardware and software system's key properties and analyze its behavior [5]. Using formal methods of mathematics, formal verification is the act of proving or disproving the correctness of intended algorithms with respect to a certain formal specification or property [6]. There are two well-established ways of formal verification [7]. The first one is theorem proving using manual proof and automated proof assistant including Isabelle, HOL, Coq, NUPRL, PVS. Another one is model checking using tools including SPIN, TLA+, UPPAAL. How to apply formal methods and techniques to real-time systems, especially in schedule constraints and algorithms?

PAR Method and **PAR Platform**, *short for PAR*, is a practicable formal method and its supporting IDE (Integrated Development Environment). PAR was firstly proposed by Prof. Jinyun Xue in 1997 [8], and its initial foundation is *Partition-And-Recur* approach for developing efficient and correct algorithmic programs. Next it evolved into a systematic formal method and a series of supporting tools based on MDD (Model-Driven Development) and generic mechanism [9–11]. PAR has been successfully applied to design many complex algorithms and programs with complicated data structure, including travel tree algorithms [12], graph algorithms [13], Knuths famous hard problem of cyclic permutation [14,15], an abstract Hopcroft-Tarjan planarity algorithm [16] and a Knuth's challenging program that converts a binary fraction to decimal fraction with certain condition [17–19]. Furthermore, PAR has also frequently used to develop several safety-critical systems, such as shuttle transportation problems [20], population classification in fire evacuation [21] and earthquakes [22], emergency railway transportation planning [23], active services support for disaster rescue [24], airline passenger profiling [25], student information management system [26], multimedia database applications [27] etc.

The paper firstly enlarges PAR's application to real-time systems. The main contribution is that we ont only have formally described some schedule constraints for uniprocessor and multiprocessor systems using Radl Specification Language of PAR, but also formally proved the correctness of EDF (Earliest Deadline First) program, written in Apla abstract modelling language of PAR, and then the EDF Apla abstract program would be automatically generated into C++, Java executable programs with Apla2C++ and Apla2Java Generator in PAR Platform. Formal specification of scheduling constraints could be used to verify that real-time systems completely and accurately satisfy properties. Meanwhile, the correctness of scheduling algorithm is guaranteed by using formal verification techniques.

The rest of the paper is structured as follows: Sect. 2 reviews some foundational knowledge about PAR and its transformation rules. Our original research work about formal specification and verification of real-time scheduling is elaborated in Sects. 3 and 4. Finally, conclusion and future work are discussed in Sect. 5.

2   Background Knowledge

A methodology of programming, called PAR (Partition-And-Recur), developed by Professor Jinyun Xue in 1997 [8]. With more than 20 years work of our research team, PAR evolved into a practicable formal method called PAR method and its supporting IDE, called PAR Platform.

2.1   PAR Method and PAR Platform

PAR pays special attention on the formal specification, derivation, verification and generation of algorithm programs, software components and database applications. PAR consists of the following three parts:

▶ **PAR Method:** a unified approach for processing quantification problem, a approach for processing non-quantification problem, a set of quantifier transformation rules.

▶ **Modeling Languages:** requirement modeling language *SNL*, specification and algorithm modeling language *Radl*, abstract program modeling language *Apla*.

▶ **PAR Platform:** a set of automatic transformation tools between requirement model, algorithm model, abstract program model and executable program.

PAR embodies the main idea of Model-driven Engineering (MDE), and preliminarily archives MDE's goal of model transformation and code generation. The architecture of PAR Platform is show in Fig. 1. There are two ways to generate codes. (1) *The first way is for processing quantification problem.* PAR Platform can transform *SNL requirement model* to *Radl specification model*, then to *Radl algorithm model*, and to *Apla abstract program model*, finally to *executable program*. (2) *The second way is for processing non-quantification problem.* Users can directly design *Apla* program manually and give its formal proof, then transform it to executable program.

2.2   Quantifier Transformation Rules

Specification and algorithm modeling language *Radl* of PAR was designed for the description of algorithm specifications, transformation rules for deriving algorithms and algorithms itself.

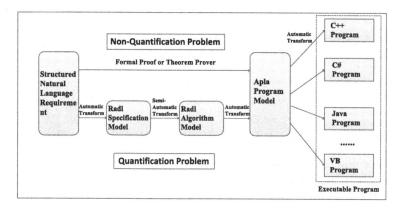

Fig. 1. Architecture of PAR platform

Most of transformation rules have quantifier properties [13,28]. Let small theta θ be an binary operator, and big theta Θ be the quantifier of operator θ, then,

$$(\Theta\ i : r(i) : f(i)) \tag{1}$$

Means the quantity of $f(i)$ where i range over $r(i)$. We write the quantifier of binary operator $+, \bullet, \wedge, \vee, \Diamond$ (minimum), $\Box$ (maximum), $\cap$ (intersection), $\cup$ (union) and $\uparrow$ as $\sum, \prod, \forall, \exists, \blacklozenge, \blacksquare, \bigcap, \bigcup$ and $\uparrow$. Obviously operator $+, \bullet, \wedge, \vee, \Diamond$, $\Box, \cap, \cup$ are associative and commutative and their quantifier Θ have following properties:

(a) Cartesian Product

$$(\Theta\ i,j : r(i) \wedge s(i,j) : f(i,j)) = (\Theta\ i : r(i) : (\Theta\ j : s(i,j) : f(i,j))) \tag{2}$$

(b) Range Splitting

$$(\Theta\ i : r(i) : f(i)) = (\Theta\ i : r(i) \wedge b(i) : f(i))\ \theta\ (\Theta\ i : r(i) \wedge \neg b(i) : f(i)) \tag{3}$$

(c) Singleton Splitting

$$(\Theta\ i : 0 \leq i < n+1 : f(i)) = (\Theta\ i : 0 \leq i < n : f(i))\ \theta\ f(n) \tag{4}$$

(d) Range Disjunction

$$(\Theta\ i : r(i) \vee s(i)\theta\ f(i)) = (\Theta\ i : r(i) : f(i))\ \theta\ (\Theta\ i : s(i) : f(i)) \tag{5}$$

Obviously, binary operation $\wedge, \vee, \Diamond(min)$, $\Box(max)$ and $\cup$ are idempotent.

(e) Generalized Commutativity

$$(\Theta\ i : r(i) : (\Theta\ j : s(j) : f(i,j)) = (\Theta\ j : s(j) : (\Theta\ i : r(i) : f(i,j)) \tag{6}$$

(f) Generalized Associativity

$$(\Theta\ i : r(i) : s(i)\theta\ f(i)) = (\Theta\ i : r(i) : s(i))\ \theta\ (\Theta\ i : r(i) : f(i)) \tag{7}$$

(g) Generalized Distribution

If binary operation θ and $\odot$ satisfy the following laws,

(I) $a \odot b = b \odot a$

(II) $(a \ \theta \ b) \odot c = (a \odot c)\theta \ (b \odot c)$

(III) $IE \odot c = IE$ (IE is the identity element of operation θ)

$$(\Theta \ i : r(i) : g \odot f(i)) = g \odot (\Theta \ i : r(i) : f(i)) \tag{8}$$

2.3   A Unified Approach for Processing Quantification Problem

Algorithmic program is an algorithm described with an implemented or abstract modeling programming language. According to PAR method, deriving an algorithmic program can be divided into six steps, which presented as follows.

▶ **Step 1.** Describe the formal functional specification of an algorithmic problem $\{Precondition AQ : Postcondition AR\}$ using *Radl*;

▶ **Step 2.** Partition the problem into a number of subproblems each of which has the same structure with the original problem but smaller in size;

▶ **Step 3.** Formally derive the algorithm from the formal functional specification. The algorithm is described using *Radl* and represented by recurrence-relations and initialization [8];

▶ **Step 4.** Develop loop invariant directly based on new definition and our two strategies of loop-invariant [29] for developing loop-invariant straightforward;

▶ **Step 5.** Based on the loop-invariant, transform *algorithm specification* $\{Precondition AQ : Postcondition AR\}$ to *program specification* $\{Precondition PQ : Postcondition PR\}$, and transform the *Radl algorithm* to *Apla abstract program* manually or automatically;

▶ **Step 6.** Automatically transform the *Apla abstract program* to an *executable program*, say C++, Java, Scala, etc. using Generators in PAR Platform.

Based on Dijkstra' s weakest precondition theory, loop invariant development strategies and the above six steps of deriving and developing algorithmic program in PAR, we also have put forward an approach of how to mechanically verify algorithmic programs using Isabelle proof assistant in our previous paper [12,30]. Different from model checking using MSVL [31,32] with framed temporal logic [33], our approach focuses on formal derivation and verification with theorem proving technology and tools.

3   Formal Specification of Schedule Constraints

Real-time systems are playing an important role in our society. In the last two decades, there has been a dramatic rise in the number of real-time systems being used in our daily lives and in industry production. Representative examples include vehicle and flight control, chemical plant control, telecommunications, and multimedia systems. These systems all make use of real-time technologies [1].

The most important attribute that sets real-time systems apart from other systems is that the correctness of systems depends not only on the computed results but also on the time at which results are produced [1]. In other words, a task in the system is required to be completed before a specific time instant which is called *deadline*. This sensitivity to timing is the central feature of system behaviors [34]. To satisfy this requirement, tasks need to be allocated sufficient resources (e.g., processor) so as to meet their deadlines. According to a SMT-based scheduling method proposed in our previous work [2], we apply the PAR platform to schedule real-time systems.

3.1   Schedule for Uniprocessor System

Assumption n tasks $\{T_1, T_2, \ldots, T_n\}$ would run on a processor, there are four arrays defined as follows.

▶ a array $r[1 \ldots n]$ store the request time $r[i]$ for each task $T_i(1 \leq i \leq n)$;
▶ a array $e[1 \ldots n]$ store the execute time $e[i]$ for each task $T_i(1 \leq i \leq n)$;
▶ a array $d[1 \ldots n]$ store the deadline $d[i]$ for each task $T_i(1 \leq i \leq n)$;
▶ a array $s[1 \ldots n]$ record the start time $s[i]$ for each task $T_i(1 \leq i \leq n)$;

3.1.1   Constraint on Start Execution Time of Tasks

As a task can only start to run after it requests, the start time of a task should be larger than or equal to the request time instant.

$$(\forall i : 1 \leq i \leq n : s[i] \geq r[i])$$

3.1.2   Constraint on Processor

A processor can execute only one task at a time. This is interpreted as: there is no overlap of the execution time of any two different tasks.

$$(\forall i, j : 1 \leq i \leq n \wedge 1 \leq j \leq n \wedge i \neq j : s[i] \geq s[j] + e[j] \vee s[j] \geq s[i] + e[i])$$

3.1.3   Constraint on Deadline

A successfully completed task should be completed before its deadline.

$$(\forall i : 1 \leq i \leq n : s[i] + e[i] \leq d[i])$$

3.2   Schedule for Multiprocessor System

Assumption n tasks $\{T_1, T_2, \ldots, T_n\}$ would run on m processors $\{P_1, P_2, \ldots, P_m\}$, besides request array, execute array and deadline array, three other Two-dimensional arrays are defined as follows.

▶ a array $r[1 \ldots n]$ store the request time $r[i]$ for each task $T_i(1 \leq i \leq n)$;
▶ a array $e[1 \ldots n]$ store the execute time $e[i]$ for each task $T_i(1 \leq i \leq n)$;
▶ a array $d[1 \ldots n]$ store the deadline $d[i]$ for each task $T_i(1 \leq i \leq n)$;
▶ a two-dimensional array $P[1 \ldots n][1 \ldots m]$ represents the relations between tasks and processors, where if $P[i][j] = 0$ means that task T_i can't be processed by processor P_j, otherwise $P[i][j] = 1$ means that task T_i can be processed by processor P_j.

▶ a two-dimensional array $D[1 \ldots n][1 \ldots n]$ represents precursor-relations among tasks, where if $D[i][j] = 0$ means that task T_j isn't a precursor of task T_i, otherwise $D[i][j] = 1$ means that task T_j is a precursor of task T_i.

▶ a two-dimensional array $s[1 \ldots n][1 \ldots m]$ represents a start time for a task processed on a processor, where task T_i could be processed by processor P_j at time of $s[i][j]$.

3.2.1   Constraint on Heterogeneous Processors

In heterogeneous systems, processors have different architectures, some tasks can only be executed on some specific processors. For tasks that cannot be executed on some processors, the start execution time of the tasks in such processors are set to $+\infty$, which means the tasks will never start to run on these specific processors.

$$(\forall i : 1 \leq i \leq n \wedge 1 \leq j \leq m \wedge P[i][j] = 0 : s[i][j] = +\infty)$$

3.2.2   Constraint on Start Execution Time of Tasks

That is, the start execution time of a task should be larger than or equal to the triggered time of function its request time instant.

$$(\forall i : 1 \leq i \leq n \wedge 1 \leq j \leq m \wedge P[i][j] = 1 : s[i][j] \geq r[i])$$

3.2.3   Constraint on Task Dependency

For a processor, if two tasks have dependency relation, task T_i can start to run only after T_j has been completed.

$$(\forall i : 1 \leq i \leq n \wedge 1 \leq j \leq n \wedge 1 \leq u \leq m \wedge 1 \leq v \leq m \wedge P[i][u] = 1 \wedge P[j][v] = 1 \wedge D[i][j] = 1 : s[i][u] \geq s[j][v] + e[j])$$

3.2.4   Constraint on Single Processor

A processor can execute only one task at a time. This is interpreted as: there is no overlap of the execution time of any two tasks.

$$(\forall i : 1 \leq i \leq n \wedge 1 \leq j \leq n \wedge 1 \leq k \leq m \wedge P[i][k] = 1 \wedge P[j][k] = 1 \wedge i \neq j : s[i][k] \geq s[j][k] + e[j] \vee s[j][k] \geq s[i][k] + e[i])$$

3.2.5   Constraint on Deadline

A successfully completed task should be completed before its deadline. In multiprocessor systems, for a task, any single processor completes it before deadline means the task has been completed successfully.

$$(\forall i : 1 \leq i \leq n \wedge 1 \leq j \leq m : s[i][j] + e[i] \leq d[i])$$

4   Formal Verification of a EDF Schedule Program

4.1   Design of a EDF Schedule Program

EDF is an dynamic priority scheduling algorithm on preemptive uniprocessor systems, which was firstly proposed by Liu and Layland [35] in 1973, and then has been proven to be an optimal scheduling algorithm on a single processor by Dertouzos [36].

A real-time system is modeled in the following sense: a collection of independent tasks $\{T_1, T_2, \ldots, T_n\}$, each task T_i characterized by a request time $r[i]$, an execution requirement $e[i]$ and a deadline $d[i]$. Tasks can be scheduled in a way that ensures all the tasks complete by their deadline. According to the EDF's scheduling strategy, a requested task with the earliest absolute deadline is firstly executed.

Based on the above scheduling strategy, we developed an EDF program by using a unified approach for processing quantification problem of PAR described in Sect. 2.3. In the following EDF program, a function *nextnode* could be used to find the earliest deadline task T_k with three conditions, (1) the task is not executed, which represents $f[k] = false$, (2) the request time is smaller than the concurrent end-time, which represents $r[k] \leqslant endt$, (3) the deadline is smaller

```
1:  program EDF;
2:  var
3:      — Omit Definition of Variables
4:  function nextnode(r:array[1..n+1,integer];f:array[1..n+1,boolean];
                        endt:integer):integer;
5:  var k,j,mindt:integer;
6:  begin
7:      mindt,k:=INF,1;
8:      do (k≤n)∧(f[k]=true) → k:=k+1;
9:      [ ] (k≤n)∧(f[k]=false) → if (r[k]≤endt)∧(d[k]≤mindt) → j:=k;mindt:=d[k];fi;
10:                                 k:=k+1;
11:     od;
12:     nextnode:=j;
13: end;
14: begin
15:     — Omit Initialization of Main Program
16:     startn,i:=1,2;
17:     do(i≤n) → if (r[i]<r[startn]) → startn:=i;
18:                 [ ] (r[i]=r[startn])∧(d[i]<d[startn]) → startn:=i;  fi;
19:                 i:=i+1;
20:     od;
21:     s[startn]:=r[startn];
22:     endtime := s[startn]+e[startn];
23:     flag[startn],i:=true,2;
24:     do(i≤n) → j:=nextnode(r,flag,endtime);
25:                 s[j]:=endtime;endtime:=endtime+e[j];flag[j]:=true;
26:                 i:=i+1;
27:     od;
28:     writeln("Output-start-time-for-each-task:");
29:     foreach(i:1≤i≤n:write(s[i],","););
30: end.
```

than min-deadline, which represents $d[k] \leqslant mindt$. The formal specification of *nextnode* function could be easier to expressed by using the *minimum* quantifier.

The *EDF Apla abstract program* can be automatically transformed into a *C++ executable language program* by using Apla2C++ Generator of PAR Platform. The transformation shows in Fig. 2.

4.2   Verification of a EDF Schedule Program

The EDF's scheduling strategy is described as that a requested task with the earliest absolute deadline is firstly executed. So *function nextnode* is the essential code in the above EDF Apla program. *Function nextnode* has three parameters, a request-time array $r : array[1..n + 1, integer]$, a flag array $f : array[1..n + 1, boolean]$ and end-time of the current task *endt*. The *Do statement* from line 8 to line 11 is the core code of *function nextnode*. Based on Dijkstra's weakest precondition theory and loop invariant development strategies of PAR method [29], formal verification the correctness of *Do statement* is given as follows.

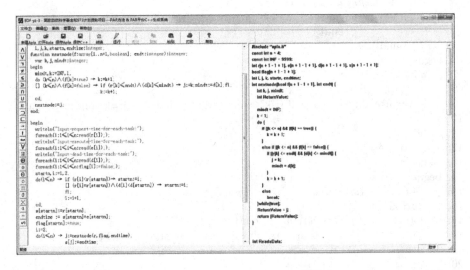

Fig. 2. Automatic transformation from Apla program (left) to C++ program (right)

A variable k is defined as the range from $[1, k)$, a variable *mindt* is a record min-deadtime from a set of $\{T_i, i \in [1, k)\}$. A initial statement "mindt, k:=INF, 1;" given before *Do statement*, where INF means $+\infty$, and the initial range $[1, 1)$ is $\emptyset$. A flag array $f : array[1..n + 1, boolean]$ record the state of tasks, where if $f[i] = false$ means that task T_i is still not executed, otherwise $f[i] = true$ means that task T_i was successfully executed and its dead-time is $+\infty$. Hence, a function $g(d[i])$ is defined as follows.

$$g(d[i]) = \begin{cases} d[i] & (f[i] = false) \\ +\infty & (f[i] = true) \end{cases} \tag{9}$$

There is a minimum quantifier $\blacklozenge$ of a binary min operator $\lozenge(a, b)$ defined in PAR. In order to describe post-condition of Do statement, a function $M[k]$ is defined as follows.

$M(k) = (\blacklozenge\, i : 1 \le i < k \wedge r[i] \le endt : g(d[i]))$

Describe the formal functional specification of Do statement in *function nextnode* $\{Q : R\}$ using *Radl* specification language of PAR.

Precondition Q: $\{(mindt = +\infty) \wedge (k = 1)\}$

Postcondition R: $\{mindt = M(n + 1)\}$

According to loop invariant development strategies of PAR method [29], we derived the following loop invariant ρ and a boundary function τ.

$\rho : mindt = M(k)$

$\tau : n - k + 1$

Same conditions C^1, C^2, C^{21}, C^{22} are signed in Do statement containing a *if statement*.

▶ *Condition* C^1 : $(k \le n) \wedge (f[k] = true)$
▶ *Condition* C^2 : $(k \le n) \wedge (f[k] = false)$
▶ *Condition* C^{21} : $(r[k] \le endt) \wedge (d[k] \le mindt)$
▶ *Condition* $C^{22} = \neg C^{21}$: $(r[k] > endt) \vee (d[k] > mindt)$

There are three branches of Do statement, and three conditions C_1, C_2, C_3 and their statements S_1, S_2, S_3 is given.

▶ *Condition* $C_1 = C^1$: $(k \le n) \wedge (f[k] = true)$
　Statement S_1 : $k := k + 1;$
▶ *Condition* $C_2 = C^2 \wedge C^{21}$:
　$(k \le n) \wedge (f[k] = false) \wedge (r[k] \le endt) \wedge (d[k] \le mindt)$
　Statement S_2 : $j := k; mindt := d[k]; k := k + 1;$
▶ *Condition* $C_3 = C^2 \wedge C^{22}$:
　$(k \le n) \wedge (f[k] = false) \wedge ((r[k] > endt) \vee (d[k] > mindt))$
　Statement S_3 : $k := k + 1;$

The condition $Guard = C_1 \vee C_2 \wedge C_3$ is calculated as follows.

▶ $Guard = C_1 \vee C_2 \wedge C_3$
$$\begin{aligned} &= C_1 \vee (C^2 \wedge C^{21}) \wedge (C^2 \wedge C^{22}) \\ &= C_1 \vee (C^2 \wedge C^{21}) \wedge (C^2 \wedge \neg C^{21}) \\ &= C_1 \vee C^2 \\ &= ((k \le n) \wedge (f[k] = true)) \vee ((k \le n) \wedge (f[k] = false)) \\ &= k \le n \end{aligned}$$

Based on Dijkstra's weakest precondition theory, we formally prove the correctness of Do statement $\{Q\}$ do $\{R\}$, several theorems expressions of weakest precondition should be verified.

(1) **Prove** $Q \Rightarrow \rho$

$Q \Rightarrow \rho$
$\equiv (mindt = +\infty) \wedge (k = 1) \Rightarrow mindt = M(k)$
$\equiv (mindt = +\infty) \wedge (k = 1) \Rightarrow mindt = M(1)$

$$[M(1) = (\blacklozenge \, i : 1 \leq i < 1 \wedge r[i] \leq endt : g(d[i]))$$
$$= (\blacklozenge \, i : false : g(d[i])) = +\infty \,]$$
$$\equiv (mindt = +\infty) \wedge (k = 1) \Rightarrow mindt = +\infty$$
$$\equiv true$$

(2) Prove $\rho \wedge C_i \Rightarrow WP(\text{``}S_i\text{''}, \rho)$

• Prove the first branch of *Do Statement* with C_1 and S_1.

$\rho \wedge C_1 \Rightarrow WP(\text{``}S_1\text{''}, \rho)$

$\equiv (mindt = M(k)) \wedge (k \leq n) \wedge (f[k] = true) \Rightarrow WP(\text{``}k := k+1;\text{''}, mindt = M(k))$

$\equiv (mindt = M(k)) \wedge (k \leq n) \wedge (f[k] = true) \Rightarrow mindt = M(k+1)$

$$[M(k+1) = (\blacklozenge \, i : 1 \leq i < k+1 \wedge r[i] \leq endt : g(d[i]))$$
$$= \Diamond(M(k), g(d[k])$$
–Using Rule of Singleton Splitting]

$\equiv (mindt = M(k)) \wedge (k \leq n) \wedge (f[k] = true) \Rightarrow mindt = \Diamond(M(k), g(d[k])$

$$[\Diamond(M(k), g(d[k]) = \Diamond(M(k), +\infty) = M(k)$$
–Using Definition of a Function $g(d[i])$**]**

$\equiv (mindt = M(k)) \wedge (k \leq n) \wedge (f[k] = true) \Rightarrow mindt = M(k)$

$\equiv true$

• Prove the second branch of *Do Statement* with C_2 and S_2.

$\rho \wedge C_2 \Rightarrow WP(\text{``}S_2\text{''}, \rho)$

$\equiv (mindt = M(k)) \wedge (k \leq n) \wedge (f[k] = false) \wedge (r[k] \leq endt) \wedge (d[k] \leq mindt) \Rightarrow WP(\text{``}j := k; mindt := d[k]; k := k+1;\text{''}, mindt = M(k))$

$\equiv (mindt = M(k)) \wedge (k \leq n) \wedge (f[k] = false) \wedge (r[k] \leq endt) \wedge (d[k] \leq mindt) \Rightarrow WP(\text{``}j := k; mindt := d[k];\text{''}, mindt = M(k+1))$

$\equiv (mindt = M(k)) \wedge (k \leq n) \wedge (f[k] = false) \wedge (r[k] \leq endt) \wedge (d[k] \leq mindt) \Rightarrow d[k] = M(k+1))$

$\equiv (mindt = M(k)) \wedge (k \leq n) \wedge (f[k] = false) \wedge (r[k] \leq endt) \wedge (d[k] \leq mindt) \Rightarrow d[k] = M(k+1))$

$$[M(k+1) = (\blacklozenge \, i : 1 \leq i < k+1 \wedge r[i] \leq endt : g(d[i]))$$
$$= \Diamond(M(k), g(d[k])$$
–Using Rule of Singleton Splitting]

$\equiv (mindt = M(k)) \wedge (k \leq n) \wedge (f[k] = false) \wedge (r[k] \leq endt) \wedge (d[k] \leq mindt) \Rightarrow d[k] = \Diamond(M(k), g(d[k])$

$$[\Diamond(M(k), g(d[k]) = \Diamond(M(k), d[i])$$
–Using Definition of a Function $g(d[i])$**]**

$\equiv (mindt = M(k)) \wedge (k \leq n) \wedge (f[k] = false) \wedge (r[k] \leq endt) \wedge (d[k] \leq mindt) \Rightarrow d[k] = \Diamond(M(k), d[k])$

$\equiv (mindt = M(k)) \wedge (k \leq n) \wedge (f[k] = false) \wedge (r[k] \leq endt) \wedge (d[k] \leq mindt) \Rightarrow d[k] = d[k]$

$\equiv (mindt = M(k)) \wedge (k \leq n) \wedge (f[k] = false) \wedge (r[k] \leq endt) \wedge (d[k] \leq mindt) \Rightarrow true$

$\equiv true$

• Prove the third branch of *Do Statement* with C_3 and S_3.

$\rho \wedge C_3 \Rightarrow WP(\text{``}S_3\text{''}, \rho)$

$$\equiv (mindt = M(k)) \wedge (k \le n) \wedge (f[k] = false) \wedge ((r[k] > endt) \vee (d[k] > mindt)) \Rightarrow WP(\text{``}k := k + 1;\text{''}, mindt = M(k))$$

$$\equiv (mindt = M(k)) \wedge (k \le n) \wedge (f[k] = false) \wedge ((r[k] > endt) \vee (d[k] > mindt)) \Rightarrow mindt = M(k + 1)$$

$$[M(k + 1) = (\blacklozenge\, i : 1 \le i < k + 1 \wedge r[i] \le endt : g(d[i]))$$
$$= \Diamond(M(k), g(d[k]))$$
$$\text{–Using Rule of Singleton Splitting}]$$

$$\equiv (mindt = M(k)) \wedge (k \le n) \wedge (f[k] = false) \wedge ((r[k] > endt) \vee (d[k] > mindt)) \Rightarrow mindt = \Diamond(M(k), g(d[k]))$$

$$[\Diamond(M(k), g(d[k])) = \Diamond(M(k), d[i])]$$
$$\text{–Using Definition of a Function} g(d[i])]$$

$$\equiv (mindt = M(k)) \wedge (k \le n) \wedge (f[k] = false) \wedge ((r[k] > endt) \vee (d[k] > mindt)) \Rightarrow mindt = \Diamond(M(k), d[k])$$

$$\equiv (mindt = M(k)) \wedge (k \le n) \wedge (f[k] = false) \wedge ((r[k] > endt) \vee (d[k] > mindt)) \Rightarrow mindt = M(k)$$

$$\equiv true$$

(3) Prove $\rho \wedge \neg Guard \Rightarrow R$

$$\rho \wedge \neg Guard \Rightarrow R$$
$$\equiv (mindt = M(k)) \wedge \neg(k \le n) \Rightarrow mindt = M(n + 1)$$
$$\equiv (mindt = M(k)) \wedge (k > n) \Rightarrow mindt = M(n + 1)$$
$$\equiv (mindt = M(k)) \wedge (k > n) \Rightarrow mindt = M(n + 1)$$
$$\equiv true$$

(4) Prove $\rho \wedge Guard \Rightarrow \tau > 0$

$$\rho \wedge Guard \Rightarrow \tau > 0$$
$$\equiv (mindt = M(k)) \wedge (k \le n) \Rightarrow n - k + 1 > 0$$
$$\equiv true$$

(5) Prove $\rho \wedge C_i \Rightarrow WP(\text{``}\tau' := \tau; S_i\text{''}, \tau < \tau')$

$$\rho \wedge C_i \Rightarrow WP(\text{``}\tau' := \tau; S_i\text{''}, \tau < \tau')$$
$$[k := k + 1; \in S_i]$$
$$\equiv \rho \wedge C_i \Rightarrow n - (k + 1) + 1 < n - k + 1$$
$$\equiv \rho \wedge C_i \Rightarrow true$$
$$\equiv true$$

The above theorems-expressions could be verified by using a generic proof assistant Isabelle/HOL.

5   Conclusion and Future Work

The goal of this paper is to apply PAR and its transformation rules to formal specification and verification of real-time scheduling. The work embodies three innovation points. (1) Formal specification of schedule constraints on uniprocessor and multiprocessor systems highlights PAR's powerful descriptive ability; (2) Based on data abstraction and function abstraction of PAR, a EDF (Earliest Deadline First) abstract program is efficiently developed using Apla modelling language, and it could be automatically generated into C++, Java executable programs with Apla2C++ and Apla2Java Generator in PAR Platform. The ratio of code-lines between EDF Apla abstract program and C++/Java executable program is approximately 1:10; (3) After developing a loop invariant using PAR's loop invariant strategies, the correctness of the EDF scheduling algorithm is guaranteed by using formal verification of Dijkstra's Weakest-Precondition theory and. In the future, we will extends PAR Method and Platform to describe, derive and verify more complicated constraints and algorithms for real-time systems.

References

1. Zhang, F., Burns, A.: Schedulability analysis for real-time systems with EDF scheduling. IEEE Trans. Comput. **58**(9), 1250–1258 (2009)
2. Cheng, Z., Zhang, H., Tan, Y., Lim, Y.: SMT-based scheduling for overloaded real-time systems. IEICE Trans. Inf. Syst. **100**(5), 1055–1066 (2017)
3. Bjørner, D., Havelund, K.: 40 Years of Formal Methods. In: Jones, C., Pihlajasaari, P., Sun, J. (eds.) FM 2014. LNCS, vol. 8442, pp. 42–61. Springer, Cham (2014). https://doi.org/10.1007/978-3-319-06410-9_4
4. Abrial, J.R.: The B book - Assigning Programs to Meanings. Cambridge University Press, Cambridge (1996)
5. Gaudel, M.C.: Formal specification techniques. In: Proceedings of International Conference on Software Engineering. ICSE, vol. 21, pp. 223–227. IEEE (1994)
6. Bjesse, P.: What is formal verification? ACM (2005)
7. Clarke, E.M., Wing, J.M.: Formal methods: state of the art and future directions. ACM Comput. Surv. **28**(4), 626–643 (1996)
8. Xue, J.: A unified approach for developing efficient algorithmic programs. J. Comput. Sci. Technol. **12**(4), 314–329 (1997)
9. Xue, J.: Genericity in PAR Platform. In: Liu, S., Duan, Z. (eds.) SOFL+MSVL 2015. LNCS, vol. 9559, pp. 3–14. Springer, Cham (2016). https://doi.org/10.1007/978-3-319-31220-0_1
10. Xu, H., Xue, J.: The research on implementation method of generic mechanism in Apla → Java program generation system. J. Jiangxi Normal Univ. (Nat. Sci. Edn.) **41**(01), 52–55+92 (2017)
11. Zhou, W., Zuo, Z., Wang, J., Shi, H., You, Z., Xie, W.: The contrastive study of generic programming in object-oriented languages. J. Jiangxi Normal Univ. (Nat. Sci. Edn.) **42**(03), 304–310 (2018)
12. You, Z., Xue, J., Zuo, Z.: Unified formal derivation and automatic verification of three binary-tree traversal non-recursive algorithms. Cluster Comput. J. Netw. Softw. Tools Appl. **19**(4), 2145–2156 (2016)
13. Xue, J.: Formal derivation of graph algorithmic programs using partition and recur. J. Comput. Sci. Technol. **13**(6), 553–561 (1998)
14. Xue, J., Gries, D.: Developing a linear algorithm for cubing a cycle permutatio. Sci. Comput. Programm. **11**, 161–165 (1988)
15. Xue, J., Yang, B., Zuo, Z.: A linear in-situ algorithm for the power of cyclic permutation. In: Preparata, F.P., Wu, X., Yin, J. (eds.) FAW 2008. LNCS, vol. 5059, pp. 113–123. Springer, Heidelberg (2008). https://doi.org/10.1007/978-3-540-69311-6_14
16. Gries, D., Xue, J.: The Hopcroft-Tarjan plannarity algorithm presentations and improvements, TR88-906, CS Department of Cornell University, pp. 1–20 (1988)

17. Knuth, D.: A simple program whose proof isn't. In: Feijen, W.H.J., van Gasteren, A.J.M., Gries, D., Misra, J. (eds.) Beauty Is Our Business: A Birthday Salute to Edsger W. Dijkstra, pp. 233–242. Springer, New York (1990). https://doi.org/10.1007/978-1-4612-4476-9_28

18. Xue, J., Davis R.: A simple program whose derivation and proof is also. In: The First IEEE International Conference On Formal Engineering Method (1997)

19. Xue, J., Davis, R.: A derivation and proof of Knuths binary to decimal program. Softw. Concepts Tools **12**, 149–156 (1997)

20. Zheng, Y., Xue, J.: A simple greedy algorithm for a class of shuttle transportation problems. Optim. Lett. **3**(4), 491–497 (2009)

21. Zheng, Y., Ling, H., Xue, J., Chen, S.: Population classification in fire evacuation: a multiobjective particle swarm optimization approach. IEEE Trans. Evol. Comput. **18**(1), 70–81 (2014)

22. Zheng, Y., Ling, H., Chen, S., Xue, J.: A hybrid neuro-fuzzy network based on differential biogeography-based optimization for online population classification in earthquakes. IEEE Trans. Fuzzy Syst. **23**(4), 1070–1083 (2014)

23. Zheng, Y., Zhang, M., Ling, H., Chen, S.: Emergency railway transportation planning using a hyperheuristic approach. IEEE Trans. Intell. Transp. Syst. **16**(1), 321–329 (2015)

24. Zheng, Y., Chen, Q., Ling, H., Xue, J.: Rescue wings: mobile computing and active services support for disaster rescue. IEEE Trans. Serv. Comput. **9**(4), 594–607 (2016)

25. Zheng, Y., Sheng, W., Sun, X., Chen, S.: Airline passenger profiling based on fuzzy deep machine learning. IEEE Trans. Neural Netw. Learn. Syst. **28**(12), 2911–2923 (2017)

26. Xia, J., Xue, J.: Design and implementation of concurrent distributed transaction in modeling language Apla. In: Conference of NCTCS 2018 (2018, to appear)

27. Zhu, X., Xue, J., Xia, J., Xiong, X.: The research on implementation method of multimedia database applications in the modeling language Apla. J. Jiangxi Normal Univ. (Nat. Sci. Edn.) **41**(01), 46–51 (2017)

28. Xue, J.: Program specification and its transformation techniques. Comput. Mod. (1993)

29. Xue, J.: Two new strategies for developing loop invariants and its applications. J. Comput. Sci. Technol. (3) (1993)

30. Xu, H., You, Z., Xue, J.: Automatic verification of non-recursive algorithm of Hanoi Tower by using Isabelle Theorem Prover. In: 17th IEEE/ACIS International Conference on Software Engineering, Artificial Intelligence, Networking and Parallel/Distributed Computing (SNPD), Shanghai, China, pp. 13–18, May 2016

31. Tian, C., Duan, Z., Zhang, N.: An efficient approach for abstraction-refinement in model checking. Theor. Comput. Sci. **461**, 76–85 (2012)

32. Zhang, N., Duan, Z., Tian, C.: A complete axiom systems for propositional projection temporal logic with cylinder computation model. Theor. Comput. Sci. **609**, 639–657 (2016)

33. Duan, Z., Yang, X., Koutny, M.: Framed temporal logic programming. Sci. Comput. Programm. **70**(1), 31–61 (2008)

34. Derler, P., Lee, E.A., Vincentelli, A.S.: Modeling cyber-physical systems. Proc. IEEE **100**(1), 13–28 (2012). (Special issue on CPS)

35. Liu, C.L., Layland, J.W.: Scheduling algorithm for multi-programming in a hard real-time environment. J. ACM **20**(1), 40–61 (1973)
36. Dertouzos, M.L.: Control robotics: the procedural control of physical processes. In: Proceedings of International Federation for Information Processing (IFIP) Congress, pp. 807–813 (1974)

Semantics

Formal Semantics and Tool Support for a Syntactically Restricted Dialect of SOFL

Johan van der Berg and Stefan Gruner(✉)

Department of Computer Science, University of Pretoria, Pretoria, South Africa
johan@vaderberg.info, sg@cs.up.ac.za

Abstract. SOFL is a well-known industrially applied software design language to be used within the framework of a formal engineering method (FEM). Though SOFL is easy to grasp and intuitively usable by practitioners, its original syntax permits the construction of 'funny' specifications (which cannot sensibly be implemented) and its semantics is not precisely defined. In the project described in this paper we have defined a restricted dialect of SOFL which can be parsed for syntactical correctness, and the semantics of which is well-defined. The static semantics of a SOFL specification can now be formally checked by means of an SMT solver, (SMT: Satisfiability 'modulo theory') whereas the dynamic semantics is provided by way of translation into a process algebra (the semantics of which is already given). Already available process algebra tools can then be used to formally check a well-constructed SOFL specification for interesting behavioural properties.

Keywords: SOFL · Restricted dialect · Formal semantics · Tool support

1 Introduction

The Structured Object Oriented Formal Language (SOFL) [14,18] is a high-level system design language to be used in the context of Formal Engineering Methods (FEM). Although essentially textual, SOFL specifications also include data flow diagrams to make such specifications more 'intuitive' and 'user-friendly' from the perspective of industrial software practitioners. Examples of SOFL's practical application can be found in [12,16,17,28]. For the sake of its 'intuitive user-friendliness', however, SOFL was never fully formalised. The language had 'grown organically' out of VDM-SL during a long period of time [14, Sect. 1.5], whereby more and more new 'features' were included whenever such inclusion appeared to be desirable at some point in time [14, Sect. 1.6]. As a result, SOFL's grammar gradually became 'cluttered' and redundant, such that there are now many different possibilities of expressing one and the same system specification, S, in syntactically many different ways with SOFL. This is especially true since 'functional', 'modular' and 'object-oriented' features became grammatically mingled into each other as the language evolved during its history.

Z. Duan et al. (Eds.): SOFL+MSVL 2018, LNCS 11392, pp. 125–145, 2019.
https://doi.org/10.1007/978-3-030-13651-2_8

Moreover: because of this long-term 'organic growth' of SOFL's grammar, it is now even possible with SOFL to construct meaningless (i.e. semantically void) system specifications that are not sensibly implementable. Only SOFL's *static* semantics has been reasonably well defined thus far [14, Chap. 17], whereas SOFL's intended *behavioural* semantics [8] was only informally described in [14, Sect. 1.5, 4.2–4]. For *safety-critical* applications, however, a specification language with un-ambiguous and fully formalized semantics is needed, such that safety-critical system properties (e.g. deadlock-freeness) can be reliably checked via suitable tool support.

In our current project, of which this paper gives a preliminary 'status report', we are working on the formalisation of SOFL's semantics—in particular its *behavioural* semantics—with the aim of also providing more 'powerful' tool support for SOFL practitioners. By means of such tools SOFL practitioners shall be enabled to prove with formal rigour that a specified system S is not only satisfiable (i.e. implementable), but also possesses desirable behavioural properties (e.g. deadlock-freeness). For this purpose, the over-rich 'organically grown' original grammar of SOFL had to be somewhat 'pruned', such that we are now actually working with a syntactically somewhat 'smaller' (i.e. more concise and less ambiguous) 'dialect' of SOFL. This modified SOFL grammar is suitable for parsing (i.e. to check a specification's syntactical correctness) by means of the usual parser tools. For all these purposes we have created (*inter alia*) an 'Eclipse' plug-in which provides support for validating the semantics of SOFL specifications: see Fig. 1. This plug-in was developed on the basis of a suitable domain-specific language (DSL) which enables the additional display of semantic information to a SOFL specification that is being written with help of our editor tool.

Figure 2 gives an overview of the tool chain via which the semantics of a SOFL specification can be analysed. First, a SOFL specification is created in the editor. The library 'Xtext' is used to parse the specification's file and to create a corresponding EMF model.[1] This EMF representation is then parsed for the correctness of its syntax (according to the modified grammar of our SOFL 'dialect'). Along the lines of [14, Chap. 17], the *static* semantics of a syntactically correct SOFL specification is then captured by means of a set of logic formulæ amenable to SMT solving: in this way, any available SMT solver can be used to prove (or disprove) the 'satisfiability' of the given SOFL specification.[2] In our case, the chosen solver is 'Z3' [21]. As far as a SOFL specification's *dynamic* semantics is concerned, we did not formally define one 'from scratch'; rather we followed a *translational* approach by 'mapping' a statically correct (i.e. type-checked) SOFL specification onto a corresponding ACP specification.[3] The Algebra of Communicating Processes (ACP) [3] is a suitable formalism with already well-defined dynamic semantics. Thereby, our 'mapping' of SOFL onto

---

[1] EMF: Eclipse Modeling Framework.

[2] For the definition of 'satisfiability' in SOFL see [14, Definition 25, p. 304].

[3] In earlier work we demonstrated the usefulness of such a 'translational' approach in the context of CSP specifications of wireless sensor networks [25].

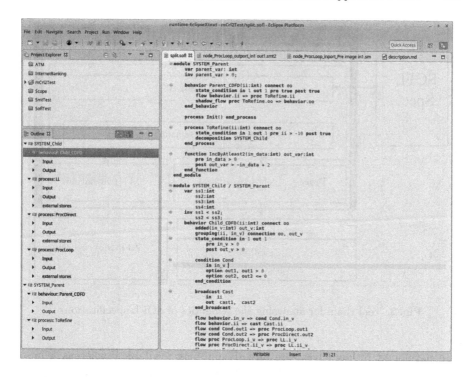

Fig. 1. Editor for syntactic and semantic analysis of SOFL specifications

ACP was guided (as much as possible) by the informal explanations and semantics descriptions found in the 'classical' SOFL book [14], although some minor deviations from the originally 'intended' SOFL process semantics turned out to be inevitable. The already existing tool suite of the 'micro Common Representation Language 2' (mCRL2) [24] can then be used to analyse the process algebraic representation (LTS: a labelled transition system) of the initially given SOFL specification for the presence or absence of interesting run-time properties, for example deadlock (Fig. 3).

Translated to ACP are only those SOFL specifications the static semantics of which is already verified. Subsequently, in our approach, the subtle relations and 'links' between static and dynamic semantics are ignored in the SOFL-to-ACP translation. As an example consider SOFL's *conditional structures* [14, Sect. 4.7] in which input data will determine on which output port some flow of data will appear. These conditional selections will be 'abstracted away' when we create an ACP representation for the operational semantics of a given SOFL specification. The resulting ACP specification is thus a 'sufficiently correct' *approximation* of the initially given SOFL specification.[4] ACP thus allows us to 'simulate' (with sufficient precision) the flow of data through SOFL's Conditional Data Flow Diagrams (CDFD). Those tools of the above-mentioned tool chain, which

---

[4] Working with approximations is very common in the field of formal methods.

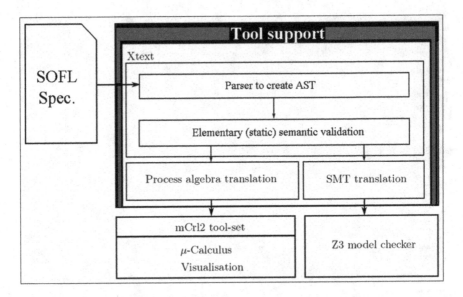

Fig. 2. Tool chain for analysing the semantics of SOFL specifications

were developed by ourselves, are already publicly available,[5] whereas a more comprehensive explanation of the underlying theoretical concepts will follow soon [2].

The remainder of this paper is organised as follows. In Sect. 2 we briefly discuss some of the most relevant related work. Section 3 outlines our modifications of the original SOFL syntax.[6] Static semantics will be considered in Sect. 4; operational semantics and property verification in Sect. 5. An example is given in Sect. 6 to illustrate the main points of our work. Section 7 concludes this paper with additional hints to future work.

2   Related Work

SOFL was already the topic of a variety of case studies [12,28] which included questions concerning SOFL's usability w.r.t. the typical 'needs' of the software engineering or system designing practitioner [30]. Though ours is not the first attempt at providing SOFL with more formal and rigorous semantics, literature on this topic is still rather scarce. As mentioned above the language's *static* semantics by Dong [7] and Liu [19, Chap. 17], which includes 'typing' rules for the proper connections between the various components of a SOFL CDFD specification, already exists, whereas the language's *behavioural* semantics was not

---

[5] https://gitlab.com/JohanVdBerg/sofl-editor.git.
[6] As we are addressing our paper to an audience of SOFL experts, we presume throughout this paper that our readers are already familiar with the contents of [14].

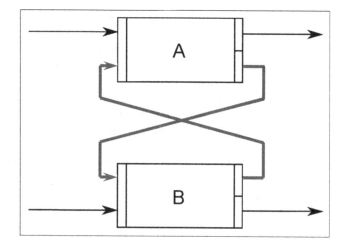

Fig. 3. Example of SOFL CDFD with possibility of deadlock

formally provided in [7] nor in [14].[7] A formal approach was taken in [8]. The generation of test data with a set of 'Functional Scenarios' (FS) was described in [11]. FS are derived from predicates by considering those predicates' structures. Thereby a FS captures a set of processes that 'fire' to produce output from input; this technique incorporates at least some 'dynamics' of a CDFD (by way of pre- and post-conditions) in the construction of a FS. The use of SMT solvers was considered in [26] to determine if a FS can be satisfied. Strictly speaking, however, the pre- and post-condition-based I/O relations of data in FS cannot fully capture the run-time dynamics of a given system, such that important properties like deadlock-freeness cannot be assessed by means of those techniques. A rigorous (albeit not tool-supported) method with Review Task Tree (RTT) diagrams was suggested to verify other logical properties (mostly static semantics) of SOFL specifications [15,20], whereas the 'internal consistency' of specifications was considered in [13]. To a limited extent also safety properties are amenable to these kinds of checking techniques. A combination of RTT and FS was described in [10]. Several support tools were created previously for working with SOFL specifications. Their user-support was typically restricted to a specification's structural syntax and (to some extent) static semantics. The tool of [19] provided visual simulations and 'animations' of data flows through CDFD by way of Message Sequence Charts (MSC). Similar simulations were shown in [9] on the basis of the above-mentioned FS. From FS execution paths a Kripke structure was created in [26] and model-checked with PROMELA/SPIN. A hierarchical meta structure of such Kripke structure is used to capture the nested structures of CDFD (with their sub-CDFD, processes and sub-processes). In [29]

---

[7] Personal communication (e-mail) by Shaoying Liu: *"In principle, SOFL specification inspection does not support formal proof simply because it is rather difficult for ordinary engineers, but for some critical applications formal proof may be valuable"* (8 Nov. 2013).

a finite state machine was created from FS. Internal consistency proof techniques are described in [6] where proof obligations stemming from FS are formulated. Operational semantics for SOFL were formally defined in [8] with help of the formalism 'Object Z'. Using a machine-checkable notation has the advantage of proof-automation for relevant properties of interest: the tool 'Ott' [23] can be used for this purpose. Noteworthy progress was also made in tool-support for a DSL of which SOFL is an instance. Xtext allows the definition of such DSL and provides a framework that enables semantic validation, code generation, and integration all in Eclipse. Thereby the library 'Xsemantics',[8] which cooperates well Xtext, assists in defining a type checker for a DSL's static semantics.

3   A New SOFL Dialect

Our new 'dialect' of SOFL has a grammar G'' based on a simplification G' of the original grammar G of [14, Appendix A]: after simplification, G' was augmented to G'' by the addition of a small number of new features which had not been part of the original G. Formally: $G' = G \cap G''$. These changes were introduced to simplify the syntactic analysis (parsing) as well as to facilitate the formal semantic analysis of specifications written in our SOFL 'dialect'. The example shown at the end of this paper sketches some of those grammatical differences; all details will appear comprehensively in [2]. Thereby, our new grammar supports specifically SOFL's user-friendly graphical CDFD notation (rather than the text-based 'explicit' specifications of [14, Sub-sect. 4.17.1 and Chap. 6]).

According to the 'classical' SOFL grammar each *process* consist of pre- and post-conditions whereby each conditioning predicate P is defined of over a *set of* ports. This, however, permits specifications in which the 'firing' rules of a process lead to strange situations. Consider, for example, a pre-condition $(x > 0) \vee (y > 0 \wedge \text{bound}(x))$ for an 'exclusive-or process', B [14, Fig. 4.3:B], where data flows x, y are connected to *different* (separate) input ports: When $y = 10$ (data available) and $x = \perp$ (no data) then the 'exclusive-or' process ought to 'fire', because: "*When either x or y is available, process B takes x or y, but not both, as input*" [14, Sect. 4.3, p. 61]. However the given pre-condition evaluates to 'false', which is in our semantics not allowed for any process to start. The dilemma in this scenario is due to the sub-condition 'bound(x)' which creates a dependency between the two (allegedly 'separate') ports. In our 'dialect' of SOFL, by contrast, a pre/post-condition will be defined individually for each input/output port *pair* to avoid the problem sketched above. The 'expressive power' of our new pre/post conditions is thus indeed somewhat limited,[9] but so we prevent cumbersome scenarios, like the one sketched above, which are not desirable in software-modelling. Our modification is consistent with [8], in which 'pre-condition = *true*' is also *demanded* before a process is allowed to 'fire', however *not* necessarily with [14, Sect. 4.3, p. 57] where it is vaguely stated that "*if the precondition is not satisfied by the input data flows, no correct output*

---

[8] https://github.com/eclipse/xsemantics.
[9] This had been noticed by one of our anonymous reviewers.

data flows are guaranteed". In other words: [14] does *not strictly prevent* 'crazy' processes from doing 'whatever they want' as soon as any kind of stimulus arrives at their input ports. By contrast: our processes (like the ones of [8]) must remain 'silent' when any given input violates a pre-condition.[10]

Demanding that a node's pre-condition must evaluate to true before it fires entails a notion of *'total' correctness*, i.e.: each process must 'terminate' in the sense of yielding post-condition-compatible output data (before this process may possibly be allowed to 'start again'). This modification removed the need to evaluate expressions in ternary logic $(t, f, \bot)$ on undefined clauses. SOFL's original use of the Logic of Partial Functions (LPF) with a third truth-value ($\bot$ or 'nil') [14, Sect. 3.6] is thus no longer needed in our approach. A disadvantage of this restriction is that predicate expressions (conditions) over dynamic data structures, for example '$\ell[1]/\text{len}(\ell) = 1$' with $\ell = []$ (hence: $\text{len}(\ell) = 0$), can no longer be evaluated any more.[11] Moreover, only *active* data flows will be used, whereby '*shadow* flows' are newly introduced in cases where no data flows are connected to any port. With help of such 'shadow flows' it can be indicated whether a process actually consumes data such that its embedding CDFD can 'terminate'. The firing rules applicable to shadow flows are the same as the ones for active data flows.

Hierarchical *refinement* of a process adds 'details' in a structured manner in order to create specifications that can ultimately serve as implementations. Problematic, however, was the way in which the additional refining data flows were defined. In the original SOFL they are simply inserted into a CDFD with only little additional information concerning their data flows.[12] Hence it was possible in the original SOFL framework to specify data flows the types of which were not sufficiently constrained, i.e.: the data *values* that a port can expect as inputs cannot be sufficiently restricted by logical predicates.[13] In our new SOFL 'dialect', by contrast, these problems can no longer occur. *Assignments* in SOFL are done in let statements and when stipulating the values of data stores. In our approach, by changing all expressions to be more 'function-like', the use of assignments to data stores is avoided. With a let statement a predicate is assigned to a variable and is substituted where the variable is used. When a value needs to be specified uniquely the corresponding predicate must be valid on states that contain only the value that is needed in such a situation.

Last but not least, the original SOFL's object-oriented *Class* concept [14, Chap. 13] turned out to be problematic, too.[14] In a SOFL Class definition the

---

[10] This, too, had been noticed by one of our anonymous reviewers.

[11] One of our anonymous reviewers has made such a remark. The list operators used in the example of above can be found in [14, Sect. 9.3].

[12] The relevant assertions on this topic can be found 'scattered' across [14, Rule 5.1, Rule 5.2, Definition 14, Definition 17, Definition 27, Definition 30 in Chap. 5 and Chap. 17].

[13] For comparison see the concept of 'Value-Space-based Sub-Typing' [22].

[14] During the historic evolution of SOFL, those object-oriented features were simply 'plugged onto' the already existing older functional features, thus 'cluttering' the entire language with much redundancy.

behaviour of its Methods must be specified, too: for this purpose CDFD are typically used again. Hence it is possible in the original SOFL framework to create semantically dubious self-references, whereby a CDFD can contain data flow of a Class type in which the very same CDFD can be used again to define Methods of that Class the Objects of which are sent as data through the channels of the CDFD. Although this claim may sound strange,[15] it can actually be proven on the basis of the grammar given in [14, Appendix A]. For this reason the Class concept has been entirely excluded from the grammar of our modified SOFL dialect.[16]

4   Static Semantics

The static semantics (including type declarations and the correct 'linking' of process via channels) of a SOFL specification will be checked by means of Xtext validation and translation into SMT-LIB. The underlying correctness definitions can be found in [14, Chap. 17], but since predicates are differently associated with ports in our dialect, some of the checks will be somewhat more complicated than in [14, Chap. 17]. However, since we do not longer use the trivalent LPF, any 'normal' SMT solver can be used to discharge the arising proof obligations.

Xtext Validation. This validation phase is convenient for the user as it provides rapid feedback if a SOFL specification is not statically consistent. For the sake of a 'swift' and 'smooth' user-experience, the checks in this phase may not be computationally costly. They merely ensure that: • data flow channels are connected correctly; • only elements 'visible' in their 'scope' are accessed; • process refinement is correct (#ports and variables used at the ports); • types are correctly used as declared.

When a process gets *refined*, a SOFL *module* and a CDFD are associated with it. As in [14] a module defines access to data stores by the processes it contains, and (possibly) additional data stores and further processes that are introduced to add further details to the refinement. Since a CDFD can add additional data flows, new ports can also be defined. Thus each port of the process being refined is mapped to a set of ports in the entire CDFD, whereby the images of these mappings are disjoint. The mapping takes a port p to a set of ports $R(p)$ that *can only be modified by adding* extra data flows to the port. When data flows are added to a port due to refinement it must be done in such a manner that no two ports in $R(p)$ are connected to the same data flow. Data flows originally connected to p are also connected to all ports in $R(p)$ resulting in the same data flow being connected to more than one port. This is an *exception* to the rule: 'the end of a data flows can only be connected to one port', but must be allowed due to the separation between the process being refined and the CDFD; note

---

[15] One of our anonymous reviewers had made a comment on this point.

[16] Strictly speaking we have thus an 'SFL' dialect *without* the Object-oriented 'O'.

that it is not allowed for data to be consumed (nor generated) twice from one data flow.[17]

A *type* in SOFL is defined by the set of data value instances that the type comprises. For standard types, like numbers, these sets of values are predefined. Nodes and data flows are regarded in our approach as instances of a new 'connection' type. Thereby, data flows connect input/output variable of nodes, such that the types of the variables and the data flows must 'match' consistently.

SMT Translation. To check the above-mentioned static semantic properties with an SMT solver, a SOFL specification must be represented logically such that the solver can 'work' with it: We do this via translation to SMT-LIB [1]. Because the verification of SMT formulæ is computationally expensive, this is done in a separate phase of the work-flow (Fig. 2). These checks are done on the basis of the notion of 'types as predicates' [27]. Thereby a (sub)type is restricted by a predicate which is used to define a (sub)set of the original set of possible data values. For a SOFL specification to be internally consistent none of these set may be empty. For the translation *only numeric types* are currently taken into account; the automatic verification of SOFL expressions with more complex data types is 'future work'. For checking such complex expressions the already existing 'manual' (semi-formal) 'review' methods [13,14, Sect. 17.4–6] can (and must) currently still be applied.[18]

Data Flows in SOFL are used to connect ports of processes in the same CDFD. In this paragraph it will be additionally assumed that a port of a process being refined and the related ports of its CDFD are also properly connected. Ports are connected in $[1\!:\!1]$ or $[m\!:\!1]$ relations. A $[m\!:\!1]$ relation is shown in Fig. 4 where predicate P is the conjunction of all predicates associated with the source ports and an invariant I_p. Condition Q is the conjunction of the predicates associated with the destination port and an invariant I_q. Invariant I_x ($x \in \{p, q\}$) is defined by the invariant of the module that contains the ports. When a port is connected to an input port of a CDFD the condition defined by that CDFD's Init process is also included in its invariant. The corresponding proof obligation, O, is thus $((\exists_{\bar{x} \in var(P)} P) \wedge (\forall_{\bar{x} \in var(P)} P \rightarrow Q))$ being satisfiable, where $\bar{x} \in var(P)$ denotes all free variables in P. This lengthy obligation formula is henceforth *abbreviated* as: $(P \rightarrow_O Q)$.

Invariants and Initialisation. Invariants are defined on SOFL *modules* and additionally constrain the pre- and post-conditions of *all* processes that belong to each module. If a module has a parent module then the invariant of the parent module is only applicable for data flows connected to input and output ports of its CDFD. When a CDFD 'fires', its Init process is invoked first. This situation is captured by a predicate that restricts the data flows connected to the input port of its CDFD.

---

[17] Shortage of page-space in this paper does not allow us to illustrate the very dense description of above with a picture; the full explanation will appear in [2].

[18] One of our anonymous reviewers had made such a remark.

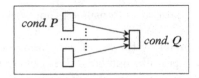

Fig. 4. Connections $[m\!:\!1]$ between ports with conditions P, Q

Processes. In our approach we cannot test statically if a process is implementable; we only check if there is any contradiction between its pre/post-conditions and the invariant of its containing module. If a contradiction is found then the entire module (with all its processes) is certainly not implementable. Refinement of a process depends on the question if a process itself is implementable: this will be assumed if the CDFD that refines the process is consistent. Predicates are also added to pre/post-conditions for data stores with only 'read' access in order to ensure that the values of stores do not inconsistently change when their accessing process 'fires'.

Structure Nodes with conditions [14, Fig. 4.19] are the only CDFD nodes that 'apply' predicates. For a condition node to be consistent its pre-condition must imply the disjunction of its output port's conditions, whereby the pairwise conjunction of its post conditions must be 'false'. SOFL's merge and un-merge structures [14, Fig. 4.20] do not apply predicates. They create product types, or split a product type into its components. The statically correct usage of these structures is checked by our above-mentioned Xtext validation.

SMT Solver. The above-mentioned proof obligations are translated into SMT-LIB format, on which the solver Z3 [21] is used. In this format our numeric types are defined by (declare-var x Real) and (declare-var x Int). *Natural* numbers are Integers with an additional constraint: (assume (> x 0)). For example, a satisfiability proof obligation $((x > 10) \to_O (-x < 0))$ under some invariant $y > 0$ is captured by the solver script:

```
(set-option : print-success false)
(set-logic ALL)
(declare-const y Int)
(declare-const x Int)
(push)
(assert( forall ((x Int) (global Int))(
=> (and (> y 0) (> x 10))
   (and (> y 0) (< (-x) 0)))))
(check-sat)
(pop)
(push)
(assert (and (> y 0) (> x 10)))
(check-sat)
(pop)
```

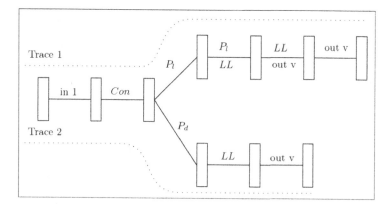

Fig. 5. LTS example of some CDFD with two behavioural traces

5   Dynamic Semantics and Property Verification

In our approach, the dynamic semantics of SOFL specifications are formally
defined by translation into ACP whereby the already existing tool mCRL2 is
used to create a corresponding LTS. In the following, the translation is explained
first with an 'exact' LTS. Thereafter we show how the exact LTS is approxi-
mated, and finally how its ACP description is generated. During this transformation an *abstraction* is created by using *tokens that represent which data flows
actually contain data*. This abstraction yields an *over-approximation* of a SOFL
specification by permitting data flows that would not normally occur. Thus: all
'behaviour' that is *absent* from the over-approximation must be absent from the
original system, too.

Exact Case. A state in an 'exact' LTS consist of: • all values 'in' the data flows
and data stores; • a label for each (sub)set of nodes that can fire; • information
about when a CDFD generates or consumes data. Figure 5 shows the LTS of
an example in which only two 'traces' are considered: the first state transition
indicates which one of the input ports consumes data. The set of nodes that fire
next is indicated by a state transition labelled with the nodes that fire. When
data is generated on an output port, a transition is created and labelled with the
port that yields the generated data. Whenever a set of nodes fire, proper access
to any connected data stores must be verified. If there is any violation, an error
state is created in the LTS (*not* Fig. 5). In Trace 1 the CDFD generates output
twice: such behaviour is not desirable, and a μ-Calculus formula will be used to
'catch' situations like these.

Approximation. The LTS used here will convert a transition to a sequence
of labels where the labels are contained in the set of labels under consideration. All sequences created from the same set are considered equivalent,
and additional labels are created to separate sequences from different sets. All

μ-Calculus formulæ use this LTS as underlying Kripke structure. All labels are order-dependent. For example: to test if both process P_l and L fire simultaneously we only need to test if either the sequence P_l, L or L, P_l appear in the formula. When these two processes need to fire at separate stages, as in the exact case, an additional transition *sep* is needed to indicate a separation between sets of nodes that fire. The sequence that needs to be tested for is now P_l, sep, L. Both these formulæ evaluate to 'true' for Trace 1 in Fig. 5.

ACP Description. When a process algebra description is created the implementation of ACP in mCRL2 is used. When an action is involved in synchronisation the action itself will be blocked to prevent any asynchronous behaviour. A number of auxiliary actions are also used to ensure a correct order of events. For example: when a set of nodes fire, all these nodes must fire first before the actions indicating the end of the firing sequence are enabled, (e.g. *sep*). Any auxiliary actions, that do not contain any information when we analyse the behaviour of a CDFD, are treated as 'internal' actions. A mCRL2 description consists of a fixed part and a part that changes depending on the underlying SOFL specification. For each data flow, node, port, and store an identifier is created as follows:

```
%%% Begin Specification-Specific Definitions:
sort FlowId = struct Child_CDFDin_v_in_vCond |
                     Condout1_out1ProcLoop | ... ;
sort NodeId = struct cdsa_node | NIChild_CDFD |
                     NICond | ... | NIProcOther;
sort PortId = struct IP0 | IP1;
sort StoreId = struct ss2 | ss3;
%%% Begin Specification-Independent Definitions:
sort NodeType = struct ... ;
sort FlowIdAction = struct ... ;
sort Phase = struct ... ;
sort Rights = struct ... ;
sort StoreMap = StoreId -> Int;
```

Mappings define connection and inclusion relations between the elements by means of rewrite rules of the form: (Predicate) -> LHS(...) = RHS, whereby the predicate is allowed to use the parameters of the LHS. A rule is applied only if its predicate evaluates to 'true'. For example, the following mappings belong to a description of a SOFL CDFD and are used by the corresponding ACP processes to simulate how data flows through the CDFD:

```
(NICast == nd_id && IP0 == pid)
        -> inPortDataFlowId(nd_id, pid) = {Child_CDFDii_iiCast};
(NICast == nd_id && IP0 == pid) -> outPortDataFlowId(nd_id, pid) = {};
(NIProcDirect == nd_id)
        -> nodeInFlowIds(nd_id) = {Condout2_out2ProcDirect};
(NICast == nd_id) -> node_write_list(nd_id) = [];
(NIProcDirect == nd_id) -> node_read_list(nd_id) = [ss3];
(NICast == nd_id) -> nodeInPorts(nd_id) = [IP0];
(node_type == exec_control) -> getNodeOfType(node_type) = [NICast,NICond];
```

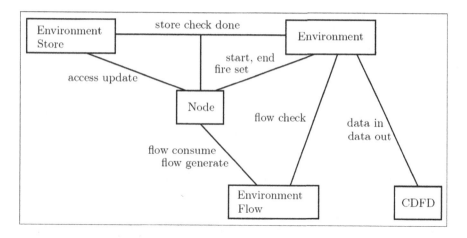

Fig. 6. ACP process types onto which SOFL entities are mapped

Five types of ACP processes are used in our approach. For each SOFL node an instance of a process `Node` is created which represents consumed data from an input port, generated data on an output port, and write-access rights needed to update data stores. An `EnvironmentFlowIds` process is created that keeps a set of all data flows that actually contain data. An `EnvironmentStore` process, which updates instances of a function of type `StoreMap = StoreId -> Int`, determines if read/write accesses are valid. The value the mapping evaluates to gives the number of processes that require a specific write-access. The process `CdfdIO` is used to generate data for a CDFD to consume and to accept data generated by a SOFL process. The process `Environment` is used to determine the type of nodes that are allowed to fire next. Interaction between the ACP process types, sketched in Fig. 6, is defined by

```
allow({flow_action, flow_consume, ...},
 comm({...
        env_flow          |node_flow           -> flow_action,
        env_flow_consume  |node_flow_consume -> flow_consume,
        ... }) ...
```

Whenever actions on the left hand side of '→' are possible simultaneously, a new action is created to represent that (and when) both actions occur. The new action's name is on the right hand side of '→'. Whenever actions are renamed, the action of the left hand side of '→' is blocked. For two concurrent processes,

$$(\Sigma_d \text{ env\_flow}(d)) \parallel (\Sigma_d \text{ node\_flow}(d))$$

where d is a parameter variable for the actions env_flow, and node_flow respectively, of the same type. The operator `comm` (of above) defines that whenever the two actions happen at the same time, and with identical parameters, then the action flow_action is added. Hence,

$$(\Sigma_d \; \text{env\_flow}(d)) \; || \; (\Sigma_d \; \text{node\_flow}(d)) \; || \; (\Sigma_d \; \text{flow\_action}(d))$$

is the newly created process. Since only the actions of type flow_action are of interest, all other actions are removed. This creates the process $(\Sigma_d \; \text{flow\_action}(d))$. This technique of 'synchronise and prevent' is used to create the ACP process that corresponds to the entities of a SOFL CDFD.

After such a synchronisation step, the actions that are not of further interest are redefined as 'internal' actions (which makes them 'invisible'). These internal actions are then removed on the basis of a *weak trace-equivalence* relation. A *trace-based semantics* was chosen in our approach because the possible sequences of actions are of highest interest; (for comparison see [25]).

Property Verification. *Access violations* on data stores are verified by identifying *error actions* in a LTS. Similar to what we know from model-checking, the output of such an analysis is a text file that contains a 'witnessing' sequence of events (i.e. a trace of nodes that 'fire' until a correctness property of interest has been violated)—for example:

```
File:_error_r_w.trc.txt
    cdsa_input(IP1)
    env_new_start
    start_fire(NIProcDirect)
    start_fire(NIProcOther)
    store_update(ss3, write_access_begin)
    store_update(ss3, write_access_begin)
    error_r_w(0, 2).
```

Other dynamic properties are verified via μ-Calculus formulæ.[19] On each label in the LTS we can use the modal 'possibility' operator $\diamond$ (<*labelname* >) as well as the modal 'necessity' operator $\square$ ([label name]). The syntax of mCRL2 also permits regular expressions with 'star' (<*labelname*∗ >) to indicate zero or more repetitions. *For example*, to check how an input port 1 in some CDFD relates to output on port 2 we can write:

```
<true*.cdsa_input(IP0).true*.cdsa_output(IP1)>true
```

and to determine if a process ProcDirect can execute infinitely often we write:

```
nu X.<true*.fire(ProcDirect)>X
```

where nu (ν) is the greatest infix operator. To determine if data can be generated more than once by a CDFD where the first output is given by IP0, we write:

```
exists cop:PortId.<true*.cdsa_output(IP1).true*.cdsa_output(cop)>true
```

---

[19] Please see Fig. 2 again for the 'general overview'. The method of generating the μ-Calculus formulæ cannot be explained in this paper due to shortage of page-space; please see [2] for the details.

6   Software Architecture and Example

As mentioned above, our new SOFL specification editor will translate SOFL specifications into their corresponding SMT-LIB files, mCRL2 descriptions, and script files, which are needed as auxiliary data structures to compute the desired semantic evaluation. In the directory 'src-gen' a folder structure is created which mirrors the inheritance of the SOFL modules and in which the translated files are stored—for example:

```
src-gen
  SYSTEM_Parent
    scripts
      prove_smt.sh
    smt_scripts
    mu_calcules_SYSTEM_Parent.sh
    trans_SYSTEM_Parent.sh
    SYSTEM_Child
      scripts
      smt_scripts
```

When a specification passes its static verification via Xtext, the above-mentioned translations are carried out. The script trans_SYSTEM_Parent.sh will create the needed LTS model, and mu_calcules_SYSTEM_Parent.sh will evaluate the corresponding μ-Calculus formulæ. The SMT scripts are then evaluated by running prove_smt.sh. Thereby our editor also generates formulæ to check the following *properties* of interest: • Can each input port of the CDFD 'trigger'? • Can a node only consume data from *one* of its input ports at any point in time? • Will the output ports of the CDFD *yield values* when their corresponding input ports can trigger? • Is there a set of nodes that can never trigger (i.e. *starvation*)? • Is there a set of nodes that can trigger infinitely often (i.e. *liveness*)?

An example of a textual SOFL specification with modified syntax is shown in Fig. 7 wherein the deviations from SOFL's original syntax are highlighted. Figure 8 shows the corresponding CDFD. Since our tool does not yet support graphical representations of CDFDs, text must be typed (like in Fig. 7) to defined a SOFL specification's control structures and data flow connections.

To get an impression of the run-time performance of checking properties of interest we sent the example specification of Fig. 7 through our tool-chain and obtained the following results:[20] • time required to compute the **LTS** models $\approx$ **18 seconds**; • time to evaluate the **SMT** formulæ $\approx$ **2 seconds**; • time to evaluate the μ-**Calculus** formulæ $\approx$ **41 seconds**. Thereby, • each input port of the CDFD was found to be able to 'fire' to generate data (values) at the corresponding output port; • no node was able to consume data from more than one input port at any given time; • no node was never able to trigger (i.e. no starvation); • two nodes of the CDFD were able to 'fire' infinitely often (liveness), namly P_l and LL.

---

[20] Intel i7-6700 CPU.

```
module SYSTEM_Parent
  var parent_var:int
  inv parent_var > 10;                    Define a shadow data flow
  behavior Parent_CDFD(indata:int | connect alt) connect oo | out_other:nat0
    state_condition in 1 out 1 pre indata>10 post true
    state_condition in 1 out 2 pre indata>=10 post true
    state_condition in 2 out 1 pre false post true
    state_condition in 2 out 2 pre false post true
    flow behavior.indata
        => proc ToRefine.indata
    ...                                   Define active flows and shadows flows
    shadow_flow behavior.alt
        => proc ToRefine.alt
  end_behavior
  process Init()
    parent_var < 100 and parent_var > 0; Define initial constrain on data stores
  end_process
  process ToRefine(indata:int | connect alt) connect oo | out_other:nat0
    ext wr parent_var
    ...
    decomposition SYSTEM_Child           Define module that refines this process
  end_process
  function IncByAtleast2(in_data:nat) out_var:nat
    pre in_data > 0  post out_var > ~in_data + 2
  end_function
end_module
module SYSTEM_Child/SYSTEM_Parent
  var ss2:int ss3:int
  inv ss1 < ss2;
  behavior Child_CDFD(in_1:int | connect alt) connect oo | out_other:nat0
    added(in_v:real) out_v:int           Adding new data input/output data flows
    grouping(in_1 | connection alt , in_v)      Data flows grouped ports
      connection oo, out_v | out_other
    ....
    condition Cond
      in in_1
      option out1, out1 > 0
      option out2, out2 <= 0
    end_condition                        Define flow control structures
    broadcast Cast
      in in_v
      out c_data_1, c_data_2
    end_broadcast
    shadow_flow behavior.alt => proc ProcOther.alt
    flow behavior.in_1 => cond Cond.in_1
    flow behavior.in_v => cast Cast.in_v
    ...
end_module
```

Fig. 7. Example: textual SOFL specification (with modified syntax)

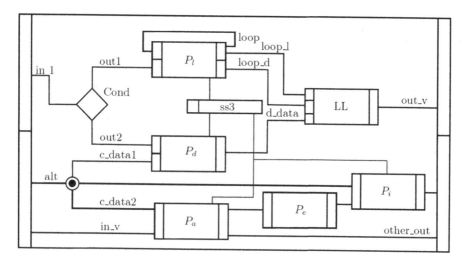

Fig. 8. CDFD graph corresponding to the textual specification of Fig. 7

7 Conclusion and Outlook to Future Work

In our almost completed project which we described in this paper we created a *new editor* that supports the *formulation and correctness-checking* of SOFL specifications. To achieve this aim a *new 'dialect'* of SOFL was defined the syntax of which differs slightly from the original syntax of [14]. Our modifications and improvements facilitate the use of an SMT solver for the verification of a SOFL specification's *static semantics* as well as the use of already existing ACP tools for the verification of a SOFL specification's *dynamic semantics*. Due to the sound formality of our techniques, safety-critical features of software systems designed with SOFL can henceforth be checked with a higher level of trustworthiness. Thereby, integration into the Eclipse environment shall make these new possibilities convenient and user-friendly for the practical software engineer who works with SOFL from day to day.

As mentioned above, our work in this project has not yet come to its full completion. In particular, our editor can still be improved by: • better integration support for Z3 and mCRL2; • running the script file through the editor (rather than off-line); • generating more 'legible' (user-friendly) reports of the analysis results; and • adding a graphical representation window of CDFDs for better 'intuition'. Moreover, our current implementation of performing types-checking (static semantics) requires explicit additional annotations in the syntax of a SOFL specification in order to provide the type information which the SMT solver needs. A more 'intelligent' type inferencing algorithm would thus be desirable for the sake of the editor's usability in practice.

Since the ternary LPF with its third truth-value ($\perp$) was removed, numeric-boolean expressions like (lst(0)/len(lst)>0) cannot always be evaluated any more. One way of circumventing this problem is to replace the given expression by (in this case):

$(\texttt{len(lst)} \neq 0 \implies (\texttt{lst(0)/len(lst)}) > 0) \vee (\texttt{len(lst)} = 0 \implies \texttt{false})$

which, though not a very elegant solution, can be justified by seeing it as the 'price' we have to 'pay' in order to 'buy' the desired precision of formality. Better tools support might also reduce this inconvenience to the practitioners in future.

As mentioned above, our restricted new dialect of SOFL does not contain all the grammatical clauses of SOFL's original syntax [14, Appendix A]. Most notable is our omission of the original SOFL's non-deterministic broadcast structures as well as the object-oriented Class types. Whereas those features had made SOFL quite 'convenient' for nowadays users (who tend to take the OO paradigm already for granted), the formal semantics of those features is subtle and difficult to define [5]: more research-time is thus needed to think very carefully about these non-trivial matters. Inclusion of Class types into our new dialect of SOFL, as well as the translation of more complex expressions to SMT-LIB, may thus be considered as 'future work'. A path in this direction might be to formally define Abstract Data Types (ADT) for those types first [5], and then to consider how to introduce user-definable data-types into the language's grammar in such a way that they remain compatible with the formally defined ADT.

In our example of above there was some process P_a that 'fired' before another process P_i, though for both processes the 'embedding' invariants defined by Init are applicable. Process P_a, however, might change the internal state of the common data store such that the invariants defined by Init might perhaps be violated when P_i 'fires'. Static analysis of pre- and post-conditions alone cannot 'capture' such a sequence of events when only the predicates of P_i are considered but the *side-effects* of P_a are ignored.[21] Thus, in future work, the firing sequences in which data stores are modified must also be considered for the formal verification of SOFL specifications: this will require a formal representation of SOFL data stores by Algebraic Data Types (ADT).

In the current phase of our project the above-mentioned translation to ACP does not yet consider all information contained in the pre/post-conditions of SOFL processes. By including all information the approximation of the behaviour of a CDFD will be closer to that of an executable 'implementation'. In this context we should also consider the possibility of constructing process *loops* in SOFL—like in *cybernetic* feedback loops or in digital electronic cirquits (e.g. flip-flops)—the formal semantics of which is not a triviality. Then, however, SOFL will become usable not only for software specifications but also for the *specification of almost any type of hardware systems* that can be characterised 'cybernetically' by some kind of 'flow' (of matter or energy or information) between 'reactors' or 'service stations'.

Last but not least, our above-mentioned run-time experiment was only small. Run-time tests with larger CDFD specifications did not yield any analysis results and were aborted after many hours of run-time. Hence, our 'academic' tool-chain

---

[21] 'Processes' in SOFL may be considered as 'functions plus side-effects', in contrast to the 'pure' functions that SOFL also allows to be specified [14, Sect. 4.17].

is not yet 'scalable'—i.e.: not yet suitable for SOFL specifications of industrially relevant size. Only 'fragments' of such large specifications can currently be checked where the level of abstraction is reasonably high (without too many details included). This shortcoming of the current version of our tool-chain illustrates of the notorious 'state space explosion problem' in automated verification, for which our tool-chain is not yet sufficiently equipped with 'smart' state space reduction methods. For larger SOFL specifications the use of the 'LTSmin' tool-set with multi-core processing [4], in combination with 'smarter' model-building and abstraction techniques, might yield some noteworthy runtime improvement. Since we cannot modify the implementation of the 'external' (third-party) tools 'mCRL2' and 'Z3' at the back-ends of our tool-chain (Fig. 2), it will be very important to further 'optimise' the internal tools of our chain from which 'mCRL2' and 'Z3' receive their input models.

Acknowledgements. During the course of our project several discussions with the following experts were especially helpful: *Shaoying Liu, Markus Roggenbach, Jan Friso Groote, Stefan Blom, Jaco v.d. Pol*, and *Christian Dietrich*. We thank the anonymous reviewers for their insightful comments on our paper's draft before the SOFL+MSVL'18 workshop, and we also acknowledge the interesting discussion contributions by various participants of the workshop following our paper's presentation in Australia.

References

1. Barrett, C., Fontaine, P., Tinelli, C.: The SMT-LIB Standard: Version 2.6. Technical report, University of Iowa (2017). www.SMT-LIB.org
2. van der Berg, J.S.: A New Dialect of SOFL: Syntax, Formal Semantics, and Tool Support. M.-Thesis, University of Pretoria (forthcoming)
3. Bergstra, J., Klop, J.: Process algebra for synchronous communication. Inf. Control **60**, 109–137 (1984)
4. Blom, S., van de Pol, J., Weber, M.: LTSMIN: distributed and symbolic reachability. In: Touili, T., Cook, B., Jackson, P. (eds.) CAV 2010. LNCS, vol. 6174, pp. 354–359. Springer, Heidelberg (2010). https://doi.org/10.1007/978-3-642-14295-6_31
5. Bruce, K.B.: Foundations of Object-Oriented Languages: Types and Semantics. MIT Press, Cambridge (2002)
6. Chen, Y.: Checking internal consistency of SOFL specification: a hybrid approach. In: Liu, S., Duan, Z. (eds.) SOFL+MSVL 2013. LNCS, vol. 8332, pp. 175–191. Springer, Cham (2014). https://doi.org/10.1007/978-3-319-04915-1_13
7. Dong, J.S., Liu, S.: An object semantic model of SOFL. In: Araki, K., Galloway, A., Taguchi, K. (eds.) IFM'99, pp. 189–208. Springer, London (1999). https://doi.org/10.1007/978-1-4471-0851-1_11
8. Ho-Stuart, C., Liu, S.: A formal operational semantics for SOFL. In: Joint Proceedings of the 4th International Computer Science Conference and 4th Asia Pacific Software Engineering Conference, pp. 52–61. IEEE (1997)
9. Li, M., Liu, S.: Automated functional scenarios-based formal specification animation. In: Proceedings of the 19th Asia-Pacific Software Engineering Conference, pp. 107–115. IEEE (2012)
10. Li, M., Liu, S.: Tool support for rigorous formal specification inspection. In: Proceedings of the 17th International Conference on Computational Science and Engineering, pp. 729–734. IEEE (2014)

11. Li, C., Liu, S., Nakajima, S.: An experiment for assessment of a functional scenario-based test case generation method. In: Proceedings of International Conference on Software Engineering and Technology, ICSET 2012, pp. 424–431 (2012)
12. Liu, S.: A Case Study of Modeling an ATM Using SOFL. Technical report, Hosei University (2003)
13. Liu, S.: A rigorous approach to reviewing formal specifications. In: Proceedings of 27th Annual NASA Goddard IEEE Software Engineering Workshop, pp. 75–81. IEEE (2002/2003)
14. Liu, S.: Formal engineering for industrial software development – an introduction to the SOFL specification language and method. In: Davies, J., Schulte, W., Barnett, M. (eds.) ICFEM 2004. LNCS, vol. 3308, pp. 7–8. Springer, Heidelberg (2004). https://doi.org/10.1007/978-3-540-30482-1_4
15. Liu, S.: Utilizing specification testing in review task trees for rigorous review of formal specifications. In: Proceedings of the 10th Asia-Pacific Software Engineering Conference, pp. 510–519. IEEE (2003)
16. Liu, S., Asuka, M., Komaya, K., Nakamura, Y.: Applying SOFL to specify a railway crossing controller for industry. In: Proceedings of the 2nd IEEE Workshop on Industrial Strength Formal Specification Techniques, pp. 16–27 (1998)
17. Liu, S., Shibata, M., Sato, R.: Applying SOFL to develop a university information system. In: Proceedings of the 6th Asia-Pacific Software Engineering Conference, pp. 404–411. IEEE (1999)
18. Liu, S., Sun, Y.: Structured methodology + object-oriented methodology + formal methods: methodology of SOFL. In: Proceedings of the 1st IEEE International Conference on Engineering of Complex Computer Systems, ICECCS 1995, pp. 137–144. IEEE (1995)
19. Liu, S., Wang, H.: An automated approach to specification animation for validation. J. Syst. Softw. **80**(8), 1271–1285 (2007)
20. Liu, S., Woodcock, J.: Supporting rigorous reviews of formal specifications using fault trees. In: Proceedings of 16th World Computer Congress Conference on Software: Theory and Practice, pp. 459–470 (2000)
21. de Moura, L., Bjørner, N.: Z3: an efficient SMT solver. In: Ramakrishnan, C.R., Rehof, J. (eds.) TACAS 2008. LNCS, vol. 4963, pp. 337–340. Springer, Heidelberg (2008). https://doi.org/10.1007/978-3-540-78800-3_24
22. Paar, A., Gruner, S.: Static typing with value-space-based subtyping. In: Proceedings of the South African Institute of Computer Scientists and Information Technologists, SAICSIT 2011, pp. 177–186. ACM (2011)
23. Sewell, P., et al.: Ott: effective tool support for the working semanticist. J. Funct. Program. **20**(1), 71–122 (2010)
24. Stappers, F.P.M., Reniers, M.A., Groote, J.F.: Suitability of mCRL2 for concurrent-system design: a 2 × 2 switch case study. In: de Boer, F.S., Bonsangue, M.M., Hallerstede, S., Leuschel, M. (eds.) FMCO 2009. LNCS, vol. 6286, pp. 166–185. Springer, Heidelberg (2010). https://doi.org/10.1007/978-3-642-17071-3_9
25. Steyn, T.J., Gruner, S.: A new optional parallelism operator in CSP for wireless sensor networks. In: Proceedings of the South African Institute of Computer Scientists and Information Technologists, SAICSIT 2017, pp. 303–310. ACM (2017)
26. Tian, C., Liu, S., Duan, Z.: Abstract model checking with SOFL hierarchy. In: [16], pp. 71–86 (2013)
27. Wadler, P.: Propositions as types. Commun. ACM **58**(12), 75–84 (2015)
28. Wang, J., Liu, S., Qi, Y., Hou, D.: Developing an insulin pump system using the SOFL method. In: Proceedings of the 14th Asia-Pacific Software Engineering Conference, pp. 334–341. IEEE (2007)

29. Wang, X., Liu, S.: Development of a supporting tool for formalizing software requirements. In: Liu, S. (ed.) SOFL 2012. LNCS, vol. 7787, pp. 56–70. Springer, Heidelberg (2013). https://doi.org/10.1007/978-3-642-39277-1_5
30. Zainuddin, F.B., Liu, S.: An approach to low-fidelity prototyping based on SOFL informal specification. In: 19th Asia-Pacific Software Engineering Conference, pp. 654–663. IEEE (2012)

On Semantics for *Mediator*:
A Coalgebraic Perspective

Ai Liu, Shun Wang, Yi Li, and Meng Sun[✉]

Department of Informatics and LMAM, School of Mathematical Sciences,
Peking University, Beijing, China
{shaoai,wshun94,liyi_math,sunm}@pku.edu.cn

Abstract. *Mediator* is a component-based modeling language where components and systems can be modeled separately and precisely. This paper aims to analyze the behavior of *Mediator* systems from a coalgebraic perspective, which is directly derived from the operational semantics of *Mediator*. Such a coalgebraic approach induces suitable notions of equivalence and refinement for *Mediator*.

Keywords: *Mediator* · Coalgebra · Operational semantics · Bisimulation · Refinement

1 Introduction

Mediator, a component-based modeling language proposed in [9], can be used for different types of systems. It provides a formalism for both low-level automata-based behavior units and high-level system layouts. An automaton can be viewed as an entity which is implemented through encapsulations of interfaces, while a system is implemented by gluing components or automata through operators and can perform complex interaction and communication behavior among components.

This paper aims to analyze the behavior of *Mediator* models with an eye towards integrating it into the study of coalgebra. Coalgebras are suitable for specifying the behavior of systems and data structures that are potentially infinite. Compared to algebraic specification which deals with functional behavior using inductive data types generated by constructors, coalgebraic specification has a strong focus on behavior modeled by coinductive process types that are observable by selectors, much in the spirit of component-based programming languages. We present a coalgebraic semantics for the *Mediator* language, which agrees with its operational semantics. Such a coalgebraic semantics allows uniform treatments of bisimulation [12], refinement [17] and operational semantics of *Mediator* models.

The motivation of this work is that software systems (components, connectors, etc.) can be naturally modeled as coalgebras, like UML [15] or Reo [16]. One obvious advantage of the coalgebraic view on *Mediator* is that it induces

© Springer Nature Switzerland AG 2019
Z. Duan et al. (Eds.): SOFL+MSVL 2018, LNCS 11392, pp. 146–165, 2019.
https://doi.org/10.1007/978-3-030-13651-2_9

a simple and intuitive notion of behavior equivalence on *Mediator* components and systems, which can be characterized as bisimulation between coalgebras. We also provide a notion of refinement for *Mediator*, which indicates whether the behavior of one system is simulated by another, so that we can replace the former by the latter.

In this paper, we focus on *automaton*, which is the basic behavior unit in *Mediator*. We present three contributions here. First, we redefine the operational semantics of *Mediator* from the perspective of observers, based on the operational semantics of *Mediator* in [9]. Second, we construct two types of operators to integrate automata into systems. The coalgebraic model of *Mediator* can be naturally induced by the operational semantics. There exists an algorithm that flattens a hierarchical system into a typical automaton in [9], while we propose a way to construct systems by combining automata and define the coalgebraic semantics of systems through some operators. Third, we specify the notions of bisimulation and refinement for *Mediator*. Following some notions of bisimulation in [10,14], we discuss some equivalence relations for *Mediator* models. Moreover, coalgebraic methods help us to propose a general notion of refinement for *Mediator* models.

The rest of the paper is structured as follows. Section 2 simply reviews the *Mediator* language. Section 3 defines the operational semantics for *Mediator*. Section 4 proposes the coalgebraic model for *Mediator* and two types of operators. Section 5 describes equivalence and refinement for *Mediator*. Section 6 summarizes the results and discusses some directions for future work.

2   *Mediator*

The *Mediator* language provides a rich-featured type system and a two-step modeling approach through *automata* and *systems*. In this section we present a basic introduction for the core notations in *Mediator*, more details can be found in [9]. In *Mediator*, models are constructed as automata and systems, both of which are called *entities*. Entities communicate through *ports*.

2.1   Automata

As the basic behavior unit in *Mediator*, an *automaton* consists of four parts: *templates*, *interfaces*, *local variables* and *transitions*, which are interpreted respectively as follows.

1. *Templates.* Templates of an automaton include a set of parameter declarations. A parameter can be either a type (common type or parameter type) or a value. Concrete values or types are supposed to be provided when the automaton is instantiated (i.e. declared in systems).
2. *Interfaces.* Interfaces consist of directed ports and describe how automata interact with their contexts. An port P can be regarded as a structure with three fields: a data value field $P.\text{value}$ indicating the current value of P, two corresponding Boolean fields `reqRead` and `reqWrite` indicating whether there is any pending *read* or *write* requests on P.

3. *Local Variables.* Each automaton contains a set of local variables. Types of these variables are supposed to be *initialized*.
4. *Transitions.* Behavior of an automaton is defined by guarded transitions. Each transition consists of a boolean term *guard* and a sequence of statements. Transitions are ordered by their priority. For example, if multiple transitions are activated at the same time, the one that has highest priority will be fired. On the other hand, non-deterministic firing is also supported by encapsulating part of the transitions through **group**.

Currently, *Mediator* supports two types of statements:

1. *Assignment* statements, each including an expression and an optional assignment target, evaluate the expressions and assign the results to their targets if possible.
2. *Synchronizing* statements, labeled with **sync**, are the flags requiring synchronized communication with other entities.

According to the existence of synchronizing statement (i.e. external communication through ports), transitions are classified as either *internal* transitions or *external* ones.

An automaton A is denoted by 3-tuple $A = \langle Ports, Vars, Trans_G \rangle$ as mentioned in [9], where $Ports$ is a set of ports, $Vars$ is a set of local variables, (the set of port variables are denoted by $Adj(A)$, which can be obtained from $Ports$ directly) and $Trans_G$ is a sequence of transition groups. There exists an approach to generate a new group of transitions with no dependency on priority from $Trans_G$ in [9], so we assume that $Trans_G$ is only a group in the following pages.

A concrete example is included to help understand the *Mediator* language:

Example 1. Consider an automaton A, as shown in Fig. 1, containing a circular linked list c formalized as an array of integers, with the head pointer defined as an integer $x \in \{0, 1, \ldots, length - 1\}$, an input port IN whose type is **int** and an output port OUT whose type is **int**. Given an input value i, the head pointer may move i position(s) bidirectionally, either to the right or left, and the value pointed to by the head pointer is then to be output.

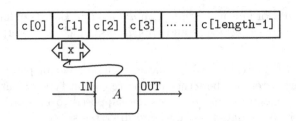

Fig. 1. The model of the automaton in Example 1

The following code fragment describes the behavior of A, with two external transitions formally specified.

```
1  automaton <length:int, c:int [length]> query (IN:in int init 0,
2    OUT:out int init 0)        # port variables are initialized to 0
3    {
4     variables{
5       x:(int 0...length-1) init 0;
6         }
7     transitions{
8       (IN.reqWrite && IN.reqRead && OUT.reqWrite && OUT.reqRead)->{
9         sync IN;                           # synchronize the port IN
10        x:=(x+IN.value) mod length;        # move rightwards
11        OUT.value:=c[x];
12        sync OUT;                          # synchronize the port OUT
13        }
14      (IN.reqWrite && IN.reqRead && OUT.reqWrite && OUT.reqRead)->{
15        sync IN;
16        x:=(x-IN.value) mod length;        # move leftwards
17        OUT.value:=c[x];
18        sync OUT;
19        }
20     }
21   }
```

2.2 Systems

As the textual representation of hierarchical entities to organize sub-entities (automata and simpler systems), *systems* are composed of:

1. *Components.* Entities can be placed and instantiated in systems as components. Each component is considered as a unique instance and executes in parallel with other components and connections.
2. *Connections.* Connections are used to connect *(a) the ports of the system itself, (b) the ports of its components, and (c) the internal nodes.* Inspired by the Reo project [2,3], complex connection behavior can also be determined by other entities.
3. *Internals.* Sometimes we need to combine multiple connections to perform more complex coordination behavior. Internal nodes, declared in `internals` segments, are untyped identifiers which are capable to weld two ports with consistent data-flow direction.

Systems also have *templates* and *interfaces* which have exactly the same forms as in automata. Actually, *Components, Connections* and *Internals* are supposed to run as automata in parallel. They intercommunicate through synchronizing ports of them.

3 Operational Semantics of *Mediator*

This section mainly discusses the underlying labeled transition system (LTS) of a *Mediator* automaton. First, we formalize the concept of *configuration*, which refers to the state of a *Mediator* automaton. Next, we define *normal guarded transition* and *observable action*. Then, we provide a way to transform an arbitrary guarded transition into a normal one. Finally, we give the operational semantics of *Mediator* automata based on labeled transition systems.

3.1   Configurations

A configuration of a *Mediator* automaton can be viewed as a state, which is described as a pair of variable evaluations. To start with, we introduce the notion of *evaluation* on a set of variables.

Definition 1 (Evaluation [9]**).** *An evaluation v on a set of variables V is defined as a function $v : V \to \mathbb{D}$ that satisfies $\forall x \in V, v(x) \in Dom(type(x))$, where $Dom(T)$ is the valued domain of type T and*

$$\mathbb{D} = \bigcup_{x \in V} Dom(type(x)).$$

We denote the set of all possible evaluations on V by $EV(V)$ and the domain of an evaluation v by $dom(v)$.

Here we introduce two operators on evaluations:

- *Restriction Operator* | : An evaluation can be restricted to a sub-evaluation by the restriction operator. Suppose $v \in EV(V)$ and $V' \subseteq V$, the restriction of evaluation v on V', denoted by $v|_{V'}$, is defined as

$$v|_{V'}(x) = v(x), \ \forall x \in V'.$$

- *Composition Operator* ∘: Given two evaluations v_1, v_2, their composition is an evaluation

$$v_1 \circ v_2(x) = \begin{cases} v_1(x) & x \in dom(v_1) \\ v_2(x) & x \in dom(v_2) - dom(v_1) \end{cases}.$$

Moreover, given a bijection function $f : V_1 \to V_2$, for any $v \in EV(V_2)$, there exists an evaluation $v * f \in EV(V_1)$, defined as $v * f(x) = v(f(x))$.

Definition 2 (Configuration [9]**).** *A configuration of an automaton $A = \langle Ports, Vars, Trans_G \rangle$ is defined as a pair (v_{loc}, v_{adj}), where $v_{loc} \in EV(Vars)$ is an evaluation on local variables and $v_{adj} \in EV(Adj(A))$ is an evaluation on port variables. We use $C_A = EV(Vars \cup Adj(A))$ to denote the set of all configurations of A.*

3.2   Normal Automata

In *Mediator*, it is assumed that ports of an automaton A can be classified into two sets: P_{in}^A represents the set of input ports of A and P_{out}^A represents the set of output ports of A. Hence we divide all synchronizing statements into two sets:

$$Syn_I = \{\text{sync } p_1, \ldots, p_n | j \neq k \to p_j \neq p_k \text{ and } p_i \in P_{in}^A, \forall 1 \leq i, j, k \leq n\}$$

and

$$Syn_O = \{\text{sync } p_1, \ldots, p_n | j \neq k \to p_j \neq p_k \text{ and } p_i \in P_{out}^A, \forall 1 \leq i, j, k \leq n\}.$$

Here we abbreviate any permutation of sync $p_1, \ldots,$ sync p_n into the synchronizing statement sync $p_1, \ldots, p_n \in Syn_I$, like in [9]. It is analogous for sync $p_1, \ldots, p_n \in Syn_O$.

Definition 3 (Normal Guarded Transitions). *A guarded transition t of the automaton $A = \langle Ports, Vars, Trans_G \rangle$ is normal, if it is one of the following shapes:*

- $t = g \to s$, *where s is an assignment statement.*
- $t = g \to [s_1, s_2]$, *where $s_1 \in Syn_I$ and s_2 is an assignment statement.*
- $t = g \to [s_1, s_2]$, *where s_1 is an assignment statement and $s_2 \in Syn_O$.*
- $t = g \to [s_1, s_2, s_3]$, *where $s_1 \in Syn_I$, $s_3 \in Syn_O$ and s_2 is an assignment statement.*

Actually, the first shape corresponds to the internal transitions, while the others correspond to the external transitions.

Definition 4 (Normal Automata). *$A = \langle Ports, Vars, Trans_G \rangle$ is a normal automaton iff all guarded transitions are normal.*

From the perspective of observers, when executing sync $p_1, \ldots, p_n \in Syn_O$, the automaton A sends $v \in EV(p_1.value, \ldots, p_n.value)$ to the environment, denoted by $!v$. Oppositely, when executing sync $p_1, \ldots, p_n \in Syn_I$, the automaton A receives $v \in EV(p_1.value, \ldots, p_n.value)$ from the environment, denoted by $?v$. Especially, when a normal guarded transition with the shape $g \to [s_1, s_2, s_3]$, where $s_1 = \text{sync } p_1, \ldots, p_n \in Syn_I$ and $s_3 = \text{sync } q_1, \ldots, q_m \in Sync_O$, the receiving action and the sending action come in pair, denoted by $(?v_1, !v_2)$, where $v_1 \in EV(p_1.value, \ldots, p_n.value)$ and $v_2 \in EV(q_1.value, \ldots, q_n.value)$.

Definition 5 (Observable Actions). *Given a normal automaton A, for convenience, we denote the set of the data fields of the output port variables by $PV_{out}^A = \{p_i.value | p_i \in P_{out}^A\}$ and the set of the data fields of the input port variables by $PV_{in}^A = \{p_i.value | p_i \in P_{in}^A\}$. Now we can define the set of all observable actions by*

$$\begin{aligned}
Act_A = \ & \{?v | \varnothing \neq dom(v) \subseteq PV_{in}^A\} \\
& \cup \{!v | \varnothing \neq dom(v) \subseteq PV_{out}^A\} \\
& \cup \{(?v_1, !v_2) | \varnothing \neq dom(v_1) \subseteq PV_{in}^A \text{ and } \varnothing \neq dom(v_2) \subseteq PV_{out}^A\}.
\end{aligned}$$

Proposition 1. *Suppose $g \to [s_1, \ldots, s_n]$ is a guarded transition of the automaton A, it can be equally rearranged to a guarded transition $g \to [s'_1, \ldots, s'_n]$, satisfying that $\exists 1 \le i < j \le n$, $s'_1, \ldots, s'_{i-1}$ are in Syn_I, $s'_i, \ldots, s'_j$ are assignment statements and $s'_{j+1}, \ldots, s'_n$ are in Syn_O.*

Proof. Because of the requirement that any assignment statements including reference to an input (output) port should be placed after (before) its corresponding synchronizing statement, we can adjust sequence $[s_1, \ldots, s_n]$ by moving all synchronizing statements in Syn_I (Syn_O) to the head (end) of the sequence in their original order, and leaving other statements unchanged. The relative positions of synchronizing statements are ensured to be maintained in each movement, so the rearrangement is decidable.   □

Intuitively, an arbitary guarded transition can be normalized based on the above conclusions. In the following context we present the main results.

Theorem 1. *Suppose $t = g \to [s_1, \ldots, s_n]$ is a guarded transition, satisfying that $\exists 1 \le i < j \le n$, $s_1, \ldots, s_{i-1}$ are in Syn_I, $s_i, \ldots, s_j$ are assignment statements and $s_{j+1}, \ldots, s_n$ are in Syn_O, it can be equally converted to a normal guarded transition t'. In detail, the shape of t' is determined by the values of i and j:*

- $t' = g \to s'$, *if* $i = 1 \wedge j = n$.
- $t' = g \to [s'_1, s'_2]$, *where* $s'_1 \in Syn_I$, *if* $1 < i < j = n$.
- $t' = g \to [s'_1, s'_2]$, *where* $s'_2 \in Syn_O$, *if* $1 = i < j < n$.
- $t' = g \to [s'_1, s'_2, s'_3]$, *if* $1 < i < j < n$.

Proof. Multiple synchronizing statements may join in one by merging $s_1, \ldots, s_{i-1}$ to $s'_1 \in Syn_I$, and merging $s_{j+1}, \ldots, s_n$ to $s'_3 \in Syn_O$. The rest of assignment statements $s_i, \ldots, s_j$ can be replaced by their composition $s'_2 = s_j \circ \cdots \circ s_i$.   □

Theorem 2. *An arbitary guarded transition $t = g \to [s_1, \ldots, s_n]$ can be reformed to a normal guarded transition.*

Proof. From Proposition 1 , we can rearrangement $t = g \to [s_1, \ldots, s_n]$ to $t' = g \to [s'_1, \ldots, s'_n]$, which satisfies the conditions in Theorem 1. Then the conclusion can be drawn by Theorem 1.   □

3.3   Automaton as Labeled Transition System

With the key language elements properly formalized, now we introduce the operational semantics of automata based on *labeled transition system*.

Definition 6. *A labeled transition system is a tuple $(S, \Sigma, \to, s_0)$ where S is a set of states, s_0 is an initial state, Σ is a set of actions and $\to \subseteq S \times \Sigma \times S$ is a set of transitions. For simplicity, we use $s \xrightarrow{a} s'$ to denote $(s, a, s') \in \to$.*

Suppose $A = \langle Ports, Vars, Trans_G \rangle$ is a normal automaton, its semantics can be captured by a LTS $(C_A, \Sigma_A, \rightarrow_A, c_0^A)$ where

- C_A is the set of all configurations of A.
- $c_0^A \in C_A$ is the initial configuration where all `reqReads` and `reqWrites` are initialized as `false`, and other variables are initialized with their default value.
- $\Sigma_A = Act_A \cup \{i\} \cup \{\tau\}$ is the set of actions, where i denotes the internal transition and τ denotes the silent action performed by the environment.
- $\rightarrow_A \subseteq C_A \times \Sigma_A \times C_A$ is the set of transitions obtained by the following rules:

Rule 1 (Silent action)

$$\frac{p \in P_{in}^A}{(v_{loc}, v_{adj}) \xrightarrow{\tau} (v_{loc}, v_{adj}[p.reqWrite \mapsto \neg p.reqWrite])}$$

$$\frac{p \in P_{out}^A}{(v_{loc}, v_{adj}) \xrightarrow{\tau} (v_{loc}, v_{adj}[p.reqRead \mapsto \neg p.reqRead])}$$

The above two rules indicate the property that, in *Mediator* automata, the reading status of an output port and the writing status of an input port may be changed by the environment at any moment. For a Boolean variable y, note that

$$(v_{loc}, v_{adj}[y \mapsto \neg y])(x) = \begin{cases} \neg (v_{loc}, v_{adj})(x) & x = y \\ (v_{loc}, v_{adj})(x) & otherwise \end{cases}.$$

Rule 2 (Internal action)

$$\frac{t = g \rightarrow s \wedge (v_{loc}, v_{adj}) \models g}{(v_{loc}, v_{adj}) \xrightarrow{i} s \circ (v_{loc}, v_{adj})}$$

In this rule, an internal transition may be triggered if the guard condition is satisfied by the configuration, denote by $(v_{loc}, v_{adj}) \models g$. The new configuration is obtained by applying s to the original one, which is denoted by $s(v_{loc}, v_{adj})$.

Rule 3 (External action)

$$\frac{t = g \rightarrow [s_1, s_2] \wedge (v_{loc}, v_{adj}) \models g \quad s_1 = \text{sync } p_1, \ldots, p_n \wedge v \in EV(\{p_1.value, \ldots, p_n.value\})}{(v_{loc}, v_{adj}) \xrightarrow{?v} s_2 \circ (v_{loc}, v \circ v_{adj})}$$

Triggering an external transition, where only some input ports are synchronized with the environment, the automaton should receive an evaluation on these input port values and then update the configuration.

$$\frac{t = g \rightarrow [s_1, s_2] \wedge (v_{loc}, v_{adj}) \models g \quad s_3 = \text{sync } p_1, \ldots, p_n \wedge v \in EV(\{p_1.value, \ldots, p_n.value\})}{(v_{loc}, v_{adj}) \xrightarrow{!v} s_1 \circ (v_{loc}, v_{adj})}$$

$$s_1 \circ (v_{loc}, v_{adj})|_{\{p_1.value, \ldots, p_n.value\}} = v$$

Triggering an external transition, where only some output ports are synchronized with the environment, the automaton should firstly update the configuration and then send an evaluation on these output port values to the environment it interacts with.

$$t = g \rightarrow [s_1, s_2, s_3] \wedge (v_{loc}, v_{adj}) \models g$$

$$s_1 = \text{sync } p_1, \ldots, p_n \wedge v_1 \in EV(\{p_1.value, \ldots, p_n.value\})$$

$$s_3 = \text{sync } p_1', \ldots, p_m' \wedge v_2 \in EV(\{p_1'.value, \ldots, p_m'.value\})$$

$$\overline{(v_{loc}, v_{adj}) \xrightarrow{(?v_1, !v_2)} s_2 \circ (v_{loc}, v_1 \circ v_{adj})}$$

$$s_2 \circ (v_{loc}, v_1 \circ v_{adj})|_{\{p_1'.value, \ldots, p_m'.value\}} = v_2$$

Triggering an external transition, where some input ports and some output ports are synchronized with the environment, the automaton should receive an evaluation on these input port values, update the configuration and send an evaluation on these output port values.

4   The Coalgebraic View

A coalgebraic semantics of *Mediator* can be naturally induced by its operational semantics. This leads to a definition of automata as coalgebras $(C, \overline{\alpha} : C \rightarrow \mathcal{P}_f(C)^\Sigma, c_0)$, where the state space C represents the set of configurations of the corresponding automaton, Σ represents the set of actions, $\mathcal{P}_f$ is the finite powerset functor and the dynamics $\overline{\alpha}$ is determined by the operational semantics.

4.1   *Mediator* Automata as Coalgebras

Given a normal automaton A, one configuration can satisfy one or more guard conditions so that multiple transitions may be triggered. Besides, different transitions may have the same observable action. These lead to non-determinism. We wish to consider an automaton with bounded non-determinism, in which from an arbitrary configuration, only a finite number of transitions are possible. Such behavioral pattern can be modeled using finite powerset functor $\mathcal{P}_f$, which specifies bounded non-determinism intuitively.

We define a functor

$$\mathcal{T}_\Sigma(X) = \mathcal{P}_f(X)^\Sigma$$

where the parameter Σ refers to an alphabet. The model of automaton A is a $\mathcal{T}_{\Sigma_A}$-coalgebra $(C_A, \overline{\alpha} : C_A \rightarrow \mathcal{T}_{\Sigma_A}(C_A), c_0^A)$ with C_A as the state space, Σ_A as the set of actions and c_0^A as the initial configuration. Note that $\overline{\alpha}$ is the curried version of α, that is, for $\alpha : C_A \times \Sigma_A \rightarrow \mathcal{P}_f(C_A)$, $\overline{\alpha} : C_A \rightarrow \mathcal{P}_f(C_A)^{\Sigma_A}$ is the unique mapping such that $\alpha(c, a) = \overline{\alpha}(c)(a)$. The dynamics α is defined according to different execution branches:

– Silent action τ,

$$\alpha(c, \tau) = \{c[p.reqRead \mapsto \neg p.reqR\dot{e}ad]| \ p \in P_{out}^A\}$$
$$\cup \ \{c[p.reqWrite \mapsto \neg p.reqWrite]| \ p \in P_{in}^A\}.$$

– Internal action i,

$$\alpha(c, i) = \{c'| \ (c, i, c') \in \to_A\}.$$

– External action $a \in Act_A$,

$$\alpha(c, a) = \{c'|(c, a, c') \in \to_A\}.$$

In particular, when the automaton A is in configuration $c \in C_A$ but can not perform an action $a \in \Sigma_A$, we use $\alpha(c, a) = \varnothing$ to depict this case.

Given two T_Σ-coalgebras $(U, \overline{\alpha} : U \to T_\Sigma U, u_0)$ and $(V, \overline{\beta} : V \to T_\Sigma V, v_0)$, a function: $h : U \to V$ is a homomorphism of T_Σ-coalgebras, if $T_\Sigma h \cdot \overline{\alpha} = \overline{\beta} \cdot h$ and $h(u_0) = v_0$. Especially, $T_\Sigma h \cdot \overline{\alpha} = \overline{\beta} \cdot h$ if and only if $\mathcal{P}_f h \cdot \alpha = \beta \cdot (h \times \mathrm{id})$, which means below diagram commutes.

$$
\begin{array}{ccc}
U \times \Sigma & \xrightarrow{\ h \times \mathrm{id}\ } & V \times \Sigma \\
\Big\downarrow{\alpha} & & \Big\downarrow{\beta} \\
\mathcal{P}_f U & \xrightarrow[\mathcal{P}_f h]{} & \mathcal{P}_f V
\end{array}
$$

4.2   Composition

We will provide some basic operators and an approach to build up *Mediator* systems by joining one or more entities in this part. Each operator contains a pair of port names $(port_1, port_2)$ as parameters, indicating the data-flow is from $port_1$ to $port_2$ and satisfying the types of their port values are the same. To avoid data-conflict, it is assumed that a port occurs in at most one operator.

There are two kinds of operators: selfing operators and crossing operators. A selfing operator links an output port of an automaton with one of its input ports, while a crossing operator links an output port of an automaton with an input port of the other automaton.

Selfing Operator. Given a *Mediator* automaton A with the coalgebraic semantics $(C_A, \overline{\alpha} : C_A \to P_f(C_A)^{\Sigma_A}, c_0^A)$, the selfing operator linking $p_1 \in P_{out}^A$ and $p_2 \in P_{in}^A$ is denoted by $\mathsf{slink}(p_1, p_2)$ and the semantics of the updated automaton $\mathsf{slink}(p_1, p_2)(A)$ is

$$[\![\mathsf{slink}(p_1, p_2)(A)]\!] = (C_A, \overline{\alpha'} : C_A \to P_f(C_A)^{\Sigma_A}, c_0^A),$$

where the dynamics $\overline{\alpha'}$ is defined according to the following cases (We assume that f is a bijection from $\{p_2.value\}$ to $\{p_1.value\}$ below.):

Case 1 (Silent action)

$$\alpha'(c,\tau) = \alpha(c,\tau) - \{c[p_1.reqRead \mapsto \neg p_1.reqRead]\}$$
$$- \{c[p_2.reqWrite \mapsto \neg p_2.reqWrite]\}$$

Once two ports p_1 and p_2 are linked, we cannot observe any information. The reading status of p_1 and the writing status of p_2 can no longer be changed by the environment.

Case 2 (Internal action)

$$\alpha'(c,i) = \alpha(c,i) \cup \bigcup_{v \in EV(p_1.value)} \bigcup_{c' \in \alpha(c,!v)} \alpha(c', ?v * f),$$

The original internal transitions remain unchanged. A transition involving a sending action through p_1 and a transition involving a receiving action through p_2 could be integrated into an internal transition.

Case 3 (External action)
The following expressions specify the observable behavior according to the types of external actions:

$$\alpha'(c, ?v) = \alpha(c, ?v) \cup \bigcup_{V \subseteq dom(v)} \bigcup_{v_1 \in EV(p_1.value)} \bigcup_{c_1 \in C_1} \alpha(c_1, ?(v_1 * f) \circ v|_{dom(v)-V})$$

$$\alpha'(c, !v') = \alpha(c, !v') \cup \bigcup_{V \subseteq dom(v')} \bigcup_{v_1 \in EV(p_1,value)} \bigcup_{c_2 \in C_2} \alpha(c_2, (?v_1 * f, !v'|_{dom(v)-V}))$$

$$\alpha'(c, (?v, !v')) = \alpha(c, (?v, !v')) \cup \bigcup_{V \subseteq dom(v)} \bigcup_{V' \subseteq dom(v')} \bigcup_{v_1 \in EV(p_1.value)} \bigcup_{c_3 \in C_3} \alpha(c_3, a)$$

where $C_1 = \alpha(c, (?v|_V, !v_1))$, $C_2 = \alpha(c, (!v_1 \circ v'|_V))$, $C_3 = \alpha(c, (?v|_V, !v_1 \circ v'|_{V'}))$ and $a = (?(v_1 * f) \circ v|_{dom(v)-V}, !v'|_{dom(v')-V'})$.

In order to avoid deadlock, we assume $p_1.value \notin dom(v')$ and $p_2.value \notin dom(v)$. Note that $(?v, !\epsilon)$ corresponds to $?v$ and $(?\epsilon, !v')$ corresponds to $!v'$, where ϵ is the empty evaluation. These describe all situations where two external transitions could be integrated into one external transition.

Proposition 2. *Given a Mediator automaton A with $p_1, p_3 \in P_{out}^A$ and $p_2, p_4 \in P_{in}^A$, the order of the selfing operators $\mathsf{slink}(p_1, p_2)$ and $\mathsf{slink}(p_3, p_4)$ to be applied does not matter, i.e.,*

$$\mathsf{slink}(p_1, p_2)(\mathsf{slink}(p_3, p_4)(A)) = \mathsf{slink}(p_3, p_4)(\mathsf{slink}(p_1, p_2)(A)).$$

Crossing Operator. Two *Mediator* automata A_1 and A_2, whose semantics are $[\![A_1]\!] = (C_1, \overline{\alpha_1} : C_1 \to \mathcal{P}_f(C_1)^{\Sigma_1}, c_0^1)$ and $[\![A_2]\!] = (C_2, \overline{\alpha_2} : C_2 \to \mathcal{P}_f(C_2)^{\Sigma_2}, c_0^2)$, can be composed into a *Mediator* automaton by a crossing operator. The crossing operator linking $p_1 \in P_{out}^{A_1}$ and $p_2 \in P_{in}^{A_2}$, is denoted by $\mathsf{clink}(p_1, p_2)$ and the semantics of the composed automaton $\mathsf{clink}(p_1, p_2)(A_1, A_2)$ is

$$[\![\mathsf{clink}(p_1, p_2)(A_1, A_2)]\!] = (C_1 \times C_2, \overline{\alpha'}, c_0^1 \times c_0^2),$$

where the dynamics $\overline{\alpha'}$ is defined according to the following cases (We assume that f is a bijection from $\{p_2.value\}$ to $\{p_1.value\}$ below.):

Case 1 (Silent action)

$$\alpha'((c_1, c_2), \tau) = ((\alpha_1(c_1, \tau) - \{c_1[p_1.reqRead \mapsto \neg p_1.reqRead]\}) \times \{c_2\})$$
$$\cup (\{c_1\} \times (\alpha_2(c_2, \tau) - \{c_2[p_2.reqWrite \mapsto \neg p_2.reqWrite]\}))$$

Case 2 (Internal action)

$$\alpha'((c_1, c_2), i) = (\alpha_1(c_1, i) \times \{c_2\}) \cup (\{c_1\} \times \alpha_2(c_2, i)) \cup \bigcup_{v \in U} (\alpha_1(c_1, !v) \times \alpha_2(c_2, ?v * f)),$$

where $U = EV(p_1.value)$. An external transition of A_1 where only p_1 is to be synchronized and an external transition of A_2 where only p_2 is to be synchronized should be integrated into an internal transition in the composed automaton.

Case 3 (External action)
For convenience, we denote $V_1 = dom(v) \cap PV_{in}^1$, $V_1' = dom(v') \cap PV_{out}^1$, $V_2 = dom(v) - V_1$ and $V_2' = dom(v') - V_1'$. In order to avoid deadlock, we require $p_1.value \notin dom(v')$ and $p_2.value \notin dom(v)$. There are three situations where an external transition of A_1 and an external transition of A_2 should be integrated into an external transition of the composed automaton.

$$\alpha'((c_1, c_2), ?v) = \begin{cases} (\alpha_1(c_1, ?v) \times \{c_2\}) \cup S_1 & dom(v) \subseteq PV_{in}^1 \\ (\{c_1\} \times \alpha_2(c_2, ?v)) \cup S_2 & dom(v) \subseteq PV_{in}^2 \\ S & otherwise \end{cases}$$

where

$$S_1 = \bigcup_{v_1 \in EV(p_1.value)} \alpha_1(c_1, (?v, !v_1)) \times \alpha_2(c_2, ?v_1 * f),$$

$$S_2 = \bigcup_{v_1 \in EV(p_1.value)} \alpha_1(c_1, !v_1) \times \alpha(c_2, ?(v_1 * f) \circ v),$$

$$S = \bigcup_{v_1 \in EV(p_1.value)} \alpha_1(c_1, (?v|_{V_1}, !v_1)) \times \alpha_2(c_2, ?(v_1 * f) \circ v|_{V_2}).$$

$$\alpha'((c_1, c_2), !v') = \begin{cases} (\alpha_1(c_1, !v') \times \{c_2\}) \cup S_1' & dom(v') \subseteq PV_{out}^1 \\ (\{c_1\} \times \alpha_2(c_2, !v')) \cup S_2' & dom(v') \subseteq PV_{out}^2 \\ S' & otherwise \end{cases}$$

where

$$S_1' = \bigcup_{v_1 \in EV(p_1.value)} \alpha_1(c_1, !v_1 \circ v') \times \alpha_2(c_2, ?v_1 * f),$$

$$S_2' = \bigcup_{v_1 \in EV(p_1.value)} \alpha_1(c_1, !v_1) \times \alpha_2(c_2, (?v_1 * f, !v')),$$

$$S' = \bigcup_{v_1 \in EV(p_1.value)} \alpha_1(c_1, !v_1 \circ v'|_{V_1'}) \times \alpha_2(c_2, (?v_1 * f, !v'|_{V_2'})).$$

$$\alpha'((c_1, c_2), (?v, !v'))$$

$$= \begin{cases} (\alpha_1(c_1, (?v, !v')) \times \{c_2\}) \cup S_1'' & dom(v) \subseteq PV_{in}^1 \wedge dom(v') \subseteq PV_{out}^1 \\ (\{c_1\} \times \alpha_2(c_2, (?v, !v'))) \cup S_2'' & dom(v) \subseteq PV_{in}^2 \wedge dom(v') \subseteq PV_{out}^2 \\ S'' & otherwise \end{cases}$$

where

$$S_1'' = \bigcup_{v_1 \in EV(p_1.value)} \alpha_1(c_1, (?v, !v' \circ v_1)) \times \alpha_2(c_2, ?v_1 * f),$$

$$S_2'' = \bigcup_{v_1 \in EV(p_1.value)} \alpha_1(c_1, !v_1) \times \alpha_2(?(v_1 * f) \circ v, !v'),$$

$$S'' = \bigcup_{v_1 \in EV(p_1.value)} \alpha_1(c_1, (?v|_{V_1}, !v_1 \circ v'|_{V_1'})) \times \alpha_2(c_2, (?(v_1 * f) \circ v|_{V_2}, !v'|_{V_2'})).$$

Given two automata and some links in *Mediator*, the order of connecting those links does not matter. In the coalgebraic view, operators correspond to links. The first link to be connected corresponds to a crossing operator, while the remained links correspond to selfing operators. No matter which link is firstly connected, the results will be the same.

Proposition 3. *Given two Mediator automata A and A', with $p_1, p_2 \in P_{out}^A$ and $p_1', p_2' \in P_{in}^{A'}$,*

$$\mathsf{slink}(p_1, p_1')(\mathsf{clink}(p_2, p_2')(A, A')) = \mathsf{slink}(p_2, p_2')(\mathsf{clink}(p_1, p_1')(A, A')).$$

5 Equivalence and Refinement for *Mediator*

With the development in [4, 6, 11], we can define the notions of equivalence and coalgebraic refinement for *Mediator*. Actually, they both involve a question whether a configuration is simulated by the other one. If the simulation is reversible, these two configurations are equivalent on some level. Otherwise, one may be regarded as a refinement of the other.

5.1 Bisimulation

This subsection is organized with a further study of bisimulations toward automata. The notion of bisimulation aims to characterize an equivalence on system manners from observers' perspective. In *Mediator* automata, a bisimulation is represented by pairs of configurations as a binary relation. We say two states s, t are strong bisimilar (in symbol, $s \sim t$) if they are related by a strong bisimulation.

Definition 7 (Strong Bisimulation). *Given two LTSs induced by Mediator automata $(C_A, \Sigma_A, \rightarrow_A, c_0^A)$ and $(C_B, \Sigma_B, \rightarrow_B, c_0^B)$, a relation $\mathcal{R} \subseteq C_A \times C_B$ is a strong bisimulation if (i) $(c_0^A, c_0^B) \in \mathcal{R}$; (ii) there exists a port renaming bijection $\psi : Adj(B) \rightarrow Adj(A)$ such that:*

- For $(s, t) \in \mathcal{R}$, if $s \xrightarrow{a} s'$, there exists $t' \in C_B$ such that $t \xrightarrow{a'} t' \wedge (s', t') \in \mathcal{R}$, where a, a' satisfy: if $a \in \{\tau, i\}$, then $a' = a$, otherwise

$$a' = \begin{cases} ?v * \psi & a = ?v \\ !v * \psi & a = !v \\ \langle ?v * \psi, !v' * \psi \rangle & a = \langle ?v, !v' \rangle \end{cases} \tag{5.1}$$

- For $(s, t) \in \mathcal{R}$, if $t \xrightarrow{b} t'$, there exists $s' \in C_A$ such that $s \xrightarrow{b'} s' \wedge (s', t') \in \mathcal{R}$, where b, b' satisfy: if $b \in \{\tau, i\}$, then $b' = b$, otherwise

$$b' = \begin{cases} ?v * \psi^{-1} & b = ?v \\ !v * \psi^{-1} & b = !v \\ \langle ?v * \psi^{-1}, !v' * \psi^{-1} \rangle & b = \langle ?v, !v' \rangle \end{cases} \tag{5.2}$$

In some cases, we only consider whether the observable transitions are equivalent, which means we ignore the effects of the silent action τ and the internal action i. For this purpose, the strong bisimulation can be relaxed to the weak bisimulation, where the internal action τ and the silent action i are hidden from the environment. The concrete definition of weak bisimulation is as follows:

Definition 8 (Weak Bisimulation). *Given two LTSs induced by Mediator automata $(C_A, \Sigma_A, \to_A, c_0^A)$ and $(C_B, \Sigma_B \to_B, c_0^B)$, a relation $\mathcal{R} \subseteq C_A \times C_B$ is a weak bisimulation if (i) $(c_0^A, c_0^B) \in \mathcal{R}$; (ii) there exists a port renaming bijection $\psi : Adj(A) \to Adj(B)$ such that:*

- *For $(s, t) \in \mathcal{R}$ and an observable action $a \in Act_A$, if $s \xrightarrow{\{\tau, i\}^*} \bullet \xrightarrow{a} \bullet \xrightarrow{\{\tau, i\}^*} s'$, there exists $t' \in C_B$ such that $t \xrightarrow{\{\tau, i\}^*} \bullet \xrightarrow{a'} \bullet \xrightarrow{\{\tau, i\}^*} t' \wedge (s', t') \in \mathcal{R}$ where a and a' satisfy the Eq. (5.1);*
- *For $(s, t) \in \mathcal{R}$ and an observable action $b \in Act_B$, if $t \xrightarrow{\{\tau, i\}^*} \bullet \xrightarrow{b} \bullet \xrightarrow{\{\tau, i\}^*} t'$, there exists $s' \in C_A$ such that $s \xrightarrow{\{\tau, i\}^*} \bullet \xrightarrow{b'} \bullet \xrightarrow{\{\tau, i\}^*} s' \wedge (s', t') \in \mathcal{R}$ where b and b' satisfy the Eq. (5.2).*

Before we introduce the coalgebraic bisimulation for *Mediator* automata, we consider the functor $\mathcal{F}_\Sigma(-) = \mathcal{P}_f(\Sigma \times -)$, which can be reversibly and naturally transformed to the functor $\mathcal{T}_\Sigma(-) = \mathcal{P}_f(-)^\Sigma$. In order to clarify their equivalence, we need to prove that there exists a natural isomorphism between $\mathcal{F}_\Sigma$ and $\mathcal{T}_\Sigma$. Define a natural transformation $\eta : \mathcal{F}_\Sigma \Rightarrow \mathcal{T}_\Sigma$. Given a state space C, $\eta_C : \mathcal{P}_f(C)^\Sigma \to \mathcal{P}_f(\Sigma \times C)$ is a function such that for $f \in \mathcal{P}_f(C)^\Sigma$,

$$\eta_C(f) = \{(a, c') | a \in \Sigma, \ c' \in f(a)\}.$$

Actually, the natural transformation η has an inverse $\mu : \mathcal{T}_\Sigma \Rightarrow \mathcal{F}_\Sigma$, making $\mathcal{F}_\Sigma \mathcal{T}_\Sigma = \mathcal{T}_\Sigma \mathcal{F}_\Sigma = \mathcal{Id}$. The formal definition of $\mu_C : \mathcal{P}_f(\Sigma \times C) \to \mathcal{P}_f(C)^\Sigma$ is

$$\mu_C(S)(a) = \{c_{a,1}, ..., c_{a,m}\},$$

where

$$S = \bigcup_{a \in \Sigma' \subseteq \Sigma} \{(a, c_{a,1}), (a, c_{a,2}), ..., (a, c_{a,m})\} \in \mathcal{P}_f(\Sigma \times C).$$

Therefore a natural isomorphism between $\mathcal{F}_\Sigma$ and $\mathcal{T}_\Sigma$ has been found.

Hence a coalgebraic $\mathcal{T}_\Sigma$-bisimulation can be reversibly and naturally transformed to a coalgebraic $\mathcal{F}_\Sigma$-bisimulation, which is in correspondence with the strong bisimulation. First we recall the abstract definition of $\mathcal{F}_\Sigma$-bisimulation in coalgebraic terms.

Given two $\mathcal{F}_\Sigma$-coalgebras $(U, \alpha : U \to \mathcal{F}_\Sigma U, u_0)$ and $(V, \beta : V \to \mathcal{F}_\Sigma V, v_0)$. A coalgebraic $\mathcal{F}_\Sigma$-bisimulation between them is a relation $\mathcal{R} \subseteq U \times V$, if there exists a coalgebra $(R, \gamma : R \to \mathcal{F}_\Sigma R, (u_0, v_0))$ making the following diagram commute.

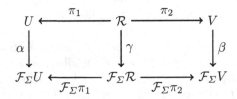

Next we show the relationship between the strong bisimulation and the coalgebraic $\mathcal{F}_\Sigma$-bisimulation.

Theorem 3. *Given a $\mathcal{F}_{\Sigma_A}$-coalgebra $(C_A, \alpha : C_A \to \mathcal{F}_{\Sigma_A}(C_A), c_0^A)$ and a coalgebraic bisimulation relation $\mathcal{R} \subseteq C_A \times C_A$, for any two configurations $s, t \in C_A$,*

$$(s, t) \in \mathcal{R} \text{ if and only if } s \sim t.$$

Proof. Suppose $\mathcal{R}$ is a coalgebraic bisimulation relation. An equivalence class of a configuration c is denoted by $[c]_\mathcal{R} = \{c' | (c, c') \in \mathcal{R}\}$, which contains all the configurations that are related to c. The quotient space of C_A under $\mathcal{R}$ by $C_A/\mathcal{R}$ is the set

$$C_A/\mathcal{R} = \{[c]_\mathcal{R} | c \in C_A\}$$

comprising all the equivalence classes of configurations.

Intuitively, the following diagram on the left side commutes according to the definition of equivalence, where $q : C_A \to C_A/\mathcal{R}$ represents the quotient mapping that maps a configuration to its equivalence class under $\mathcal{R}$.

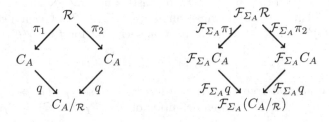

The right diagram is obtained by applying $\mathcal{F}_{\Sigma_A}$ to the left one. Since $\mathcal{F}_{\Sigma_A}$ preserves weak pullbacks, the right diagram is therefore a weak pullback diagram. Now we combine the right diagram above with the one mentioned in the coalgrbraic bisimulation (setting the state space to C_A and the functor to $\mathcal{F}_{\Sigma_A}$), and we obtain the following commutative diagram.

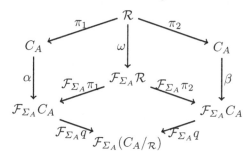

Two configurations s, t are related by a coalgebraic $\mathcal{R}$-bisimulation, i.e., $(s, t) \in \mathcal{R}$ if and only if

$$\mathcal{F}_{\Sigma_A} q \cdot \alpha(s) = \mathcal{F}_{\Sigma_A} q \cdot \beta(t)$$

$\equiv$ { unfold the expressions }

$$\mathcal{F}_{\Sigma_A} q(\{(a, s') | (a, s') \in \alpha(s)\}) = \mathcal{F}_{\Sigma_A} q(\{(a, t') | (a, t') \in \beta(t)\})$$

$\equiv$ { definition of $\mathcal{F}_{\Sigma_A}$ on homomorphisms }

$$\mathcal{P}_f(id \times q)(\{(a, s') | (a, s') \in \alpha(s)\}) = \mathcal{P}_f(id \times q)(\{(a, t') | (a, t') \in \beta(t)\})$$

$\equiv$ { definition of $\mathcal{P}_f$ }

$$\{(a, q(s')) | (a, s') \in \alpha(s)\} = \{(a, q(t')) | (a, t') \in \beta(t)\}$$

$\equiv$ { definition of q }

$$\{(a, [s']_\mathcal{R}) | (a, s') \in \alpha(s)\} = \{(a, [t']_\mathcal{R}) | (a, t') \in \beta(t)\}$$

$\equiv$ { definition of set }

$$\forall (a, [s']_\mathcal{R}) = (a, [t']_\mathcal{R}) \ where \ (a, s') \in \alpha(s) \ and \ (a, t') \in \beta(t)$$

$\equiv$ { definition of equivalence class }

$$\forall s \xrightarrow{a} s' \ \exists t' \ s.t. \ t \xrightarrow{a} t' \wedge (s', t') \in \mathcal{R} \ and \ vise \ versa.$$

$\equiv$ { definition of strong bisimulation }

$$s \sim t$$

$\square$

Theorem 4. *Given a $\mathcal{T}_{\Sigma_A}$-coalgebra $(C_A, \alpha : C_A \to \mathcal{T}_{\Sigma_A}(C_A), c_0^A)$ and a coalgebraic bisimulation relation $\mathcal{R} \subseteq C_A \times C_A$, for any two configurations $s, t \in C_A$,*

$$(s, t) \in \mathcal{R} \ if \ and \ only \ if \ s \sim t.$$

Proof. The conclusion follows by Theorem 3 and the property that natural isomorphisms preserve coalgebraic bisimulations.   □

Example 2 (continued). Example 1 gives the pseudocode of elements detection in a circular linked list. Now we take further steps to discuss one possible bisimulation $\mathcal{R}$ for a concrete list $c = [0, 1, 0, 1]$. Intuitively, we define $\mathcal{R}$ according to the parity of position variable x that occurs in configurations, i.e., we let

$$\mathcal{R} = \{((x := i, v_{adj}^1), (x := i + 2, v_{adj}^2)) | v_{adj}^1 = v_{adj}^2, i = 0, 1\}$$
$$\cup \{((x := i + 2, v_{adj}^1), (x := i, v_{adj}^2)) | v_{adj}^1 = v_{adj}^2, i = 0, 1\}.$$

Here we show two possible transition schemes, with the corresponding configurations $\mathcal{R}$-bisimilar. Note that IN.reqRead, IN.reqWrite, OUT.reqRead and OUT.reqWrite are always maintained true in each transition so that we omit their evaluations by *.

$$(x := 0, IN.value := Null, \quad — \ \mathcal{R} \ — \quad (x := 2, IN.value := Null,$$
$$OUT.value := Null, *) \qquad\qquad OUT.value := Null, *)$$

$$(?IN.value := 1, \Big\downarrow \qquad\qquad\qquad\qquad\qquad\qquad \Big\downarrow (?IN.value := 1,$$
$$!OUT.value := 0) \qquad\qquad\qquad\qquad\qquad\qquad !OUT.value := 0)$$

$$(x := 1, IN.value := 1, \qquad\qquad\qquad\qquad (x := 3, IN.value := 1,$$
$$OUT.value := 0, *) \qquad\qquad\qquad\qquad OUT.value := 0, *)$$
$$\text{or} \qquad\qquad — \ \mathcal{R} \ — \qquad\qquad \text{or}$$
$$(x := 3, IN.value := 1, \qquad\qquad\qquad\qquad (x := 1, IN.value := 1,$$
$$OUT.value := 0, *) \qquad\qquad\qquad\qquad OUT.value := 0, *)$$

5.2   Refinement

Similarly, we can define refinement based on coalgebraic morphisms. Given two coalgebraic models, besides the function between their state spaces, we need a preorder to define the notion of refinement. Then we can use the refinement relation to detect whether a configuration is simulated by the other one on some level, decided by the preorder.

Definition 9 (Forward Morphism). *Given an extended polynominal functor $\mathcal{G}$ on Set and two $\mathcal{G}$-coalgebras $(U, \alpha : U \to \mathcal{G}U, u_0)$ and $(V, \beta : V \to \mathcal{G}V, v_0)$. A forward morphism $h : \alpha \to \beta$ w.r.t. refinement preorder $\leq$ is a homomorphism from U to V such that $\mathcal{G}h \cdot \alpha \leq \beta \cdot h$. Diagrammatically,*

$$\begin{array}{ccc}
U & \xrightarrow{\ \ h\ \ } & V \\
\alpha \downarrow & & \downarrow \beta \\
\mathcal{G}U & \xrightarrow{\ \mathcal{G}h\ } \mathcal{G}h(\mathcal{G}U) \leq & \mathcal{G}V
\end{array}$$

For two *Mediator* components (systems) p, q, we say p is a behavior refinement of q (denoted by $q \trianglelefteq p$) if there exist two components r and s such that $p \sim r$, $q \sim s$, and there exists a forward morphism $h : r \to s$.

Now we discuss about a concrete refinement preorder $\sqsubseteq$ for $\mathcal{T}_{\Sigma_A}$-coalgebras. Given a $\mathcal{T}_{\Sigma_A}$-coalgebra $(C_A, \overline{\alpha} : C_A \to \mathcal{T}_{\Sigma_A}(C_A), c_0^A)$, $\mathcal{T}_{\Sigma_A}(C_A)$ can be regarded as the set of functions from Σ_A to $\mathcal{P}(C_A)$. Given two elements $f, g \in \mathcal{T}_{\Sigma_A}(C_A)$,

$$f \sqsubseteq g \ if \ \forall a \in \Sigma_A, f(a) \subseteq g(a).$$

It can be easily proved that $\sqsubseteq$ is a preorder. With $\sqsubseteq$, we can get the following lemmas.

Lemma 1. *Removing a port which is not involved in any transition from an automaton is a refinement:*

$$(C_A', \overline{\alpha'} : C_A \to \mathcal{T}_{\Sigma_A}(C_A), c_0^A) \trianglelefteq (C_A, \overline{\alpha} : C_A \to \mathcal{T}_{\Sigma_A}(C_A), c_0^A),$$

if p is a port of A, such that $C_A' = EV(V)$, where

$$V = Vars \cup Adj(A) - \{p.value, p.reqRead, p.reqWrite\},$$

and $\forall a \in \Sigma_A, \alpha'(c|_V, a) = \alpha(c, a)|_V$.

Lemma 2. *Removing any transition from an automaton is a refinement:*

$$(C_A, \overline{\alpha'} : C_A \to \mathcal{T}_{\Sigma_A}(C_A), c_0^A) \trianglelefteq (C_A, \overline{\alpha} : C_A \to \mathcal{T}_{\Sigma_A}(C_A), c_0^A),$$

if $\exists t \in Trans_G$, for $\forall c \in C_A, a \in \Sigma_A$,

$$\alpha'(c, a) = \begin{cases} \alpha(c, a) - t(c, a) & if \ \forall t' \neq t, t'(c, a) \neq t(c, a) \\ \alpha(c, a) & otherwise \end{cases},$$

where $t(c, a) = \{c'\}$ if from the configuration c the automaton does the action a in the transition t and results in the configuration c', otherwise $t(c, a) = \varnothing$.

Now we continue our example of the circular linked list to make better sense of refinement.

Example 3 (continued). Reconsider the circular linked list $[0, 1, 0, 1]$. In Example 2, we detect its elements in a bidirectional manner. Intuitively, elements detection in a specific direction is a refinement of it. This can be implemented by deleting an external transition from the group of transitions. Suppose the forward morphism is identity, and the following schemes depict some part of the refinement relation. The left one is a refinement process of the right one.

$$(x := 0, IN.value := Null,$$
$$OUT.value := Null, *)$$

$$(?IN.value := 1,$$
$$!OUT.value := 0)$$
$$\downarrow$$

$$\{(x := 1, IN.value := 1,$$
$$OUT.value := 0, *)\}$$

$$(x := 0, IN.value := Null,$$
$$OUT.value := Null, *)$$

$$(?IN.value := 1,$$
$$!OUT.value := 0)$$
$$\downarrow$$

$$\{(x := 3, In.value := 1,$$
$$OUT.value := 0, *),$$
$$(x := 1, In.value := 1,$$
$$OUT.value := 0, *)\}$$

$$\quad - \quad \subseteq \quad -$$

6   Conclusion and Future Work

A coalgebraic approach to abstract *Mediator* automata is proposed in this paper to help us discuss equivalence and refinement for *Mediator* models. We defined the coalgebraic semantics for *Mediator* automata, which is induced by the operational semantics we redefined. We showed how to integrate several automata into one automaton. We discussed the strong bisimulation and the weak bisimulation for *Mediator* automata based on labeled transition systems. We proved the strong bisimulation is equivalent to the coalgebraic bisimulation. Last but not least, we discussed the refinement relation.

With the improvement of *Mediator* language, we will modify our coalgebraic model to abstract it more precisely. An interesting direction for future work is to define coalgebraic trace semantics for *Mediator* automata, like probabilistic systems in [7,8]. Bisimulation is sometimes considered too strict, while trace equivalence is coarser. Moreover, a coalgebraic perspective on minimization and determinization of *Mediator* automata is worth considering, like in [1,5,13].

Acknowledgement. The work was partially supported by the National Natural Science Foundation of China under grant nos. 61772038, 61532019, 61202069 and 61272160.

References

1. Adámek, J., Bonchi, F., Hülsbusch, M., König, B., Milius, S., Silva, A.: A coalgebraic perspective on minimization and determinization. In: Birkedal, L. (ed.) FoSSaCS 2012. LNCS, vol. 7213, pp. 58–73. Springer, Heidelberg (2012). https://doi.org/10.1007/978-3-642-28729-9_4
2. Arbab, F.: Reo: a channel-based coordination model for component composition. Math. Struct. Comput. Sci. **14**(3), 329–366 (2004)
3. Baier, C.: Probabilistic models for Reo connector circuits. J. UCS **11**(10), 1718–1748 (2005)
4. Dorsch, U., Milius, S., Milius, S., Schröder, L., Wißmann, T.: Efficient coalgebraic partition refinement. In: CONCUR. LIPIcs, vol. 85, pp. 32:1–32:16. Schloss Dagstuhl - Leibniz-Zentrum fuer Informatik (2017)

5. Goy, A.: Trace semantics via determinization for probabilistic transition systems. CoRR abs/1802.09084 (2018)

6. Jacobs, B.: Invariants, bisimulations and the correctness of coalgebraic refinements. In: Johnson, M. (ed.) AMAST 1997. LNCS, vol. 1349, pp. 276–291. Springer, Heidelberg (1997). https://doi.org/10.1007/BFb0000477

7. Kerstan, H., König, B.: Coalgebraic trace semantics for probabilistic transition systems based on measure theory. In: Koutny, M., Ulidowski, I. (eds.) CONCUR 2012. LNCS, vol. 7454, pp. 410–424. Springer, Heidelberg (2012). https://doi.org/10.1007/978-3-642-32940-1_29

8. Kerstan, H., König, B.: Coalgebraic trace semantics for continuous probabilistic transition systems. Log. Methods Comput. Sci. 9(4), 1–34 (2013)

9. Li, Y., Sun, M.: Component-based modeling in mediator. In: Proença, J., Lumpe, M. (eds.) FACS 2017. LNCS, vol. 10487, pp. 1–19. Springer, Cham (2017). https://doi.org/10.1007/978-3-319-68034-7_1

10. Milner, R.: Communication and concurrency. PHI Series in Computer Science. Prentice-Hall, Englewood cliffs (1989)

11. Rodrigues, C.J., Oliveira, J.N., Barbosa, L.S.: A single complete relational rule for coalgebraic refinement. Electr. Notes Theor. Comput. Sci. **259**, 3–19 (2009)

12. Rutten, J.: Universal coalgebra: a theory of systems. Theor. Comput. Sci **249**, 3–80 (2000)

13. Silva, A., Bonchi, F., Bonsangue, M.M., Rutten, J.J.M.M.: Generalizing determinization from automata to coalgebras. Log. Methods Comput. Sci. **9**(1:09), 1–27 (2013)

14. Sokolova, A., de Vink, E.P., Woracek, H.: Coalgebraic weak bisimulation for action-type systems. Sci. Ann. Comp. Sci. **19**, 93–144 (2009)

15. Sun, M., Aichernig, B.K., Barbosa, L.S., Naixiao, Z.: A coalgebraic semantic framework for component based development in UML. Electr. Notes Theor. Comput. Sci. **122**, 229–245 (2005)

16. Sun, M., Arbab, F., Baier, C.: Synthesis of Reo circuits from scenario-based interaction specifications. Sci. Comput. Program **76**, 651–680 (2011)

17. Meng, S., Barbosa, L.S.: On refinement of generic state-based software components. In: Rattray, C., Maharaj, S., Shankland, C. (eds.) AMAST 2004. LNCS, vol. 3116, pp. 506–520. Springer, Heidelberg (2004). https://doi.org/10.1007/978-3-540-27815-3_38

Blockchain

A Blockchain Implementation of an Attendance Management System

Jingyao Tu, Zhenhua Duan$^{(\boxtimes)}$, Cong Tian$^{(\boxtimes)}$, Nan Zhang$^{(\boxtimes)}$, and Ying Wu

ISN Lab and ICTT, Xidian University, Xi'an, China
{zhhduan,ctian,nzhang}@mail.xidian.edu.cn

Abstract. An attendance management system (AMS) is a useful system for personal management in organizations. The existing AMSs include traditional manual method, smart-card identification, fingerprint recognition, face recognition and so on. An awkward problem with these systems is that the recorded data could be forged by malicious users. Fortunately, the blockchain is emerging which can be used to decentralize management and protect sensitive data. In this paper, we present a blockchain architecture for the AMS and its implementation in detail.

Keywords: Attendance management system · Blockchain ·
Unforgeable · Decentralization · Authentication

1 Introduction

Attendance management is one of the important activities in the personnel management of large organizations. The existing mainstream AMSs include traditional method, rifd identification [18], fingerprint recognition [8], face recognition [1], iris identification [9] and so on. However, these systems suffer from a threaten that the recorded data could be forged by malicious users, hence resulting in serious data security problem.

The emerging blockchain technology was originated with "Bitcoin: a peer-to-peer electronic cash system" in 2008 [11]. In fact, the blockchain is an unforgeable, distributed digital ledger system supported by peer-to-peer (P2P) network, consensus algorithm, encryption algorithm and other related technologies. The blockchain technology has excellent unforgeable and fully traceable security characteristics as well as decentralization features [16]. It is regarded as a supporting technology to build a valuable and trusted network in the future [19]. In addition, the blockchain is also an effective solution to solve problems such as unsecure data storage in untrusted network [17], which meets the needs of AMSs.

This paper presents a blockchain architecture for the AMS. We improve the classical blockchain architecture and design our AMS as a four-layer structure including data layer, network layer, consensus layer and application layer. The

---

The research is supported by National Natural Science Foundation of China under Grant Nos. 61420106004, 61572386, 61732013 and 61751207.

Z. Duan et al. (Eds.): SOFL+MSVL 2018, LNCS 11392, pp. 169–182, 2019.
https://doi.org/10.1007/978-3-030-13651-2_10

data layer uses digital signature cryptographic algorithms and hash function SHA-256 to save block data and some other information. The network layer implements a P2P network to make nodes communicate with each other for handling block and record data. In the consensus layer, we implement a consensus algorithm POW to make nodes achieve a consensus on the update of the blockchain. Finally, the application layer mainly provides functions for users such as check-in, check-out and query operations. In particular, we also provide a supervisory module to manage the permission of nodes. As a small-scaled AMS application, we have developed a blockchain system and implemented our design.

The contributions of the paper are two-fold: (1) we design a blockchain architecture to implement an AMS system; (2) we apply our AMS in a small-scaled scenario with about 100 students in 4 labs.

The paper is organized as follows. The next section briefly introduces blockchain and its related technologies. The Sect. 3 presents the blockchain architecture of a four-layer design. Section 4 indicates the implementation of main modules in the system. Section 5 shows testing results of the AMS. Finally, Sect. 6 summarizes the paper and discusses the future research.

2   Introduction to Blockchain

2.1   Blockchain Related Technologies

Hash Function. Hash function is a one-way function that means one cannot derive the input from the output. It can be used to map data with arbitrary size to data with a fixed size. The result is randomness and unpredictable. It is hard to map two different data to the same result.

The popular hash function is SHA series algorithms. Among them, the commonly used ones are SHA-1, SHA-224, SHA-256, etc. Except SHA-1, the suffix numbers represent the number of bits in output. The hash algorithm used in this paper is SHA-256 [6].

Asymmetric Key. The asymmetric key uses a public key and a private key for data storage and transmission. The public key can be released publicly while the private key is only known to the user and kept by the user himself.

Asymmetric key has two functions. When the public key encrypts data and the corresponding private key decrypts data, this process is called asymmetric encryption. Whereas the private key encrypts a hashed data and the corresponding public key decrypts data, this process is called digital signature. The latter is used to certify if data is tempered or forged and if data is sent by a specific user.

In the existing asymmetric cipher systems, RSA and elliptic curve algorithms are widely used. Because the elliptic curve algorithm can achieve the same security by using fewer bits comparing with RSA [10], our system adopts the elliptic curve algorithm.

Merkle Tree. A merkle tree is a hash binary tree [13]. It can be used to induce and check the integrity of large-scale data quickly. Generating a complete Merkle tree requires hashing the node recursively and inserting the newly generated hash node into the Merkle tree until only one hash node is left. The left hash node is the digital fingerprint of the entire nodes collection, also known as Merkle tree root. We use the binary merkle tree as show in Fig. 1.

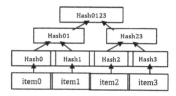

Fig. 1. Merkle tree   **Fig. 2.** P2P structure

Peer-to-Peer Network. A P2P network is a distributed computer network. The "peers" are computer systems which are connected each other. In a P2P network, there is no central server. Peers are equally privileged and equipollently participated in a network. Actually, peers are both servers and clients [12]. A P2P network structure is shown in Fig. 2.

Proof-of-Work. Satoshi Nakamoto proposes proof-of-work (POW) algorithm in [11]. In POW, nodes in a P2P network hold their own candidate blocks which have the same order. In these candidate blocks, each node should find a suitable hash value less than the difficulty goal (see Sect. 3) for its own candidate block to make it legal. However, it is not guaranteed that the effort a node pained can get success since a hash value is randomness, unpredictable and the finding process is competed with other nodes. As a result, the fastest generated legal block is broadcasted to other nodes. Once the new block is verified by other nodes, it is connected to their local blockchains. Meanwhile node who generates the new block is awarded with the bitcoin (BTC) and other candidate blocks become invalid.

2.2 Blockchain Structure

A blockchain is composed of lots of blocks connected in chronological order. Each block contains a certain number of items and a block header. In BTC, items mean transactions between two BTC users. Each block header includes a hash value of its previous block header. Thus one can trace from the newest block to the first block. Meanwhile, each header has a merkle tree root which contains all records in the block. A blockchian structure is indicated in Fig. 3.

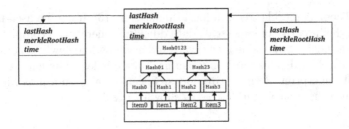

Fig. 3. Blockchain structure

2.3 Blockchain Security

In a blockchain, a block connects to its previous block by the recorded hash value of the previous block header. Once there is any modification in a block, it can easily be detected since its hash value is changed and unmatched with recorded one in its next block. If one wants to forge a block, he has to modify all the blocks upto the newest one. However, even so one can modify a complete local blockchain, he is still not able to modify all local blockchains distributed over the network. Therefore, the records stored in a blockchain are unforgeable and secure [7].

3 The Design of the AMS

3.1 Requirements Analysis

There are administers and ordinary users in the AMS. Except for managing registration of users and querying attendance data, administers are treated as ordinary users. Accordingly, all operations from administers are also recorded in the blockchain. After registration, ordinary users can check-in, check-out and query data.

3.2 System Design

Architecture Design. The system architecture is designed as a four-layer structure: data layer, network layer, consensus layer and application layer. The application layer mainly provides a user-oriented interactive interface. The consensus layer implements the POW algorithm. Records and blocks are broadcasted and verified in the Network layer. The data layer adopts cryptographic algorithms to save block data. The architecture is shown in Fig. 4.

Types of Nodes. There are two types of nodes in the AMS for two kinds of users: full nodes for ordinary users and supervisory nodes for administers. A full node not only generates, broadcasts and verifies attendance records and blocks but also saves a whole copy of a blockchain. A supervisory node is used for

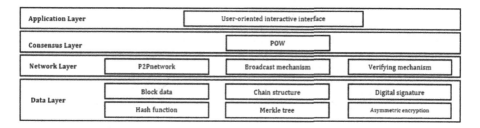

Fig. 4. Architecture design

system supervision. A user need register into the blockchain network under the supervision of an administer at the first time. Very often a user can do his own business such as check-in, check-out and query. Whereas, a supervisory node saves a whole local blockchain if any. The functional modules of each node are designed as shown in Fig. 5.

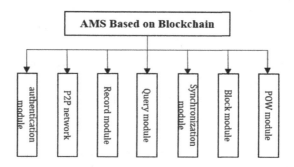

Fig. 5. Functional modules

P2P Network. The network used in our AMS is a typical P2P network. This P2P network has two types of nodes: full nodes and supervisory nodes. A full node can join or exit the P2P network dynamically but should connect to at least one node, usually a supervisory node while a supervisory node should online all the time. The P2P structure is shown in Fig. 6. In practice, we can set the number of supervisory nodes according to specific scenarios.

3.3 Data Structure

Block Data Structure. A block is a basic unit of blockchain. Its data structure is indicated in Table 1.

LastHash represents the hash value of the previous block header of a block. It is the unique identification of a block. *Merkle* saves the merkle tree root which contains all records in a block. It is the fingerprint of records in a block;

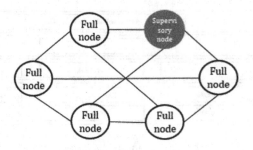

Fig. 6. A P2P structure

Table 1. Block data structure

Variable field	Length	Type
lastHash	32	Byte array
Merkle	32	Byte array
time	4	10 Byte array
difficulty	1	Byte
nonce	4	Byte array
cumulativeDifficulty	4	Byte array
blockNumber	3	Byte array
recordCount	2	Byte array
data	Uncertain length	Byte array

time represents the time when a block generates; *difficulty* denotes a difficulty goal to create a block; *nonce* is a random number which is initialized to 0. When a node creates a block, the node tries various *nonce* to make hash value of its block so that a hash value less than the *difficulty* can be found. The *cumulativeDifficuly* is an accumulative difficulty value from the first block to the current block. The *blockNumber* is the order of the block in a blockchain. It is useful to determine the location of a block. The *recordCount* indicates the the number of records in a block. The first eight fields in the table are called block header. The *data* is the body of a block which contains all records of the block.

A block header is a significant basis to verify records and blocks. In a block, the block header binds with the block body by *merkle* while in adjacent blocks, they connect to each other by *lastHash*.

Record Data Structure. A record is a basic unit of data storage. Its data structure is shown in Table 2.

The *address* is a location ID. We use MAC address of the computer for each ordinary user as his attendance location. The *state* represents an attendance state value which is 1, 2, 3 and 4 respectively denoting check-in, check-out, user's

Table 2. Record data structure

Variable	Length	Type
address	6	Byte array
state	1	Byte
orderStamp	3	Byte array
time	4	Byte array
lockScript	32	Byte array
unlockScript	80–160 (Uncertain)	Byte array

register and the query of administers. The *orderStamp* indicates the order of a record in one's all history records; *time* shows the time of a generated record; *lockScript* is the unique identification of an ordinary user; it is the hash value of one's public key. The *unlockScript* contains the digital signature of a record and public key of the user. These fields are useful to verify a record.

3.4   Main Work Flow

The process of an AMS running on a full node is shown in Fig. 7. The full node initializes the system including parameter settings, network connection, user's register and so on. Subsequently, the full node synchronizes its local blockchain with other nodes. Further, this full node tries to generate blocks and listens to the network. Once the full node receives and verifies a new block, it saves and broadcasts this new block to the network. Finally, the full node updates its local blockchain and starts to generate a new block.

4   Implementation of Core Functions

4.1   Supervisory Module

The AMS creates a pair of secret keys (a public key and a corresponding private key) for each user when the user logs on the AMS at the first time. Afterwards, a user should hand his public key to an administer to be identified. Then the administer certifies the user's identification and generates a register record for the user. The registered record is broadcasted to the network since it is the first record of the user. Since then other nodes receive and verify the registered record so that the user is accepted by the blockchain network. In addition, the administer hash the user's public key to get the unique identification *lockScript* of the user. Finally, the administer saves the mapping relationship between the user and his *lockScript*. No other users except for administers know these mapping relationships. This grantees the anonymity of users and the supervision of administers.

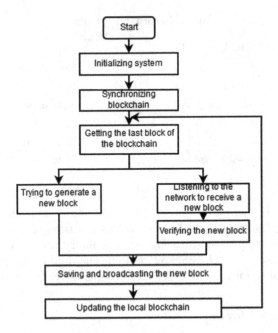

Fig. 7. Main work flow

4.2   Record Module

Record Generation. To generate a new record, the AMS gets one's MAC address to fill the field of *address* and generates a value for *lockScript* by means of hashing the user's public key. Further, the system writes a value for *orderStamp* according to the order of the user's last record and records the current time to *time*. Finally, the system utilizes the user's private key to generate a digital signature for other fields, leading to a new record.

Record Pool. Each full node has a record pool to save records not only generated by itself but also received from the network. A record pool includes three lists: an unidentified list, an identified list and an ending list. The three lists respectively record related information: unverified attendance records, verified attendance records and the last record of each user.

When receiving or generating a new record, a node writes the new record into its unidentified list. Then the node verifies this new record. If the new record is legal, it is moved from the unidentified list into the identified list otherwise it is abandoned by the record pool. Finally, the node replaces the user's last record by the new record to update the ending list.

Record Verification. A full node verifies a new record according to the following steps. At first, it verifies the *lockScript* and *unlockScript* fields. To do so, the values of *lockScript* and *unlockScript* are checked to see whether the following hold: (1) *lockScript* is equal to the hash value of the public key in *unlockScript*; (2) the decrypted digital signature in *unlockScript* equals to the concatenation of the record's *address*, *time* and *orderStamp*. Secondly, the system checks the *orderStamp* as follows: if it is the next index of the user's latest record's index, the *orderStamp* is legal otherwise it is illegal. Thirdly, the *time* is verified by two steps: (1) checking if *time* is greater than the *time* of latest record; (2) verifying if *time* is within the range of the allowable error of the system. Usually, we set the allowable error during system initialization. As a result, a legal record is put into the identified list and the ending list updates otherwise an illegal record is denied.

4.3 Block Module

We use $block_i$ and $block_{i+1}$ to respectively denote a blockchain's lastest block and a new block.

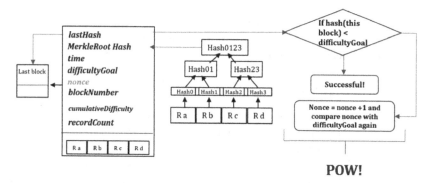

Fig. 8. Block generation

Block Generation. To generate a new $block_{i+1}$, we do the following: at first the AMS fills the field of *lastHash* according to the $block_i$'s hash value; secondly, the value of $block_{i+1}$'s *blockNumber* is set to the value of $block_{i+1}$'s *blockNumber* plus 1; thirdly, the system takes records from its identified list to fill the *data* field and counts these records to write *recordCount*; fourthly, the system constructs a merkle tree using these records to generate a merkle root for *merkle*; fifthly, the system executes a function for computing difficulty so as to write *difficulty*; sixthly, *cumulativeDifficulty* is assigned the total value of $block_i$'s *cumulativeDifficulty* and $block_{i+1}$'s *difficulty*; finally, the system finds a *nonce* by means of POW algorithm to make $block_{i+1}$ legal and records the current time to *time*. A block generating process is shown in Fig. 8.

POW. The POW algorithm is used to find out a *nonce* for a block header so as to make the hash value of a block header less than the value of *difficulty*. The *nonce* is initialized to 0 and increased by 1 after each unsuccessful effort. Further, a new current time for *time* is required with each attempt. If a *nonce* is beyond 2^{32}, it is reset to 0 again.

Block Verification. Each node verifies a new block independently and applies the same check standards. When receiving a new block($block_{i+1}$), a node usually verifies all its fields in the block to see if the following conditions are satisfied.

(1) The hash value of the block head is less than the *difficulty*. (2) The *difficulty* is less than its *cumulativeDifficulty*. (3) The *time* of the new block is behind the time of the latest and within the allowable error. (4) The new *blockNumber* equals the latest block's *blockNumber* plus one. (5) The *cumulativeDifficulty* is greater than *cumulativeDifficulty* of the latest block. (6) The *lastHash* is equal to the hash value of the latest block header. (7) All records in the new block are verified by record verification. (8) The node regenerates a merkle tree using all its records and the merkle tree root is equal to *merkle*.

As a result, if a new block satisfies all the above conditions, it is legal and connected to the local blockchain of a node. It is worthy pointing out that any errors in the verification steps could lead the new block to be rejected.

4.4 Synchronized Module

A node needs to synchronize its local blockchain in one of the following scenarios: (1) it has joined the blockchain network for the first time; (2) the node was offline before and joins the network again; (3) the AMS fails because of some unexpected errors; or (4) its local blockchain gets error. To synchronize the local blockchain, the node broadcasts a synchronized request to the blockchain network and other nodes send the specific requested blocks to the node. Once the node receives the blocks received from the network, it verifies these blocks and saves the verified blocks to its local blockchain.

5   System Demonstration

5.1   Demonstration Overview

The demonstration is mainly to show some new features of the blockchain AMS. It includes three parts: (1) users query attendance records independently; (2) administers query all attendance records; (3) one hacker forges an attendance record and attempts to hand it to the AMS.

5.2   Environment and Parameter Settings

The running environment and parameter settings of nodes are shown in Tables 3 and 4 below.

Table 3. Environment settings

Nodes	CPU	RAM	Bandwidth	System	Java
No. 1 and no. 2 full nodes	Intel i7-4790	4G	40 Mbps	Windows10	Jdk1.8.181
No. 3 full node	intel i7-8550	8G	40 Mbps	Windows10	Jdk1.8.181
Supervisory node	intel i7-8550	4G	40 Mbps	Windows7	Jdk1.8.066

Table 4. Parameter settings

Parameters	Values
The average time of block generation	600 s
The error time when generated blocks	50 s
Cache size of block	1000 blocks
Difficulty adjustment interval	10 blocks
Unit of difficulty adjustment	1 bit
Elliptic curve parameter	secp160r

5.3   Demonstrations

User Query. Users query their own records independently in the blockchain AMS. They can also see attendance records of others though they do not know who these attendance records belong to. Since users in the blockchain AMS are identified by their public keys and only administers know the mapping relationships between public keys and users. A user query case is shown in Fig. 9.

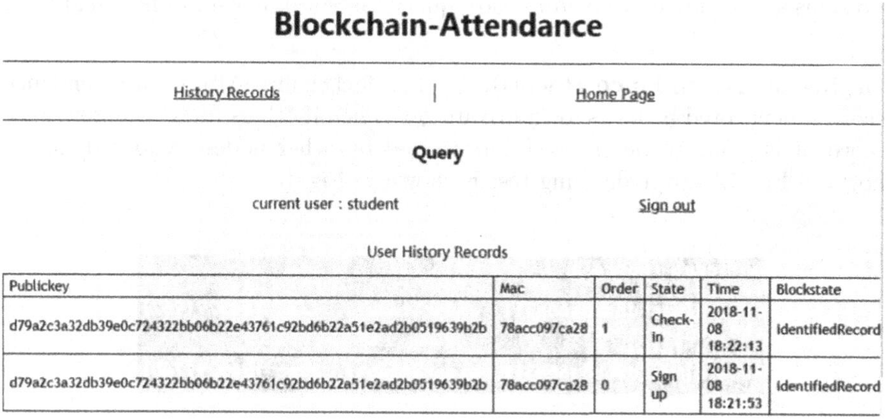

Fig. 9. User query. One can query his own history data in his home page, also he can see other's history records. However, he doesn't know whose records they are.

Admin Query

current admin : admin01   Sign out

Name	Publickey	Mac	Order	State	Time	Block
admin01	6ee1903819beab6faac3d933b971c35f2a7686a41c0a81da85b399f158cbcb34	78acc097ca28	4	Admin Login	2018-11-08 18:22:48	ident
student	d79a2c3a32db39e0c724322bb06b22e43761c92bd6b22a51e2ad2b0519639b2b	78acc097ca28	2	Check-out	2018-11-08 18:22:26	ident

Fig. 10. Admin query: administers can query all the history records and know whose records they are.

Admin Query

current admin : admin01   Sign out

BlockNumber	LastHash	BlockTime	RecordCount	Nonce
861	8af7e39cf84522ec9ba4e6dbe234b299fc47fa4d2baed669fa79d80b395eba70	2018-11-08 18:09:21	1	456708931
860	76ab7d9ba6e9f79086d2280ff7206b60923c74160121aa6e09977e5f7f998b73	2018-11-08 17:56:19	0	119735585
859	11323637887af9e7902cccf3cc685ef71c76c79d67d2868308cba318b1f98c20	2018-11-08 17:52:52	0	53389425

Fig. 11. Admin query2: administer query the history blocks.

Administers Query. Administers can only query all attendance data but they are not permitted to modify any data. Meanwhile their activities such as queries and signs are recorded. Two administer query cases are shown in Figs. 10 and 11.

Forging an Attendance Record. In the blockchain AMS, each attendance record is encrypted by users' own private key. Then if others forge an attendance record, it is going to be checked and refused by other nodes. A forged case is shown in Fig. 12 and a checking test is shown in Fig. 13.

```
an legal record
record info:
Record{mac=d8cb8a66e311, orderStamp=1, time=1545291962}
the faking record
record info:
Record{mac=d8cb8a66e311, orderStamp=1, time=1545291740}
```

Fig. 12. A forged record: the time field of an legal record is forged and broadcasted to the blockchain network.

```
receive record
record info:
Record[mac=d8cb8a66e311, orderStamp=1, time=1545291740]
invalid record
```

Fig. 13. Verifying the forged record: other nodes receive the forged record and verify it.

6   Conclusion

This paper presents a blcokchain AMS. It implements the basic functions of AMS and takes advantages of blockchain to prevent attendance data from modifying. Further, We design a supervisory module to help supervise the AMS.

The system satisfies a small-scale application. However, it remains to be verified in complex application scenarios. The system can be improved in the following aspects: (1) developing a more strict way of attendance; (2) improving the existing POW; and (3) proposing simplified nodes and extending the P2P network.

At present, the system uses a MAC address as an attendance location. This can cause a risk since one could check-in instead of other individuals. So it is better to take more strict ways such as fingerprint recognition or face identification to reduce this risk. Further, the POW algorithm we use in the AMS is energy-consuming and slow. In the future, we will improve the POW algorithm so that a fast energy-saving algorithm could be adopted. Moreover, we will propose simplified nodes to provide a light AMS which does not need save a whole blockchain. Finally, we will construct an effective P2P network [4] so as to improve the performance of the network.

As a software system, the blockchain AMS also needs to be tested or verified since bugs can be hidden in the system. Therefore, we plan to apply MSVL based technique to verify the system [2,3,15]. Further, we will also protect the security and privacy of the blockchian AMS by means of MSVL techniques [5,14] so that the data cannot be forged by hackers.

References

1. Chintalapati, S., Raghunadh, M.V.: Automated attendance management system based on face recognition algorithms. In: Proceedings of the IEEE International Conference on Computational Intelligence and Computing Research, pp. 1–5. IEEE (2014)
2. Duan, Z.: Temporal logic and temporal logic programming. Science Press (2005)
3. Duan, Z., Tian, C., Zhang, L.: A decision procedure for propositional projection temporal logic with infinite models. Acta Informatica 45(1), 43–78 (2008)
4. Duan, Z., et al.: Two-layer hybrid peer-to-peer networks. Peer-to-Peer Netw. Appl. 10(6), 1304–1322 (2017)
5. Duan, Z., Yang, X., Koutny, M.: Framed temporal logic programming. Sci. Comput. Program. 70(1), 31–61 (2008)

6. Gilbert, H., Handschuh, H.: Security analysis of SHA-256 and sisters. In: Matsui, M., Zuccherato, R.J. (eds.) SAC 2003. LNCS, vol. 3006, pp. 175–193. Springer, Heidelberg (2004). https://doi.org/10.1007/978-3-540-24654-1_13

7. Iansiti, M., Lakhani, K.R.: The truth about blockchain. Harvard Bus. Rev. **95**(1), 118–127 (2017)

8. Kamaraju, M., Kumar, P.A.: Wireless fingerprint attendance management system. In: Proceedings of the IEEE International Conference on Electrical, pp. 1–6. IEEE (2015)

9. Khatun, A., Haque, A.F., Ahmed, S., Rahman, M.M.: Design and implementation of iris recognition based attendance management system. In: Proceedings of the International Conference on Electrical Engineering and Information Communication Technology, pp. 1–6. IEEE (2015)

10. Lauter, K.E.: The advantages of elliptic curve cryptography for wireless security. IEEE Wirel. Commun. **11**(1), 62–67 (2004)

11. Nakamoto, S.: Bitcoin: a peer-to-peer electronic cash system (2008). http://www.bitcoin.org/bitcoin.pdf

12. Peng, Z., Duan, Z., Qi, J.J., Cao, Y., Lv, E.: HP2P: a hybrid hierarchical P2P network. In: Proceedings of the International Conference on the Digital Societ, p. 18. IEEE (2007)

13. Szydlo, M.: Merkle tree traversal in log space and time. In: Cachin, C., Camenisch, J.L. (eds.) EUROCRYPT 2004. LNCS, vol. 3027, pp. 541–554. Springer, Heidelberg (2004). https://doi.org/10.1007/978-3-540-24676-3_32

14. Tian, C., Duan, Z., Duan, Z.: Making cegar more efficient in software model checking. IEEE Trans. Softw. Eng. **40**(12), 1206–1223 (2014)

15. Tian, C., Duan, Z., Zhang, N.: An efficient approach for abstraction-refinement in model checking. Theoret. Comput. Sci. **461**, 76–85 (2012)

16. Xie, H., Wang, J.: Study on block chain technology and its applications. Netinfo Secur. **9**, 192–195 (2016)

17. Xu, R., Zhang, L., Zhao, H., Peng, Y.: Design of network media's digital rights management scheme based on blockchain technology. In: Proceedings of the IEEE International Symposium on Autonomous Decentralized System, pp. 128–133. IEEE (2017)

18. Zhi, M., Mahinderjit Singh, M.: RFID-enabled smart attendance management system. In: Park, J., Pan, Y., Kim, C., Yang, Y. (eds.) Future Information Technology - II. LNEE, vol. 329, pp. 213–231. Springer, Dordrecht (2015). https://doi.org/10.1007/978-94-017-9558-6_26

19. Zyskind, G., Nathan, O., Pentland, A.: Decentralizing privacy: using blockchain to protect personal data. In: Proceedings of the 2015 IEEE Security and Privacy Workshops (SPW), pp. 180–184. IEEE Computer Society (2015)

State-of-the-Art and Future Trends of Blockchain Based on DAG Structure

Chong Bai$^{(\boxtimes)}$

Instrument Science and Technology, Xidian University,
Xi'an 710071, People's Republic of China
shuyaott@163.com

Abstract. Blockchain is a decentralized storage technology rose rapidly recent years, it has the advantages of decentralization, untamperability and unforgeability, high safety and reliability, and has attracted vast attentions from governments, financial institutions, technology enterprises and capital markets. Blockchain has numerous application scenarios and huge development potential, Bitcoin is the most representative one of it. Primarily, the first generation blockchain and the second generation blockchain and their respective representative crypto-currencies: Bitcoin and Ether are introduced briefly. Next, a new type of blockchain based on DAG (Directed Acyclic Graph) structure is illustrated, it is considered to be the possible evolution route of the next generation blockchain. Furthermore, two influential applications of DAG blockchain systems: IOTA and Byteball are introduced. Finally, Conclusion and forecast of blockchain are discussed.

Keywords: Blockchain · DAG · IOTA · Byteball

1 Introduction

In recent years, as the market value of Bitcoin increasing continually, blockchain, which Bitcoin is based on, is gradually known. As a distributed network architecture and storage technology, blockchain has the advantages of decentralization, unforgeability and high reliability. Current crypto-currencies are based on blockchain architecture practically. Since the birth of crypto-currencies, blockchain has gone through two generations of development. The representative application of the first generation blockchain is Bitcoin, which created a decentralized crypto-currency worldwide firstly. The second generation blockchain [1], known as "Ethereum", added the concept of "Smart Contract", started the era of crypto-currencies combined with smart contract. Over the past two years, a new blockchain based on DAG structure was proposed. Compared with the preceding two generations of blockchain, the DAG blockchain adopts asynchronous communication mechanism and concurrent processing algorithm, improves system scalability greatly, and sets off a revolution of development of the next generation blockchain.

The remainder of this paper is organized as follows. Section 2 reviews the first generation blockchain and Bitcoin. Section 3 presents the second generation blockchain-Ethereum and Ether as its token. Section 4 illustrates the DAG blockchain

© Springer Nature Switzerland AG 2019
Z. Duan et al. (Eds.): SOFL+MSVL 2018, LNCS 11392, pp. 183–196, 2019.
https://doi.org/10.1007/978-3-030-13651-2_11

and its two typical applications: IOTA and Byteball. Section 5 concludes the paper and foresees the future trend of blockchain.

2 The First Generation Blockchain

2.1 Overview of the First Generation Blockchain

Blockchain originated from a paper: "Bitcoin: A peer-to-peer electronic cash system" [2] proposed by Satoshi Nakamoto in 2008, in this paper the concept of blockchain was proposed firstly, and specific implementation scheme was given. Blockchain is considered as a specific data structure that blocks were arranged in time order and constructed in chains; data in blocks cannot be tampered with and cannot be forged. It can store simple, sequential data that can be validated easily in system [3].

2.2 Bitcoin

Bitcoin is a crypto-currency based on the first generation blockchain, it is also the most successful blockchain application so far. According to the real-time statistical data of Bitcoin transactions globally, by July 23rd, 2018, at 10:36 a.m. the number of Bitcoin transactions in the last 24 h were 236813, with a total market value more than 133 billion US dollars [4]. Referring to the GDP ranking of countries in the world in 2017, Bitcoin is ranking fifty-fifth [5], higher than Hungary's GDP nationwide. The real-time exchange rate of Bitcoin to US dollars was 1 to 7731.27; the price of Bitcoin has soared more than 3 million times, compared with the value in May 2010, when a Florida programmer bought a 25 US dollars pizza coupon with 10,000 BTC. The real-time transaction data of Bitcoin were shown in Fig. 1 below.

Fig. 1. Bitcoin real-time transaction data

Bitcoin is a crypto-currency essentially, its generation does not depend on any central authority, but a process called "Mining" figuratively, nodes of the Bitcoin network engaged in mining are called miners. Miners compete with each other to calculate a mathematical problem that the index of difficulty can be adjusted, miner who solved the mathematical problem in the shortest time broadcast the result and related information to Bitcoin network. After the other miners receive the broadcast, they verify the validity of the information, check whether the information do not exist in previous blocks, if all the check pass, the miner who solved the mathematical problem in the shortest time gains the right to update blockchain in current cycle, which is ten minutes in average. During this cycle, this miner packs all the unconfirmed transactions into a new block, and links it to the main chain of blockchain chronologically, and gains a certain number of Bitcoin as reward. If the verification result is invalid, the calculate result and information will be discarded and all miners will compete again to mining.

Bitcoin uses PoW (Proof of Work) consensus algorithm to ensure the generation of new blocks, maintain the stable growth of blockchain. The block structure of Bitcoin is shown in Fig. 2 below [6].

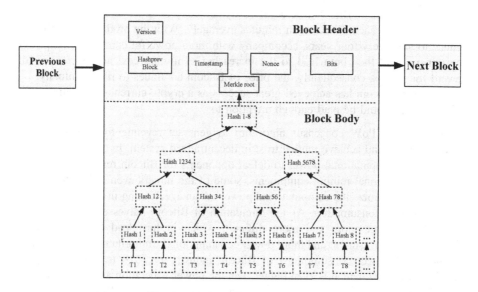

Fig. 2. The block structure of Bitcoin

Blocks are connected each other in chronological order, each block consists of block body and block header. Block body contains all the unconfirmed transactions collected by miners. The hash function calculates the message of each transaction respectively (T1 represents transaction 1). Afterwards, every two hash value of the transaction combined to generate a new hash value. This process is repeated again to form the "Merkle tree" structure until only one hash value is left, which is called "Merkle root", and it will be written into the corresponding block header.

Block header contains six parameters: Version, HashprevBlock, Timestamp, Bits (mining difficulty), Merkle root and Nonce (random value), a target value will be calculated (Target) through Bits for mining [7].

The process of mining essentially is executing double hash operations for data of block header, which is equal to solve the following inequation (1):

$$SHA256(SHA256(Version + HashprevBlock + Timestamp + Merkleroot + Bits + Nonce)) < Target \tag{1}$$

On the left side of the inequation, the first five parameters have constant values, the value of Target on the right side is also a constant which can be calculated through the value of Bits. The value of Nonce need to be solved to satisfied the inequation. The initial value of Nonce is set to zero, and the double hash value is calculated, if the calculate result bigger than the value of the Target, value of Nonce add one and continue calculate, if the result still bigger than Target, Nonce value add one and calculate again, this process repeat until the calculate result smaller than the value of Target, this indicates the success of mining.

The parameter of Bits can be adjusted dynamically in order to stabilize the generation period of each block in ten minutes averagely. With the production of Bitcoin reduce to half every four years, accompany with more powerful computational power the miners own, they both lead to the increasing of mining cost and decreasing of reward for miners, consequently, the price of Bitcoin continues to rise eventually.

Although Bitcoin has achieved great success as a crypto-currency, its deficiencies are clear and should be paid enough attention to.

1. Bitcoin uses PoW consensus algorithm to generate revenue for miners, assure transactions and achieve mutual trust in decentralized system. In order to get more powerful computational power to defeat opponents for Bitcoin reward, miners use more professional mining equipments, some of the miners even united to mining pools to maximize the computational power advantage, mining in large scale cause huge power consumption. As the circulation of Bitcoin halves every four years, mining become more and more difficult, which in turn lead to more mining equipments investment and more power consumptions. Authoritative statistical data show that power consumptions of Bitcoin industry in 2018 is estimated up to 731.2 TWh [8], which is even bigger than the power generation amount of Kuwait in 2017 (711 TWh) [9], the average power consumption of each Bitcoin transaction are 900 KWh. Huge amount of power was wasted do nothing but calculate hash value and random number search.

2. The PoW consensus algorithm used in Bitcoin will face "51% attack" problem inevitably, it means that miners in Bitcoin network may carry out malicious attacks, forge data if they manage to get more than half computational power of the whole network. Although it's nearly impossible to obtain such huge computational power and the cost of attack are much more than the reward after the attack is implemented.

3. The transaction speed of Bitcoin network is too slow, with only 7 transactions per second [10], while Alipay's peak trading volume is up to 256 000 per second during the "Double Eleven Shopping Festival" in 2017 [11], the gap between Bitcoin and mainstream payment platform is considerable large in this respect, extensions of the application of Bitcoin were limited due to its low transaction speed.

4. The hash algorithm Bitcoin used is susceptible to meet hash collision, although the probability is very low. With the promotion of hardware performance and the development of new computing technologies such as the birth of quantum computer, the probability of hash collision increasing continuously, and the hash algorithm facing the risk of being cracked.

The first generation blockchain is used mainly in field of crypto-currencies, it adopts decentralized architecture, without any central authorities, transactions were conducted and confirmed through all the nodes of the network, Bitcoin can be generated and circulated globally, this brand-new crypto-currency is entirely different from the conventional currencies. Although drawbacks still exist in technical aspects and the performance needs improvement, the prosperity of crypto-currencies is irreversible, increasingly important role crypto-currencies will act under the tide of globalization.

3   The Second Generation Blockchain

3.1   Overview of the Second Generation Blockchain

The first generation blockchain made a decentralized crypto-currency come true for the first time and depicted a grand blueprint for a unified global currency, brought us endless imaginations that crypto-currencies would trigger the "Dominoes effect" and lead to a revolution in monetary field as a pioneer, and then the evolvements of social formation and operation mode, change our life drastically.

However, the first generation blockchain is only focused on crypto-currencies. The need to extend it to the fields beside crypto-currencies and construct decentralized applications across fields has led to the birth of the second generation blockchain.

The second generation blockchain, also known as "Ethereum", was first put forward by Vitalik in 2014 [12].

Compared with the first generation blockchain, the most prominent characteristic of Ethereum is "Smart Contract", which is also the core content of Ethereum. The concept of smart contract was first proposed by Nick early in 1994 [13], in which the main principles smart contract operate were given, but there was no suitable operating platform until the birth of Ethereum.

Smart Contract is a code fragment built in blockchain application, a variety of rules and operations are set in advance and trigger mechanisms are contained in the code. Once the conditions are met, the code executed automatically and implemented according to the agreed rules.

Transactions on Ethereum are information transferred during different accounts, information can be crypto-currencies or content valuable. There are two kinds of accounts on Ethereum: ordinary accounts and contract accounts, ordinary accounts contain Ether (the token used in Ethereum), transactions of Ether can be executed during ordinary accounts. Unlike ordinary accounts, contract accounts contain not only Ether, but also smart contracts, specific addresses (where Ethereum launch smart contracts) are reserved for storing contract accounts. Contract accounts cannot be executed on their own unless called by ordinary accounts, which is the only way smart contracts can be executed. A series of functions can be realized after being called, include transferring of Ether, mining for new Ether, even creation of new smart contracts.

All nodes in the Ethereum network run their Ethereum Virtual Machine (EVM) respectively and execute PoW algorithm to validate and generate blocks. The PoW algorithm used on Ethereum is called "Ethash", which is different from the PoW algorithm of Bitcoin, some modifications were made and can be regarded as a variant of the standard hash algorithm.

Ethereum is an open source platform on which anyone can launch their own smart contracts and conduct transactions. Congestions and chaos may occur in the network, even more, malicious attacks may be launched if the situations are not regulated properly. Given to this consideration, users must to pay to run their procedures on Ethereum, the payment are described as "gas", the gas amount offered by users are defined as Eq. (2):

$$Gas = gasprice * gaslimit \tag{2}$$

Gasprice denotes the price per unit gas, while gaslimit shows the amount of gas users offered, gasprice and gaslimit are defined by users, they both determine the maximum transaction fees available. Each transaction need a certain gas amount to operate, if the gas amount offered exceeds the required gas amount, the transaction will be executed normally and the extra gas will be returned to user's account after the transaction is completed. Otherwise, the transaction will be terminated and reverted to its pre-transaction state. Due to effort was done by miners even if the transaction is cancelled, the gas been used to execute transaction will not be returned, but the Ether (Token circulated on Ethereum) will be returned normally if there has Ether transferring in the transaction.

Practically, miners are prone to choose the transactions with higher transaction fees, in order to ensure the success of transactions, and make sure transactions can be confirmed more quickly, users often offer excessive gas than required gas amount.

The emergence of gas ensures transactions to be conducted orderly in one hand, it is also in accordance with the Turing completeness of the programming language of Ethereum in another hand, the programming language operated on Ethereum supports a variety of complex logic operations, and dead loop is prohibited for it. Gas makes this goal come true to prevent abnormality of procedures or malicious attacks, finite gas supplies bound to make the procedures run out in a finite time.

Several remarkable application platforms were founded based on Ethereum these years. In August 2014, the first smart contract client in the world called "Bithalo" [14] was launched officially, users can carry out services such as deposit, crypto-currencies exchange, goods exchange and email services by the client; besides, Amir Kafshdar Goharshady proposed a decentralized storage and query system about credit report in May 2018, in which the smart contract was built, it can store and report credit data safely and credibly [15], it's the first approach that can be able to perform real-world credit reporting tasks without a central authority.

3.2   Ether

Ether is the crypto-currency circulated in Ethereum to pay transaction fees and service charges, it is the second largest crypto-currency in the world. By July 23th, 2018, at 10:36 a.m. the total market value of Ether has reached 47.9 billion US dollars [16], which is equivalent to one third of the total market value of Bitcoin at the same time. With the establishment of Enterprise Ethereum Alliance (EEA) in 2017 [17], there will be more applications based on Ethereum published in future, and the market value of Ether will continue to rise. Trading data of Ether are shown in Fig. 3 below:

Fig. 3.   Real-time trading data of Ether

The differences between Ether and Bitcoin are listed below:

1. Unlike the fact that the circulation of Bitcoin halves every four years, the circulation of Ether remains invariable, with annual circulation is 0.26 times the total amount of the pre-sale Ether.
2. The generation period of each Bitcoin block is ten minutes in average, while the generation time of Ethereum block is much faster, up to fifteen seconds in average, this notable difference result in different performance in transaction speed.
3. Bitcoin and Ether have different roles as crypto-currencies. Bitcoin has the same value preservation and property hedging function as gold since its birth, especially in the Cyprus Debt Crisis in 2013 [18], in which Bitcoin played a great role in preventing property from shrinking. While Ether is the "fuel" required to conducted smart contracts on Ethereum platform, ensure the execution of smart contracts. The value of Bitcoin lies in result, while the value of the Ether rests in process.

The first generation blockchain focused on the field of crypto-currencies, gave birth to the subversive application like Bitcoin. The second generation blockchain added the concept of smart contract, expanded the scope of blockchain from the field of crypto-currencies to more application scenes, led to profound changes in financial, economic, science-technology and even political fields, guiding whole society moving forward to industry 4.0 era [19, 20].

4 DAG Blockchain

4.1 DAG Introduction

DAG (Directed Acyclic Graph) is an important concept of data structure theory in computer science subject, due to its unique topological structure, DAG is usually used to deal with dynamic programming problems, such as the shortest path tracing, data compression and other fields.

DAG was proposed in blockchain as part of consensus algorithm in 2013, when a scholar in Hebrew University of Israel proposed a GHOST (Greedy Heaviest-Observed Sub-Tree) protocol, which aimed to improve transaction performance of Bitcoin, consequently, lifted the transaction speed of Bitcoin from 7 transactions per second to 200 transactions per second [21].

In 2015, Sergio Demian Lerner published a paper "Dag Coin: a cryptocurrency without blocks", in which the concept of DAG-chain [22] was first proposed.

DAG is a way of storing data along with one direction, no circular structure was founded in it. Start from one node of DAG, proceeding along a directed arrow, it is impossible to return to the starting node. Structure of DAG is shown in Fig. 4 below.

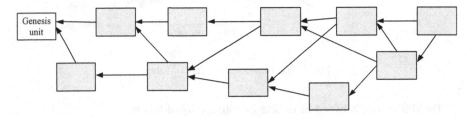

Fig. 4. DAG structure diagram

In Fig. 4, the order of time flows from left to right, each box represents a transaction, this is different from traditional blockchain structure. The arrows between boxes represent a certain validation relationship between them, when a new transaction wants to join the network, it is necessary for it to validate previous two transactions firstly.

In the DAG network, each new transaction validates its parent transaction directly, and validates the parent transaction of the parent transaction indirectly. After multiple direct and indirect validations, genesis unit leftmost can be reached. Each transaction contains the hash value from the genesis unit to its father unit. As time goes by, all nodes are interconnected, forming a tangle structure. As long as the data of any node in the whole network is altered, the hash value of the whole network will be changed, so it is very difficult to tamper with the network.

Gossip algorithm [23] is used in DAG network to ensure the final consistency of states between different transactions. Although it cannot guarantee the consistency of the states of the network all the time, the final data consistency of them will be obtained in a certain moment at last. All nodes of the network will be agreed after a period of time even some of them offline or new nodes join in.

DAG network adopts asynchronous communication mechanism, which can improve the scalability of blockchain (throughput and transaction speed) greatly. The more transactions involved in the network, the faster the transaction will be confirmed. However, the excellent performances are at the cost of period consistency, asynchronous communication and gossip algorithm obtain data synchronization of the DAG network at some certain time points. Before these points, attackers can use data inconsistency to initiate Double Spend attack. Furthermore, attackers can take advantage of the characteristics of parallel transactions of DAG network to forge a shadow chain to replace the main chain and implement attack.

Two influential blockchain applications based on DAG structure: IOTA and Byteball are introduced below.

4.2 IOTA

IOTA is a distributed ledger system designed for Internet of Things (IoT), which is used to meet the micro-payment demands between a large number of machines, it expands the P2P (Peer-to-Peer) trading mode of Bitcoin to M2M (Machine-to-Machine) mode, built the blueprint of machine economy through the way exempting transaction fees between objects. IOTA is also the crypto-currency circulated in IOTA system. By July 28th, 2018, IOTA was the ninth largest crypto-currency in the world, with a total market capitalization of 27.7 billion US dollars [24], and is still growing rapidly.

In IOTA network, if a node wants to initiate a new transaction, it is necessary for it to validate other two transactions in the network firstly, and point to the two transactions. New transactions are validated continually and added to the network, cause the network expanding. The IOTA network is shown in Fig. 5 below [25].

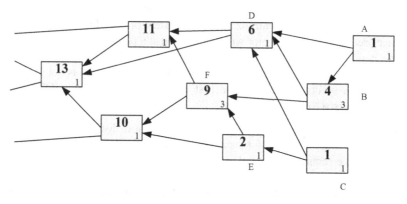

Fig. 5. Tangle structure of IOTA diagram

Figure 5 comes from the IOTA white paper. Transactions on the right side validate the transactions on the left side, the whole network expands from left to right. For the rightmost transactions, such as A and C, they have not been validated yet and called tips.

In IOTA network, two important concepts are defined, they are the own weight and the accumulative weight of a transaction. If a node in the network wants to initiate a new transaction, it should validate two transactions in the network firstly and implement PoW. The PoW algorithm used in DAG network is a ternary algorithm, which is designed by the author of the SHA-3 algorithm, it is also the first ternary hash algorithm in the world [26]. PoW workload the node implemented are proportional to the own weight of the transaction. The value of own weight of a transaction can be defined as 3^N (N is a non-negative integer), own weight is marked in the lower right of each box in Fig. 5.

In addition to own weight, each transaction has accumulated weight, which is defined as the sum of the own weight of a transaction itself and the own weight of all the other transactions validate the transaction directly and indirectly. Accumulated weight is indicated in black bold number in the upper part of each box in Fig. 5. For example, the transaction F is validated by transaction B and transaction E directly, and validated by transaction A and transaction C indirectly, the accumulative weight of transaction F is the sum of the own weight of the four transactions and the own weight itself, that is $3 + 1 + 3 + 1 + 1 = 9$.

The new transaction (assume T0) validates two transactions in the network and implement PoW, then T0 is joined to the network. Subsequent transaction T1 validates T0 directly in same way, the accumulative weight of T0 will increase. Afterwards, the new transaction T2 and T3 continue validates T0 indirectly, the accumulative weight of T0 increases gradually. The more times T0 were validated (no matter directly or indirectly), the bigger the accumulative weight will be. When accumulative weight exceeds a certain threshold value, the transaction T0 will be finally confirmed.

In the early days of IOTA, in order to ensure the reliability of the accumulative weight value, IOTA founded a role called "Coordinator", which is essentially a closed source network node maintained by IOTA authority. The coordinator releases a transaction every minute, as an auxiliary way to validate new transactions. Lots of controversy existed for the centralized characteristics of coordinator in the industry. IOTA declared that the coordinator will be removed at a proper time in future officially, but there is no exact time scheme yet.

Although IOTA has significant advantages in the field of IoT, it is not perfect. As a crypto-currency, security is always the first essential users concern, IOTA's performance is not satisfactory in this aspect.

1. Serious flaws the hash algorithm adopted by IOTA was discovered in July 2017 by an academic organization of Massachusetts Institute of Technology, these flaws threatened the security of digital signature and PoW algorithm of IOTA. It urged IOTA upgraded the hash function finally [27].
2. IOTA has no transaction fees, unlike Bitcoin has mining incentive, so it facing the possibility of denial of service attacks and spam attacks.
3. The existence of the coordinator mechanism makes IOTA highly controversial about centralization, and there is a risk of regression to the centralized system.

4.3 Byteball

Byteball is also a distributed ledger system based on DAG structure. Byte is the token circulated in Byteball network. It aims at popularizing Bitcoin, eliminating defects which hamper the widespread use of Bitcoin, and even replacing banknotes such as US dollar and Euro, becoming the crypto-currency worldwide [28].

In Byteball system, new transactions contain hash value of earlier transactions, the hash value is used to validate the previous transactions in the network and establish its own partial order [29]. By including hash value of parent transactions, new transactions confirm all parent transactions directly and its parent transactions of parent transactions indirectly. With more transactions join in, transaction number will increase rapidly like snowballs, this is the reason the system is named Byteball.

In the system, "witnesses" and "main chain" are introduced innovatively. Witnesses are the individuals or organizations who have high reputation, participate actively in maintaining the development of the Byteball network. The total number of witnesses is twelve, witnesses validate new transactions continually, add them into the network and increase the network volume. There are many paths from a certain transaction to genesis transaction, during those paths an optimal path can be found, this path is main chain, which is stable and credible as long as there are no more than a certain percentage of witnesses who have collaborated with attackers to launch attacks.

The witnesses are not unalterable, system will weed out the witnesses whose reputation is lower and replace them with the more prestige candidates regularly by specific screening mechanism, so as to maintain the stability and reliability of the witnesses. There is a similarity between the witness mechanism and the DPOS (Delegated Proof of Stake) [30] consensus algorithm.

The witnesses and the main chain are actually a consensus mechanism, which play the role of consensus algorithm. Byteball can avoid occurrence of "double spending" and "shadow chain attack" via this consensus mechanism.

In Byteball system, transactions fees are the same to the storage capacity of transactions themselves, part of the transactions fees is obtained by validaters who validate the transactions, and the other part is obtained by the witnesses.

The main functions of Byteball are integrated into its App, which is called Byteball wallet. On which services available include payment, P2P chatting, market forecast, insurance and betting business [31].

5 Summary and Prospect

Using DAG structure in bockchain can solve the deficiencies of low throughput and slow transaction speed of traditional blockchain. Characterized by the inherent advantages of parallel processing and multi-thread operation, DAG structure is very suitable for large-scale transaction scenes. However, it still has some drawbacks, such as do not support strong consistency and security performance has not been validated massively, and need to be corrected and improved gradually. Improvements about security of DAG blockchain are urgent and significant. The latest researches about security are as follows:

1. Researchers of Tsinghua University proposed a paper: "Scaling Nakamoto Consensus to Thousands of Transactions per Second" [32], in which a DAG blockchain system called "Conflux" was introduced. The core of Conflux is its consensus protocol that allows multiple participants to contribute to the Conflux blockchain concurrently while still being provably safe. The consensus algorithm divides the Conflux network into several "epochs" according to the time sequence, sub-main chain of each epoch is determined respectively afterward, all the sub-main chains make up the main chain finally. As long as the main chain keeps clear and stable, majority of conventional security problems will be eliminated in the network.

2. Blockchain start-ups "DAG Labs" developed a DAG blockchain system called SPECTRE [33], in order to avoid transaction conflicts brought by parallel processing and ensure the consistency of information contained in the new generated blocks, all users voting to determine the architecture of the whole network. The order of transactions is determined by users. Including order of the parent transactions and the order the parent transactions of the parent transactions. The network expands following this order, new transactions are also joined to the network in the prescribed order, and the growth logic of the transactions is determined by majority of users in the network. This method ensures that the amount of honest blocks is more than the amount of malicious blocks, eliminates the possibility of 51% attacks. On the premise of high availability of network, the vote mechanism ensures stable transaction sequence in the network and avoids security problems caused by system conflicts.

The DAG blockchain has broken through the limitation of linear processing ability of traditional blockchain, and has made qualitative improvement in system throughput and transaction speed. Great interests have been shown both at home and abroad, and a number of influential DAG blockchain systems have been developed, in addition to those mentioned above, a general blockchain programming platform "Nerthus" [34] was published in 2017, it combined smart contract with DAG, constructed the "DAG + Ethereum" model of blockchain system. The system released beta version in the first quarter of 2018, and plans to hold the first Nerthus Application Developer Conference in the first quarter of 2019. The future of the system is worth looking forward to.

Besides, many DAG blockchain systems are emerging, such as Nano [35], Hash-Graph [36] and Hycon [37]. ITC [38] from China is also a matter of great concern.

With the rise of DAG blockchain, it is often compared with traditional blockchain. In fact, the relationship between them are neither simply advanced or not, nor replaced or be replaced. After nearly a decade of development, the traditional blockchain has already had a stable ecosystem, the security performance has been fully validated and formalized verification methods are available for safety of the traditional blockchain [39–43]. So far, the traditional blockchain and the DAG blockchain still are focusing on their respective specialties. The traditional blockchain concentrates on the cryptocurrencies industry, while DAG blockchain flourishes in the field like IoT. However, the possibility of integration between them and the development of hybrid mode of "Blockchain + DAG" will not be ruled out. There are already some DAG systems exploring in this area. Within the foreseeable years, with the maturity of 5G technologies and the popularization of neural network and artificial intelligence, the traditional blockchain and the DAG blockchain will learn and merge with each other. The integration of them will be accelerated and the completion of blockchain ecosystem will be promoted, to embrace the age of parallel society driven by blockchain [44].

References

1. Jacynycz, V., Calvo, A., Hassan, S.: Betfunding: a distributed bounty-based crowdfunding platform over Ethereum. Adv. Intell. Syst. Comput. **474**, 403–411 (2016)
2. Nakamoto, S.: Bitcoin: a peer-to-peer electronic cash system (2008)
3. Yuan, Y., Wang, F.Y.: Blockchain: the state of the art and future trends. Acta Autom. Sin. **42**, 481–494 (2016)
4. https://www.blockchain.com/explorer
5. http://www.8pu.com/gdp/ranking_2017.html
6. Joanna, M., Eric, F., Maroun, C.: On blockchain security and relevant attacks. In: 2018 IEEE Middle East and North Africa Communications Conference, pp. 7–12, Lebanon (2018)
7. Duan, X.N., Yan, Z.W., Geng, G.G., Yan, B.P.: Research and trend analysis on blockchain consensus algorithm. E-Sci. Technol. Appl. **8**, 43–51 (2017)
8. Bitcoin Energy Consumption Index. https://digiconomist.net
9. BP Statistics Review of World Energy (2017). https://www.bp.com
10. Gobel, J., Krzesinski, A.E.: Increased block size and bitcoin blockchain dynamics. In: 27th International Telecommunication Networks and Applications Conference, pp. 414–419 (2017)
11. http://finance.sina.com.cn/roll/2017-11-11/doc-ifynrsrf3747270.shtml
12. Vitalik, B.: Ethereum: A Next-Generation Cryptocurrency and Decentralized Application Platform. https://bitcoinmagazine.com
13. Nick, S.: Smart Contracts Glossary. www.fon.hum.uva.nl
14. David, Z., Sean, D., Alec, H., Peggy, S., Giovanni, M. http://bithalo.org
15. Amir, K.G., Ali, B., Krishnendu, C.: Secure credit reporting on the blockchain. In: The 2018 IEEE International Conference of Blockchain (2018)
16. https://Etherscan.io/stat/supply
17. Christie, H.: Startups, Banks and tech giants launch enterprise Ethereum alliance. https://bitcoinmagazine.com
18. http://www.8btc.com/article/60256
19. Fu, B.L., Shu, Z., Liu, X.G.: Blockchain enhanced emission trading framework in fashion apparel manufacturing industry. Sustainability **10**, 1105 (2018)
20. Yan, Y.X., Duan, B., Zhong, Y., Qu, X.S.: Blockchain technology in the internet plus: the collaborative development of power electronic devices. In: 43rd Annual Conference of the IEEE-Industrial-Electronics-Society (IECON). IEEE, pp. 922–927 (2017)
21. https://www.hibtc.org
22. Sergio, D.L.: DagCoin: a cryptocurrency without blocks. https://bitslog.wordpress.com
23. Robbert, V.R., Dan, D., Valient, G., Chris, T.: Efficient reconciliation and flow control for anti-entropy protocols. ACM (2008)
24. https://coinmarketcap.com
25. Serguei, P.: The Tangle, Version 1.4.3. https://iota.org
26. https://www.jianshu.com
27. https://www.iotachina.com

28. IOTA VS Byteball. https://www.iotachina.com
29. Anton, C.: Byteball: a decentralized system for storage and transfer of value. https://byteball. org
30. Tiago, M.F.-C., Paula, F.-L.: A review of the use of blockchain for the Internet of Things. IEEE Access **6**, 32979–33001 (2018)
31. www.byteball.cn
32. Li, C.X., Li, P.L., Zhou, D., Xu, W., Long, F.: Scaling Nakamoto Consensus to Thousands of Transactions per Second, https://arxiv.org/abs/1805.03870
33. Yonatan, S., Yoad, L., Aviv, Z.: SPECTRE: Serialization of Proof-of-work events: confirming transactions via recursive elections. https://eprint.iacr.org/2016/1159.pdf
34. http://www.nerthus.io
35. https://raiblocks.net
36. https://www.hederahashgraph.com
37. www.hycon.io
38. https://iotchain.io
39. Chen, C., Tian, C., Duan, Z.H.: RFC-directed differential testing of certificate validation in SSL/TLS implementations. In: ICSE, pp. 859–870 (2018)
40. Tian, C., Duan, Z., Duan, Z.H.: More effective interpolations in software model checking. In: ASE, pp. 183–193 (2017)
41. Tian, C., Duan, Z.H., Duan, Z.: Making CEGAR more efficient in software model checking. IEEE Trans. Softw. Eng. **40**, 1206–1223 (2014)
42. Tian, C., Duan, Z.H.: Detecting spurious counterexamples efficiently in abstract model checking. In: ICSE, pp. 202–211 (2013)
43. Duan, Z.H., Tian, C., Zhang, L.: A decision procedure for propositional projection temporal logic with infinite models. Acta Inform. **45**, 43–78 (2008)
44. Yuan, Y., Wang, F.Y.: Parallel blockchain: concept, methods and issues. Acta Autom. Sin. **43**, 1703–1712 (2017)

Author Index

Printed in the United States
By Bookmasters